Teacher's Manual

For Christian Schools

SPELLING

By Sound and Structure

Grade 7

Rod and Staff Publishers, Inc.
P.O. Box 3, Hwy. 172
Crockett, Kentucky 41413
Telephone: (606) 522-4348

Acknowledgements

We acknowledge the everlasting God, the Lord, beside whom there is none else. His blessing made the writing and publishing of this book possible.

We express gratitude to Brother Marvin Eicher for revising and editing this textbook, to numerous ones involved in reviewing it, and to Brother Lester Miller for the artwork.

We are grateful for the teachers and students who tested this revision in their classrooms and for all those who helped to make this book possible.

Printed in U.S.A.

ISBN 978-07399-0707-8

Catalog no. 167912

4 5 6 7 — 21 20 19 18 17 16 15 14

Outline of Concepts

A Unearthing the Roots
B Affixing Affixes
C Sound, Structure, and Meaning
D Language Lineage

Introduction

The previous books in this spelling series concentrate on basic phonetic patterns. Beginning in Grade 7, the main emphasis shifts to another important factor that affects spelling, namely, the study of word elements—roots, prefixes, and suffixes.

These word elements are taught primarily to help students understand why words are spelled as they are. Knowing the meanings of roots and affixes will also be helpful in expanding the students' vocabularies, and many of the exercises are designed for that purpose. But it is good to remember that this is a spelling course first of all. How much and how strongly the meanings of the word elements should be emphasized is something that each teacher must determine for his own students. *Learning to spell* must be the primary emphasis throughout.

A large percentage of our common vocabulary is made of word elements that come from Latin. Therefore, the lessons in this book teach the meanings of numerous Latin roots, prefixes, and suffixes. This is the purpose of parts A and B of each lesson.

Each lesson also has two other parts. Part C is a review section that exercises phonetic and word-building concepts that are taught in earlier years of this course. (There is no part C in the six-week review lessons.) Part D is a section on the history of the English language. This part of each lesson explains some of the reasons for the modern spellings, pronunciations, and meanings of many English words.

In addition to parts A, B, C, and D, a Speller Dictionary has been included. This specialized dictionary has been condensed to fit the needs of the students as they do the exercises throughout the book; however, a classroom dictionary will also be needed.

A good understanding of phonics, word elements, and the history of the English language should make a significant contribution to the spelling ability of the students.

Spelling Tests

After pupils have completed the work in the spelling lesson and have studied the words in the word lists sufficiently, the spelling test should be administered. If pupils are having problems with mastering the words, a trial test given a day or two before the final test may be desirable.

Testing procedures other than the ones suggested below may be acceptable if the results accurately portray the degree of word mastery.

Administering the Spelling Test

Use the test sentences provided with each lesson. Pronounce the word once, say the sentence, and pronounce the word again.

Every sixth lesson reviews the words from the preceding five lessons. To test these lessons, use the test sentences provided if time permits. Be sure that pupils understand that they are to write only abbreviations for the specified words.

Scoring the Test

For tests from the regular lessons, you could apply 100 points and deduct 4 points for each misspelled word to get a percent grade.

Tests for Review Lessons may again be ascribed 100 points, with each word or abbreviation counting 2 points. Make sure that pupils understand that they need to write the abbreviations only for the specified words.

The basic goal of Rod and Staff spelling courses is to help pupils master the spelling of the words in the word lists. Therefore, scores from the spelling tests should be given more weight on the final grades than scores from the regular work in the lessons.

Word List

Alphabetized List of Latin Roots

This list contains all the Latin roots taught in *Spelling by Sound and Structure,* Grade 7. Each root is followed by its meaning and the number of the lesson in which it is taught.

ag, act (do, set in motion) 13
ann (year) 5
aqua (water) 31
beat (bless) 3
bi (two, twice) 11
bos (ox, cow) 27
can (dog) 27
cap (head) 25
cap, cip, cept (seize, take) 33
carn (flesh) 25
cede, ceed, cess (go, yield) 22
cent (hundred, hundreth) 11
cid (fall) 32
cid, cis (cut, kill) 32
circum (around) 21
clam (cry out) 7
cor, cord (heart) 25
corp (body) 25
cred (believe) 4
dec (ten, tenth) 11
di (day) 5
dic, dict (say) 8
doc (teach) 10
duc (lead) 20
duo (two) 11
empt, em (take, buy) 19
equ (horse) 27
fac, fic (make, do) 14
fel (cat) 27
fer, lat (bear, carry) 20
fess (speak, admit) 7
fid (trust) 4
fili (son, child) 26
fini (end, limit) 2
flex, flect (bend) 17
frater, fratr (brother) 26
grad, gress (walk, step) 23
initi (beginning, start) 2
juven (young) 28
lat (bear, carry) 20
later (side) 20
leg, lect (choose, gather) 33
leg (law) 33
lig (bind) 16
loc (place [noun]) 23
lun (moon) 5
man (hand) 25
mand (order) 33
mater, matr (mother) 26
medi (middle) 2
mill (thousand, thousandth) 11
mit, miss (send, let go) 22
monit (remind, warn) 4
mov, mob, mot (move) 13
multi (many) 11
nav (ship) 31
novem (nine) 11
oct (eight) 11
oper (work) 14
par (appear) 9
pater, patr (father) 26
pel, puls (drive, push) 15
pend, pens (hang, weigh) 19
plic, plex (fold) 17
port (harbor, gate) 31
pos, pon (put, place) 23
press (press) 17
quer, quest (ask, seek) 8
quad (four) 11
quart (fourth) 11
quin (five) 11
reg, rect (rule, straighten) 33
rupt (burst, break) 16
sacr (holy) 3
sanct (holy) 3
sci (know) 10
sect (cut) 32
semi (half) 11
sen (old) 28
sept (seven) 11
sequ, secut (follow) 20
sex (six) 11
sider, sir (star) 5
sol (sun) 5
solv, solu (loosen, free) 16
spec (look at) 9
spond, spons (pledge, answer) 8
stat, stit, sist (set up, stand) 23
sus (hog) 27
ten, tin, tain (hold) 16
tend, tens, tent (stretch) 17
tract, trah (pull, draw, drag) 15
tri (three) 11
uni (one) 11
vacc (cow) 27
ven, vent (come) 22
vert, vers (turn) 21
vid, vis (see) 9
volv, volu (roll) 21

Introduction

Have you ever heard of the word *unflattenable*? No, you will not find it in a dictionary. Nevertheless, if someone said that he had bought an *unflattenable* tire, you would immediately know what he meant, would you not?

Knowing the meanings of common roots and affixes is a great help to vocabulary building. Knowing how to spell common roots and affixes is a great help to correct spelling. In this book, therefore, two sections of each lesson (parts A and B) are devoted to the study of roots and affixes.

Part C in the lessons is a review section on phonetic and word-building concepts that are taught in earlier years of this spelling course. Part D is a section on the history of the English language. This last section explains some of the reasons for the modern spellings, pronunciations, and meanings of many English words.

Lesson 1—60 points (A–C)

LESSON 1

NEW WORDS

1. alley
2. brethren
3. briefest
4. canceled
5. embargoes
6. employees
7. engineering
8. enrolled
9. graduating
10. hoarse
11. hungrier
12. listening
13. liveliest
14. pulleys
15. quizzes
16. shepherds
17. straightened
18. tariff
19. threaten
20. vacancies

REVIEW WORDS

21. assure
22. children's
23. heretofore
24. typewriter
25. vice-president

A. UNEARTHING THE ROOTS

WORD ELEMENTS

Affixes

Prefixes	**Root**	**Suffixes**
re, com	mend	ation, s

recommendations

The diagram above shows how *word elements* are put together to make words. The basic element is the *root*; it contains the primary meaning of the word. Elements that can be attached to roots are called *affixes*. The affixes attached to the beginning of a root are *prefixes*, and those attached to the end of a root are *suffixes*.

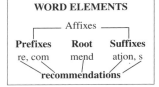

In this spelling book, you will study roots in part A of each lesson, and affixes (prefixes or suffixes) in part B of each lesson. Understanding how roots and affixes are spelled and how they are put together to form words is a great help in the study of spelling.

1. Many roots are easily recognized English words. Write the spelling words (New Words or Review Words) that have the following roots.

   a. listen e. hunger i. child
   b. straight f. quiz j. live
   c. roll g. brief k. cancel
   d. threat h. sure

2. Some words contain two roots put together. Write the spelling words with these roots.

   a. type + write b. sheep + herd

3. Some roots are less easy to recognize because they come from foreign languages. You will study a number of Latin roots in this spelling book. Write the spelling words with these roots.

   a. gin c. ploy
   b. vac d. grad

4. Write spelling words without affixes to match these clues.

   a. A homophone for *horse*.
   b. Means "narrow street between buildings."
   c. Means "before this time."
   d. Means "tax on imported goods."

A. 21 points

1. a. listening
   b. straightened
   c. enrolled
   d. threaten
   e. hungrier
   f. quizzes
   g. briefest
   h. assure
   i. children's
   j. liveliest
   k. canceled
2. a. typewriter
   b. shepherds
3. a. engineering
   b. vacancies
   c. employees
   d. graduating
4. a. hoarse
   b. alley
   c. heretofore
   d. tariff

Test Sentences

1. *brethren*	We need the advice of our *brethren*.
2. *enrolled*	Yesterday Kevin *enrolled* in our school.
3. *alley*	The narrow *alley* was littered with boxes.
4. *graduating*	Are you *graduating* from school soon?
5. *hungrier*	Soon James felt *hungrier* than ever.
6. *liveliest*	David's colt is the *liveliest* of all.
7. *listening*	Are you *listening* to this story?
8. *hoarse*	This morning I had a *hoarse* throat.
9. *briefest*	Tom's speech was the *briefest* of all.
10. *quizzes*	Brother Allen gave two *quizzes* this week.
11. *canceled*	We have *canceled* the meeting.
12. *engineering*	The bridge shows fine *engineering*.

B. AFFIXING AFFIXES

Some suffixes are *inflectional suffixes,* so called because they are used to make different inflections of words. They include the suffixes used to make plural forms, past forms, and forms of comparison.

1. Write the spelling words that are plural forms made in the following ways. If there is more than one answer, a number in parentheses tells how many words to write.
   a. By simply adding *-s*. (3)
   b. By adding *-es* after final *o*.
   c. By changing *y* to *i* and adding *-es*.
   d. By adding *-s* after *ey*.
   e. By doubling a final consonant before adding *-es*.
2. The suffix *-en* is an archaic plural ending. Which two spelling words have this suffix?
3. Write the plurals of *alley* and *tariff*.

Inflectional Suffixes

SUFFIX	MEANING	EXAMPLE
-s, -es	plural	girls, dishes
-'s	possession	child's
-s, -es	singular present	says, goes
-ed, -ing	past, progressive	cared, caring
-er, -est	forms of comparison	older, oldest

4. Write the spelling word with a suffix that shows possession.
5. Write NEW WORDS that are verb forms as described below.
   a. past forms (3)
   b. progressive (*-ing*) forms (3)
6. Write the three NEW WORDS that are forms of comparison.
7. Write the REVIEW WORD that ends with *-er* but is not a form of comparison.

B. 22 points
1. a. employees, pulleys, shepherds
   b. embargoes
   c. vacancies
   d. pulleys
   e. quizzes
2. brethren, children's
3. alleys, tariffs
4. children's
5. a. canceled, enrolled, straightened
   b. engineering, graduating, listening
6. briefest, hungrier, liveliest
7. typewriter

C. SOUND, STRUCTURE, AND MEANING

1. Write the spelling words in which you hear these sounds.
   a. /k/ and /s/ both spelled *c* (2)
   b. /ē/ spelled *ie* (2)
   c. /j/ spelled *d*
   d. /îr/ spelled *eer*
   e. /sh/ spelled *ss*
2. a. Write the NEW WORD in which double letters spell /l/ after /a/ in an accented syllable.
   b. In which NEW WORD do you see *ll* after /o͝o/ in an accented syllable?
3. Final /f/ is often spelled *ff* even in an unaccented syllable. Write the NEW WORD that illustrates this pattern.

The spelling of a compound word may be open (with a space), hyphenated (with a hyphen), or closed (with no space).

4. Write the REVIEW WORD that is
   a. a closed two-part compound.
   b. a hyphenated compound.
   c. a closed three-part compound.
5. Which spelling words have these meanings?
   a. Short oral tests.
   b. To cause to be confident.
   c. Wage earners.
6. One NEW WORD is an old plural form that is now used mainly in referring to the men in a church. Write this word.

7

C. 17 points
1. a. canceled, vacancies
   b. briefest, vacancies
   c. graduating
   d. engineering
   e. assure
2. a. alley
   b. pulleys
3. tariff
4. a. typewriter
   b. vice-president
   c. heretofore
5. a. quizzes
   b. assure
   c. employees
6. brethren

13.	*employees*	Only five *employees* worked Saturday.
14.	*pulleys*	We lifted the heavy bricks with *pulleys*.
15.	*straightened*	She *straightened* the tablecloth.
16.	*shepherds*	Angels told the *shepherds* about Jesus.
17.	*tariff*	The Dutch ship paid a heavy *tariff*.
18.	*heretofore*	Everyone *heretofore* has had a cold.
19.	*embargoes*	Nations often use *embargoes* in wartime.
20.	*typewriter*	A noisy *typewriter* disturbs my nap.
21.	*assure*	We *assure* you that we are honest.
22.	*threaten*	Do not *threaten* to hurt your puppy.
23.	*vice-president*	The *vice-president* spoke.
24.	*vacancies*	The motel had only two *vacancies* left.
25.	*children's*	Daisy was the *children's* pet goat.

D. LANGUAGE LINEAGE

GOD'S WORD NEVER CHANGES . . .

Old English, about A.D. 960

Fæðer ūre þū þe eart on heofonum, sī þīn nama gehālgod. Tō becume þīn rīce. Gewurþe ðīn willa on eorðan swā swā on heofonum. Ūrne gedæghwāmlīcan hlāf syle ūs tō dæg. And forgyf ūs ūre gyltas, swā swā wē forgyfað ūrum gyltendum. And ne gelæd þū ūs on costnunge, ac ālȳs ūs of yfele. Sōþlīce.

Wycliffe, A.D. 1382

Oure Fader that art in heuene, halewed be thi name. Thi kyngdom come to us. Thi wylle be don, as in heuene, and in erthe. Oure eche dayes breed yeue us to day. And foryeue us oure dettys, as we foryeue oure dettourys. And ne lede us not in temptacyon, but delyuere us of yuel. Amen.

Tyndale, A.D. 1534

O oure father which arte in heven, halowed be thy name. Let thy kyngdome come. Thy wyll be fulfilled, as well in erth, as it ys in heven. Geve vs thisdaye oure dayly breede. And forgeve vs oure treaspases, even as we forgeve oure trespacers. And leade vs not into temptacion: but delyver vs from evell. For thyne is the kyngedome and the power, and the glorye for ever. Amen.

King James, A.D. 1611

Our father which art in heauen, hallowed be thy name. Thy kingdome come. Thy will be done, in earth, as it is in heauen. Giue vs this day our daily bread. And forgiue vs our debts, as we forgiue our debters. And lead vs not into temptation, but deliuer vs from euill: For thine is the kingdome, and the power, and the glory, for euer, Amen.

. . . BUT MAN'S DOES

Languages change with time. Change is obvious in the excerpts above from English Bibles of the past. Yet each one expressed the unchanging, eternal Word of God to the people of its time.

Part D of each lesson discusses some of the changes that the English language has experienced. You will study the reasons for these changes and then see their influence on English as it is used today. First, however, you will study a few facts about language in general.

Exercises

1. For each word below, show how its spelling developed by giving the spellings used in the first three versions of the Lord's Prayer. *Example:* will. *Answer:* willa, wylle, wyll.
   a. Father b. heaven c. forgive d. lead
2. Writers spelled words in various ways before standard spellings were developed. The spellings *kyngdome* and *ys* appear in the excerpt from Tyndale's version. Copy a different spelling of each word from the same excerpt.
3. Long ago, *u* and *v* were different forms of the same letter. Many writers used *v* at the beginning of words and *u* within words. Give the modern spellings of *vs, deliuer,* and *euill,* which appear in the King James version as printed in 1611.

Teacher: Part D is an optional section. It may be used as an extra activity or assigned to the more able students.

D. 17 points
1. a. Fæder, Fader, father
   b. heofonum, heuene, heven
   c. forgyf, foryeue, forgeve
   d. gelæd, lede, leade
2. kyngedome, is
3. us, deliver, evil

Lesson 2—50 points (A–C)

LESSON 2

NEW WORDS

1. amateur
2. authority
3. aviator
4. circular
5. commence
6. decent
7. definite
8. director
9. employer
10. familiar
11. finance
12. infinite
13. initial
14. initiative
15. mediator
16. medieval
17. particular
18. passenger
19. superior
20. treasurer

REVIEW WORDS

21. business
22. cedar
23. medium
24. synagogue
25. transfer

A. UNEARTHING THE ROOTS

ROOT	MEANING	EXAMPLE
initi	beginning, start	initial
medi	middle	medium
fini	end, limit	finish

In this book you will study many Latin roots, which usually have three to five letters. Latin roots seldom appear alone in writing, because Latin words usually have inflectional suffixes like *-are* (an infinitive ending). So you will not find a root such as *medi* by itself in a dictionary etymology. Rather, the root is part of a Latin word like *mediare* or *medius*.

initi (in ish)

1. If a person lacks _____*, he finds it hard to begin a task. (*Note:* A star means the answer is a spelling word.)
2. An _____* is one of the beginning letters of your name.
3. If you c___* to do something, you start to do it. *Note:* The root *initi* is hard to recognize in this word. This is because the word began in Latin, became a French word, and later became an English word. You can see this by finding the word in the Speller Dictionary and reading its *etymology* (the word history in brackets).

medi

4. Three sizes of eggs are large, _____*, and small.
5. Since Christ is in the middle, between God and man, He is our _____*.
6. Things that happened during the Middle Ages are _____* events.
7. Choose from these words: *immediately, median, mediocre.*
   a. The grassy strip in the middle of an interstate highway is called the _____.
   b. If one event comes _____ after another, nothing comes in the middle, between the two events.
   c. A _____ job is of middle quality, neither very good nor very poor.

fini

8. Something _____* has clear limits; it is not general or vague.
9. God's wisdom is _____*; there is no limit to His understanding.
10. The word _____* suggests bringing a debt to an end by paying it.
11. Choose from these words: *confinement, final, fine.*
    a. A _____ test comes at the end of a school term.
    b. Prisoners are kept in _____; their freedom is strictly limited.
    c. A driver found guilty of speeding can end the matter by paying a _____.

A. 15 points

1. initiative
2. initial
3. commence
4. medium
5. mediator
6. medieval
7. a. median
   b. immediately
   c. mediocre
8. definite
9. infinite
10. finance
11. a. final
    b. confinement
    c. fine

See page 18 for test sentences.

B. AFFIXING AFFIXES

Remember that an inflectional suffix changes the inflection of a word. A *derivational suffix* usually changes a word from one part of speech to another. There are many more derivational suffixes than inflectional suffixes.

act—action (verb to noun)
stone—stony (noun to adjective)
neat—neatly (adjective to adverb)

Starting in this lesson, all the suffixes that you will study are derivational suffixes.

1. Write spelling words with the Latin suffix *-or* to match these definitions.
   a. One who directs.
   b. One who aviates.
   c. One who mediates.
   d. One who is above another person.
2. In one New Word, the Latin suffix *-or* changed to *-eur* when the word passed through French. Write this word.
3. As a noun-forming suffix, *-ar* is somewhat rare in the English language. Use that spelling to complete the following nouns.
   a. schol__ b. li__ c. calend__

Noun-forming Suffixes

SUFFIX	MEANING	EXAMPLE
-or	one who or	radiator
-ar	that which	beggar

4. The suffix *-ar* is more common as an adjective-forming suffix with the meaning "pertaining to" or "characteristic of." Write the spelling words with these meanings.
   a. Pertaining to a particle; detailed.
   b. Characteristic of a family; well known.
   c. Pertaining to a circle.
5. Write the Review Word in which final *ar* is not a suffix.
6. The Anglo-Saxon (native English) form of *-or* or *-ar* is *-er*. Write the New Words that have these meanings.
   a. One who keeps the treasury.
   b. One who employs.
   c. One who makes a passage; traveler.

B. 15 points
1. a. director
   b. aviator
   c. mediator
   d. superior
2. amateur
3. a. scholar
   b. liar
   c. calendar
4. a. particular
   b. familiar
   c. circular
5. cedar
6. a. treasurer
   b. employer
   c. passenger

C. SOUND, STRUCTURE, AND MEANING

1. Write the spelling words in which you hear these sounds.
   a. /oi/ spelled *oy* within the word
   b. final /it/ spelled *ite* (2)
   c. /iz/ spelled *usi*
2. Which spelling word has
   a. /i/ spelled *y* and /g/ spelled *gue*?
   b. the suffix *-ity* after *-or*?
3. Add the suffix *-ing* to *finance* and *transfer*.
4. Write spelling words that are synonyms of these words.
   a. proper b. pilot
   c. begin d. intercessor
5. Write the spelling word that is a homophone for *seeder.*
6. In what three ways may the last syllable of *amateur* be pronounced?
7. What is the special meaning of *infinite* in the phrase "the Infinite"? (Use the Speller Dictionary if you need help.)
8. The word *medium* has two plural forms, one English and one Latin. Write these two plurals.
9. Give another spelling of the New Word that means "of the Middle Ages."

C. 20 points
1. a. employer
   b. definite, infinite
   c. business
2. a. synagogue
   b. authority
3. financing, transferring
4. a. decent
   b. aviator
   c. commence
   d. mediator
5. cedar
6. /tûr/, /cho͝or/, or /chər/
7. God
8. mediums, media
9. mediaeval

Test Sentences

1.	*decent*	We expect *decent* manners at the table.
2.	*transfer*	Ann will *transfer* her church membership.
3.	*passenger*	The *passenger* train travels at night.
4.	*amateur*	My father is an *amateur* artist.
5.	*employer*	Ben's *employer* demands quality work.
6.	*infinite*	Who can understand God's *infinite* love?
7.	*mediator*	Jesus is the *mediator* between God and men.
8.	*authority*	We accept the *authority* of the Bible.
9.	*treasurer*	Uncle Henry is the *treasurer* of the board.
10.	*commence*	The meeting will *commence* at 7:00 P.M.
11.	*synagogue*	Jairus was a ruler of the *synagogue*.
12.	*superior*	This story is *superior* to the first one.

D. LANGUAGE LINEAGE

THE MIRACLE OF LANGUAGE

Verbal communication is a miracle. When a sheep opens its mouth, we expect to hear *Baa!*—nothing more. But when a man opens his mouth and starts talking, he may produce forty or more different sounds.

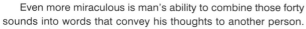

Even more miraculous is man's ability to combine those forty sounds into words that convey his thoughts to another person. Imagine one animal trying to tell another about Jesus' death on the cross nearly two thousand years ago. Both vocabulary and comprehension would be lacking. Speech is indeed a miracle of God's creation, a gift to those who are made in His own image.

There is another miracle related to language. Originally all men spoke the same language. But one day at Babel, in a single stroke of judgment, God confused man's language. Words that once were familiar now became strange. Suddenly many people had a completely new vocabulary. A miracle indeed!

From Babel's confusion, there has come a multiplicity of languages, which today totals nearly three thousand. And within those languages there are several thousand dialects. The country of India alone has about two hundred different languages and more than seven hundred dialects.

Today, English is the most widely spoken language, and Spanish is the second most widely used. Besides these, there are at least thirteen different languages that have 50 million or more speakers. Some languages have only a few thousand or even a few hundred speakers.

Exercises

1. Describe at least three miracles related to language.
2. What two things do animals lack, which make them unable to communicate as man does?
3. A language is a standardized system of words and word arrangements by which people communicate. What is a dialect? (Use a dictionary for help.)
4. Which is the most widely spoken language in the world? Which language is the second most widely used?

D. 12 points (Essay-type answers are worth 2 points each.)
1. (Any three.) Man is able to make forty or more distinct speech sounds. He is able to combine those sounds into words that have meaning. He can use words to express his thoughts to others. Man's language was confused by a single stroke of God's judgment at Babel.
2. vocabulary and comprehension
3. A dialect is a variation of a standard language that is used by a certain group of people.
4. English; Spanish

13. *circular*	The planets travel in *circular* orbits.
14. *cedar*	Put the quilt into the *cedar* chest.
15. *medieval*	Castles remind us of *medieval* times.
16. *director*	Mr. Peters is *director* of the hospital.
17. *particular*	No *particular* person came to mind.
18. *familiar*	My horse knows the *familiar* road home.
19. *initial*	The *initial* cost was ten dollars.
20. *medium*	Is the coat a *medium* or large size?
21. *aviator*	The young *aviator* climbed into his plane.
22. *initiative*	A good leader has strong *initiative*.
23. *finance*	The *finance* charge was $450.
24. *definite*	Sarah could not give a *definite* answer.
25. *business*	Do not meddle into another's *business*.

LESSON 3

NEW WORDS

1. Beatitudes
2. Calvary
3. Christendom
4. complexion
5. condemnation
6. confusion
7. discussion
8. fashionable
9. indebtedness
10. opinion
11. possession
12. resurrection
13. sacrifice
14. sacrilege
15. sanctification
16. sanctuary
17. separation
18. session
19. suggestion
20. worldliness

REVIEW WORDS

21. attack
22. freedom
23. Gethsemane
24. machinery
25. worthy

A. UNEARTHING THE ROOTS

ROOT	MEANING	EXAMPLE
sacr	holy	sacred
sanct	holy	sanctify
beat	bless	beatitude

sacr

1. Christ offered Himself as a holy ____* for our redemption.
2. Two of Aaron's sons died because they committed ____* by offering "strange fire" before the Lord.
3. Make an adjective by attaching *-ious* to *sacrilege*. (Be sure to drop the final *e*.) Remember that the word you wrote is a form of *sacrilege*. It is **not** made by joining *sac* and *religious*.
4. Choose from these words: *consecrate, sacrament, sacred.*
   a. Communion is a ____ ordinance observed in memory of Jesus' death.
   b. Christian ordinances are important, but none of them is a ____ that will make anyone holy.
   c. The blood of animals was used to ____ Old Testament priests for holy service to God.

sanct

5. The holy place in the tabernacle was called the ____*.
6. Christians are called to ____*, which is a life of holiness.
7. Choose from these words: *sanctimony, sanction, sanctity.*
   a. We respect the ____ of human life because God created man in His own image.
   b. Making a show of religion is not holiness; it is ____.
   c. God will never ____ a life of sin.

beat (bē at)

8. In Matthew 5 we can read the ____*, which are nine blessings pronounced by Jesus.
9. Choose from these words: *beatific, beatify.*
   a. A person who feels blessed may wear a ____ smile.
   b. After a person dies, the Catholic Church may ____ him by declaring him a blessed one worthy of public religious honor.

12

Lesson 3—56 points (A–C)

A. 14 points
1. sacrifice
2. sacrilege
3. sacrilegious
4. a. sacred
   b. sacrament
   c. consecrate
5. sanctuary
6. sanctification
7. a. sanctity
   b. sanctimony
   c. sanction
8. Beatitudes
9. a. beatific
   b. beatify

Test Sentences

1. *Calvary*	Jesus hung between two thieves at *Calvary*.
2. *fashionable*	Tea was served in a *fashionable* parlor.
3. *attack*	Our dog likes to *attack* woodchucks.
4. *sanctuary*	We entered the *sanctuary* reverently.
5. *condemnation*	Sin is under God's *condemnation*.
6. *freedom*	Anabaptists desired *freedom* of worship.
7. *Beatitudes*	Jesus gave the *Beatitudes* on a mountain.
8. *resurrection*	Jesus' *resurrection* gave hope.
9. *Gethsemane*	In *Gethsemane*, Jesus prayed alone.
10. *separation*	Hannah faced *separation* from Samuel.
11. *possession*	Never let a *possession* master you.
12. *machinery*	Heavy *machinery* rattled up the slope.

B. AFFIXING AFFIXES

Noun-forming Suffixes		
SUFFIX	MEANING	EXAMPLE
-ion	state of, quality or condition of, act of	confusion
-ation		adoration

1. Write spelling words with the Latin suffix *-ion* to match these definitions.
   a. An act of discussing.
   b. The condition of being separated.
   c. The state of being confused.
   d. An act of suggesting.
   e. The state of possessing.
   f. The act of resurrecting.
2. Sometimes the meaning of a derived form is not very close to the meaning of the root. Write New Words ending with *-ion* that have these meanings.
   a. The appearance of the skin, especially that of the face.
   b. The result of thinking (opining).
   c. A meeting or class period.
3. In which New Word does the suffix *-able* follow *-ion*?
4. Use the suffix *-ation* to change *condemn* and *sanctify* to nouns.
5. The English equivalent of *-ion* or *-ation* is *-ness* or *-dom*. Add *-ness* or *-dom* to these words, changing their spellings as needed.
   a. free d. Christian
   b. good e. worldly
   c. worthy f. indebted
6. The second *n* in *condemn* is silent but is heard in *condemnation*. Write the words indicated, noting the same pattern in them.
   a. hymn + al c. autumn + al
   b. solemn + ity d. column + ist

C. SOUND, STRUCTURE, AND MEANING

1. Write the spelling words in which you hear these sounds.
   a. /ksh/ spelled *xi*
   b. /ûr/ spelled *or* after /w/ (2)
   c. /g/ and /j/ both spelled *g*
2. a. In which word does *ch* spell /sh/?
   b. In which word does *ch* spell /k/?
3. Write the three words in which /sh/ is spelled *ss*. What three-letter suffix follows this spelling?
4. Write the spelling word in which /r/ is spelled *rr*. How many sets of double letters are in this word?
5. Which New Word means "a parting; division"? Which little word comes in the middle of this word—*par* or *per*?
6. Write spelling words that are proper nouns suggested by these phrases.
   a. The place of a skull.
   b. An olive grove.
   c. All professing Christians.
7. Write the spelling word that belongs with each group.
   a. departure, cleavage, division
   b. conversation, argument, conference
   c. assault, ambush, onslaught

B. 22 points
1. a. discussion
   b. separation
   c. confusion
   d. suggestion
   e. possession
   f. resurrection
2. a. complexion
   b. opinion
   c. session
3. fashionable
4. condemnation, sanctification
5. a. freedom
   b. goodness
   c. worthiness
   d. Christendom
   e. worldliness
   f. indebtedness
6. a. hymnal
   b. solemnity
   c. autumnal
   d. columnist

C. 20 points
1. a. complexion
   b. worldliness, worthy
   c. suggestion
2. a. machinery
   b. Christendom
3. discussion, possession, session; *-ion*
4. resurrection; one
5. separation; par
6. a. Calvary
   b. Gethsemane
   c. Christendom
7. a. separation
   b. discussion
   c. attack

13. *discussion*	Class *discussion* was lively today.
14. *complexion*	Sue's dark *complexion* tans easily.
15. *worthy*	Only God is *worthy* of our highest love.
16. *suggestion*	Do you have a *suggestion* to offer?
17. *opinion*	In your *opinion*, which tractor is best?
18. *session*	The morning *session* seemed to drag by.
19. *indebtedness*	His *indebtedness* made him labor earnestly.
20. *Christendom*	Not all *Christendom* honors Christ.
21. *sanctification*	Jesus is our *sanctification*.
22. *confusion*	Dan's room was a *confusion* of clutter.
23. *sacrifice*	Job offered a *sacrifice* for his sons.
24. *worldliness*	Godliness and *worldliness* cannot mix.
25. *sacrilege*	Joking about holy things is *sacrilege*.

D. LANGUAGE LINEAGE

THE ORIGIN OF WRITING

Egyptian

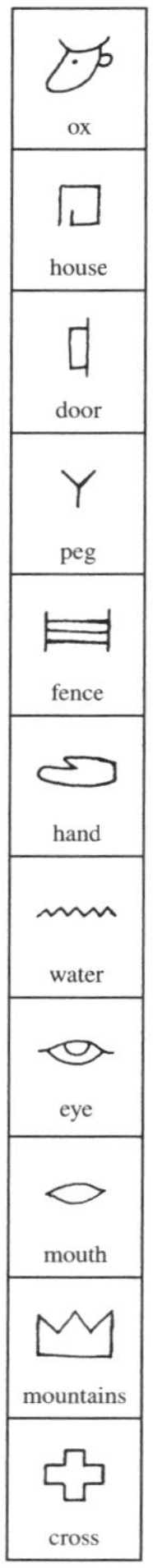

American Indian

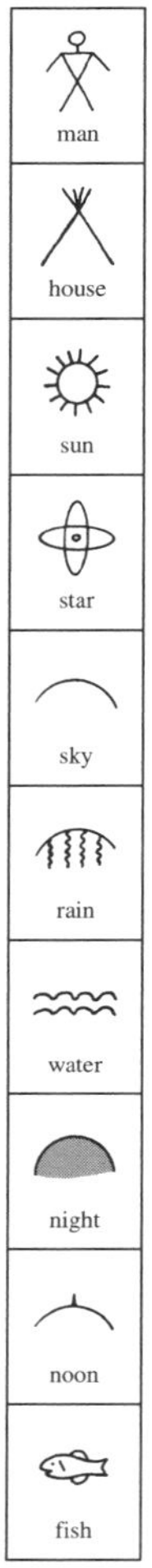

We know that from the Creation, man had the God-given gift of speech. Adam's conversation with God in the Garden of Eden shows that his speech was well developed too; it was not mere grunts and gestures as some think.

But did Adam and Eve write? There is no way of knowing. In the Bible, writing is first mentioned in connection with Moses, who lived about 1500 B.C. (Exodus 17:14). Archeologists have also found written records of the Sumerians, which are thought to precede even Abraham's time. Whether writing existed before the Flood is simply not known.

Man and his speech were created in a mature form, but the written form of language appears to have developed gradually. The earliest or least developed type of writing is called pictographic writing. It is simply the use of word pictures: drawing a tree or a cow to indicate a tree or a cow. This type of writing was used by ancient people such as the Sumerians, Babylonians, Egyptians, and Chinese. In more recent times pictographic writing was used by the American Indians.

Gradually the pictographs were simplified. They looked less and less like the objects they represented. Finally they were only symbols that were associated with certain objects, rather than actual pictures of those objects. These symbols became the forerunners of the letters that eventually were used to spell words as we do today.

Exercises

1. How is the origin of writing different from the origin of speech?
2. Describe the basic idea behind pictographic writing.
3. What are two of the problems that a person would face in using a system of pictographic writing?
4. What two things happened as ancient pictographs were simplified and no longer looked like actual pictures?

D. 12 points
1. Man and his speech were created in a mature form, but writing appears to have developed gradually.
2. A picture of an object is used to indicate that object.
3. (Sample answers.) Most words cannot be represented by pictures. A reader may not understand the meaning of a pictograph. Thousands of different pictographs would be needed.
4. The pictographs became symbols associated with objects, rather than actual pictures of objects. These symbols became the forerunners of letters that eventually were used to spell words.

LESSON 4

NEW WORDS

1. admonition
2. appearance
3. attendance
4. conference
5. confidence
6. credence
7. credential
8. credible
9. creed
10. emergency
11. faithfully
12. fidelity
13. ignorance
14. monitor
15. monument
16. nuisance
17. ordinance
18. penitence
19. residence
20. summon

REVIEW WORDS

21. cheerful
22. experience
23. independence
24. miracles
25. who'd

A. UNEARTHING THE ROOTS

ROOT	MEANING	EXAMPLE
fid	trust	confide
cred	believe	credit
monit	remind, warn	admonish

fid

1. "It is better to trust in the LORD than to put ____* in man" (Psalm 118:8).
2. "Not purloining, but shewing all good ____*" (Titus 2:10).
3. The spelling of the Latin root *fid* changed to *faith* when it passed through the French language. Write the NEW WORD that has this form of the root.
4. From 1 Timothy 5:8, copy a word that has the prefix *in-* (not), the root *fid,* and the meaning "one who does not have faith."

cred

5. Something ____* is worthy of being believed.
6. A statement of religious belief is a ____*.
7. We must not give ____* to a questionable report until it has been proven true.
8. A consistent life is a person's best ____* for having others believe that he is a real Christian.
9. Do not confuse *credible* (believable) with *credulous* (believing easily; gullible). Write the correct word for each sentence.
   a. A ____ person is easily deceived.
   b. The story of Jesus' resurrection has been established by many ____ witnesses.
   c. Father was not so ____ as to believe everything that the salesman said.

monit

10. The act of warning someone is an ____*.
11. Which NEW WORD means "an object set up to remind"?
12. Which NEW WORD originally meant "to warn secretly" and now means "to order (someone) to come"?
13. A ____* is someone who keeps watch and gives warning if something goes wrong.

15

Lesson 4—65 points (A–C)

A. 15 points
1. confidence
2. fidelity
3. faithfully
4. infidel
5. credible
6. creed
7. credence
8. credential
9. a. credulous
   b. credible
   c. credulous
10. admonition
11. monument
12. summon
13. monitor

See page 24 for test sentences.

B. AFFIXING AFFIXES

1. Write spelling words with the Latin suffix *-ance* to match these definitions.
   a. The act of attending.
   b. The quality of being troublesome.
   c. The act of appearing.
   d. The state of not knowing.
2. Which word ending with *-ance* has the meaning "ordained rule or practice"?
3. Write spelling words ending with *-ence* for these definitions.
   a. The act of conferring.
   b. The state of not depending on others.
   c. The condition of repenting.
   d. The state of residing.
   e. The condition of having had actual practice.
   f. The act of believing.
   g. The state of feeling assured.
4. Which word has the suffix *-ency* instead of *-ence*?

Noun-forming Suffixes

SUFFIX	MEANING	EXAMPLE
-ance	state of, quality or condition of, act of	appearance
-ence		penitence

To remember the spelling of a certain word, it is often helpful to think of how another form of the word is spelled.

5. The rule above applies when deciding whether the ending /əns/ should be spelled *ance* or *ence*. Which spelling word is helpful for spelling the suffix of *credence*?
6. For each word, write a spelling word that is a different form of it.
   a. resident d. confident
   b. attendant e. ignorant
   c. penitent f. independent
7. Write spelling words with these suffixes.
   a. *-ion* b. *-or* c. *-ity*

C. SOUND, STRUCTURE, AND MEANING

1. Write the spelling words in which you hear these sounds.
   a. /o͞o/ spelled *ui*
   b. /yə/ spelled *u*
   c. final /sē/ spelled *cy*
   d. /o͞o/ spelled *o*
2. Write the spelling words that have these spellings of /îr/.
   a. ir c. ear
   b. er d. eer
3. *Penitence* emphasizes being sorry for sin, but *repentance* emphasizes turning away from sin. For each Bible verse, write whether *penitence* or *repentance* applies better to the person described.
   a. 1 Kings 21:27 b. Ezra 10:6
   c. Ezekiel 33:15 d. Galatians 1:23
4. Write these spelling words. Beside each one, write a single-word synonym from the Speller Dictionary.
   a. monument c. experience
   b. nuisance d. penitence
5. Write a spelling word to match each pair.
   a. freedom, liberty
   b. counsel, warning
   c. trust, assurance
   d. believable, reliable
   e. happy, joyous
   f. loyally, steadfastly
6. One NEW WORD has the original meaning "act of sitting back" (from *re-* back and *sid* sit). Write this word.

Test Sentences

1. *ignorance* Through *ignorance* the damage was done.
2. *credential* Education is a necessary *credential* for a nurse.
3. *residence* Do I call his *residence* or his office?
4. *nuisance* Mosquitoes are a *nuisance* to us.
5. *admonition* The minister's *admonition* is heeded.
6. *monitor* Grandpa's heart *monitor* was stable.
7. *summon* Please *summon* help right away.
8. *creed* Can you explain your *creed* to an unbeliever?
9. *appearance* We appreciate your neat *appearance*.
10. *cheerful* Your *cheerful* smile brightened my day.
11. *monument* A tall *monument* honors Washington.
12. *credible* Can Matthew's strange story be *credible*?

B. 23 points
1. a. attendance
   b. nuisance
   c. appearance
   d. ignorance
2. ordinance
3. a. conference
   b. independence
   c. penitence
   d. residence
   e. experience
   f. credence
   g. confidence
4. emergency
5. credential
6. a. residence
   b. attendance
   c. penitence
   d. confidence
   e. ignorance
   f. independence
7. a. admonition
   b. monitor
   c. fidelity

C. 27 points
1. a. nuisance
   b. monument
   c. emergency
   d. who'd
2. a. miracles
   b. experience
   c. appearance
   d. cheerful
3. Persons are identified in parentheses for the teacher's reference.
   a. penitence (Ahab)
   b. penitence (Ezra)
   c. repentance (wicked man)
   d. repentance (Paul)
4. a. monument, memorial
   b. nuisance, annoyance
   c. experience, occurrence
   d. penitence, contrition
5. a. independence
   b. admonition
   c. confidence
   d. credible
   e. cheerful
   f. faithfully
6. residence

D. LANGUAGE LINEAGE

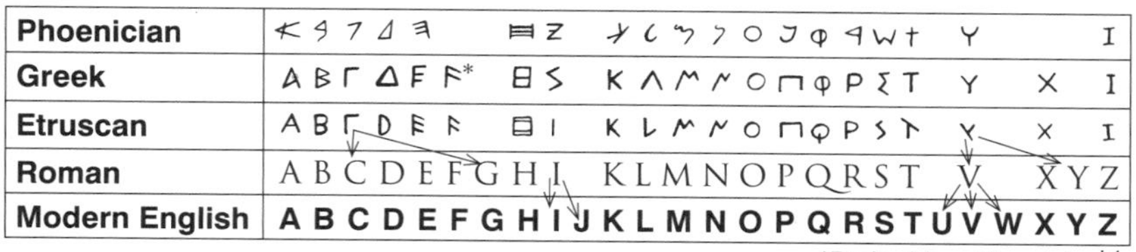
Phoenician
Greek
Etruscan
Roman
A B C D E F G H I K L M N O P Q R S T V X Y Z
Modern English
A B C D E F G H I J K L M N O P Q R S T U V W X Y Z

*Derived from Phoenician Y

DEVELOPMENT OF THE ALPHABET

As time passed, pictographic writing gradually changed from distinct pictures to more abstract characters. This led to *ideographic writing,* in which ideas as well as objects were indicated with signs or symbols. But it still took thousands of symbols to put man's speech in written form.

Next came the development of *syllabic writing,* in which a different symbol stood for each spoken syllable. The cuneiform of the Sumerians is one kind of syllabic writing. But this system still required a great number of symbols, though the number was reduced from thousands to hundreds.

The simplest form of writing is *alphabetic writing.* In this system, letters are used to stand for speech sounds in words. Alphabetic writing requires only a small number of symbols, yet any spoken word can be represented in writing.

Alphabetic writing was first used by the Phoenicians, who lived north of Palestine. No one knows for sure how they developed this method. But scholars think that Phoenician letters first stood for entire words; then someone got the idea of using each symbol for a different speech sound.

The chart above shows the development of the alphabet that we use today.

Exercises

1. For each description, write *pictographic, ideographic, syllabic,* or *alphabetic.*
   a. An object is represented by a picture.
   b. Each spoken sound in a word is represented by a symbol.
   c. An object or an idea is represented by a symbol.
   d. Each word part is represented by a symbol.
2. a. Which people were the first ones known to use alphabetic writing?
   b. According to scholars, how did they develop this method?
3. In the Modern English alphabet,
   a. which two letters come from the Greek and Etruscan Γ?
   b. which two letters come from the Roman I?
   c. which five letters come from the Phoenician Y?

D. 16 points
1. a. pictographic
   b. alphabetic
   c. ideographic
   d. syllabic
2. a. the Phoenicians
   b. Symbols that first stood for whole words came to be used as symbols for speech sounds.
3. a. C, G
   b. I, J
   c. F, U, V, W, Y

13. *experience*	Job's *experience* of suffering purified him.
14. *attendance*	Was the church *attendance* large?
15. *ordinance*	Baptism is a God-given *ordinance*.
16. *emergency*	In an *emergency*, try to think calmly.
17. *independence*	America declared *independence* in 1776.
18. *conference*	I enjoyed the *conference* for poets.
19. *miracles*	Jesus did many *miracles* of healing.
20. *faithfully*	Jesus *faithfully* cares for us.
21. *who'd*	Linda was the one *who'd* been absent.
22. *confidence*	Gideon's *confidence* was in God.
23. *penitence*	Susan knelt in *penitence* and wept.
24. *fidelity*	Christians declare *fidelity* to Christ.
25. *credence*	Jesus' life gave *credence* to His words.

Lesson 5—63 points (A–C)

LESSON 5

NEW WORDS

1. achievement
2. adjournment
3. anniversary
4. annually
5. carriage
6. commitment
7. consideration
8. desiring
9. development
10. diary
11. lunar
12. management
13. meridian
14. perennial
15. pilgrimage
16. solar
17. Colossians Col.
18. Isaiah Isa.
19. Jeremiah Jer.
20. Thessalonians Thess.

REVIEW WORDS

21. announcement
22. calendar
23. current
24. journey
25. rural

A. UNEARTHING THE ROOTS

ROOT	MEANING	EXAMPLE
ann	year	annual
di	day	diary
sol	sun	solar
lun	moon	lunar
sider, sir	star	consider

ann

1. Hannah and her husband went to Shiloh ____* to offer sacrifices (1 Samuel 2:19).
2. A date that returns every year is an ____*.
3. A ____* plant lives through the whole year. (The prefix *per-* means "through.")

di

4. The word ____* looks much like *dairy.* You can distinguish the two words by noting the *di* root in this New Word.
5. The sun reaches its ____* at noon.
6. The Latin root *di* changed to *jour* when it passed through the French language. Write the two spelling words with this root.
7. Choose from these words: *diurnal, journal.*
   a. Another name for a diary is a ____.
   b. Many wild animals are nocturnal (active at night), but a few are ____.

sol (sōl)

8. A ____* eclipse is an eclipse of the sun.
9. Choose from these words: *solarium, solstice.*
   a. The ____ was warmed by the rays of the sun.
   b. At the winter ____, the sun "stands still" in its southward course; then it begins returning north.

lun (lo͞on)

10. A ____* eclipse is an eclipse of the moon.
11. In the past, emotionally disturbed persons were called lunatics because they were thought to be disturbed by the ____.

sider, sir

12. In giving ____* to plans for the future, some people seek guidance from the stars through the heathen practice of astrology.
13. Instead of seeking God's blessing, people who use astrology are ____* a favorable sign from the stars.

A. 16 points
1. annually
2. anniversary
3. perennial
4. diary
5. meridian
6. adjournment, journey
7. a. journal
   b. diurnal
8. solar
9. a. solarium
   b. solstice
10. lunar
11. moon
12. consideration
13. desiring

Test Sentences

1. *desiring*	At Pentecost, many were *desiring* baptism.
2. *announcement*	Your *announcement* surprised us.
3. *pilgrimage*	A Christian's *pilgrimage* ends in heaven.
4. *development*	A baby's *development* is exciting.
5. *achievement*	Reading is a big *achievement.*
6. *solar*	God created our immense *solar* system.
7. *rural*	They live in a quiet *rural* area.
8. *adjournment*	The *adjournment* is at a late hour.
9. *consideration*	Take facts into *consideration.*
10. *diary*	Never read a *diary* without permission.
11. *calendar*	Check your *calendar* for the date.
12. *anniversary*	My parents' *anniversary* is today.

B. AFFIXING AFFIXES

1. Write spelling words with the Latin suffix *-ment* to match these definitions.
   a. The act of achieving.
   b. The state of being adjourned.
   c. The act of developing.
   d. The condition of being committed.
   e. The act of announcing.
2. Look at your answers to exercise 1. Two of them show that when a suffix begins with a consonant, final *e* is (dropped, retained).
3. Add *-ment* to these words.
   a. excite b. state c. advertise
4. The English equivalent of *-ment* is *-age*. Add *-age* to these words, changing their spellings as needed.
   a. pilgrim c. lever
   b. carry d. marry
5. Which spelling word has both *-age* and *-ment*?

Noun-forming Suffixes

SUFFIX	MEANING	EXAMPLE
-ment	state of, quality or condition of, act of	amazement

6. Write the spelling words that have these noun-forming suffixes.
   a. *-ar* b. *-ent* c. *-ation*
7. In which two NEW WORDS does the suffix *-ans* mean "inhabitants of"?
8. Write the spelling words that end with these adjective-forming suffixes.
   a. *-al* (2) b. *-ar* (2)
9. Which word with the suffix *-an* means "line indicating degrees of longitude"?
10. Write spelling words ending with *-ary* for these.
    a. A book for recording daily events.
    b. A date celebrated every year.

C. SOUND, STRUCTURE, AND MEANING

1. Write the spelling words in which you hear these sounds.
   a. final /ij/ spelled *iage*
   b. final /ə/ spelled *ah* (2)
   c. /ûr/ spelled *ur*; spelled *urr*
2. In which NEW WORD is /ēv/ spelled *ieve*? Observe that this word follows the "*i* before *e*" pattern.
3. Write *development* without the *-ment* suffix. Observe that neither form has an *e* after the *p*.
4. Write the plural forms of *diary, journey,* and *anniversary*.
5. For each reference, copy the abbreviation and then write the book name in full.
   a. Jer. 17:9 c. Col. 1:18
   b. Isa. 53:6 d. 2 Thess. 3:10
6. Which spelling words have these meanings?
   a. Table of days, weeks, and months.
   b. A promise; pledge.
   c. A declaration; public notification.
7. a. What is the meaning of the name Isaiah?
   b. What is the meaning of Jeremiah?
8. The names Colossians and Thessalonians are derived from what city names?

13. *perennial* Often, *perennial* flowers bloom first.
14. *lunar* Have you ever seen a *lunar* eclipse?
15. *annually* The trustees meet *annually* in April.
16. *current* May I have your *current* price list?
17. *management* Ben's choices show good *management*.
18. *carriage* The polished *carriage* rolled along.
19. *journey* Our *journey* to Alaska was interesting.
20. *meridian* The prime *meridian* crosses Europe.
21. *commitment* He made a firm *commitment* to Christ.

For numbers 22–25, write the words *and* their abbreviations.

22. *Colossians* *Col.* Paul wrote *Colossians* in prison.
23. *Isaiah* *Isa.* The prophet *Isaiah* foretold Jesus' death.
24. *Jeremiah* *Jer.* Some call *Jeremiah* the weeping prophet.
25. *Thessalonians* *Thess.* Paul exhorted the *Thessalonians*.

B. 26 points
1. a. achievement
   b. adjournment
   c. development
   d. commitment
   e. announcement
2. retained
3. a. excitement
   b. statement
   c. advertisement
4. a. pilgrimage
   b. carriage
   c. leverage
   d. marriage
5. management
6. a. calendar
   b. current
   c. consideration
7. Colossians, Thessalonians
8. a. perennial, rural
   b. lunar, solar
9. meridian
10. a. diary
    b. anniversary

C. 21 points
1. a. carriage
   b. Isaiah, Jeremiah
   c. rural; current
2. achievement
3. develop
4. diaries, journeys, anniversaries
5. a. Jer., Jeremiah 17:9
   b. Isa., Isaiah 53:6
   c. Col., Colossians 1:18
   d. 2 Thess., 2 Thessalonians 3:10
6. a. calendar
   b. commitment
   c. announcement
7. a. Salvation of God
   b. God loosens
8. Colossae and Thessalonica

D. LANGUAGE LINEAGE

THERE ARE OTHER ALPHABETS

The modern English alphabet is not the only one in existence. Below is a chart showing several others.

The ancient Hebrew alphabet is closely related to the Phoenician alphabet. It even preceded the Greek alphabet. The forms shown here are the modern Hebrew and Greek alphabets.

The Arabic alphabet was developed from the Aramaic alphabet, which was based on the Phoenician alphabet. The Koran is written with the Arabic alphabet; and because of the spread of Islam, this is one of the most widely used alphabets today.

The origin of the runic alphabet is uncertain. The oldest runic inscriptions known are thought to have been written in the A.D. 200s. This alphabet was used by people whose descendants would later develop the English language.

The Russian alphabet is a modified form of the Cyrillic alphabet used by many Slavs. The Cyrillic alphabet was developed from the Greek alphabet in the A.D. 800s. The Russian alphabet has been adapted to correspond more closely to the Roman alphabet. It has thirty-two letters.

Hebrew	א בּ ב ג ד ה ו ז ח ט י כּ כ ל מ נ ס ע פּ פ צ ק ר שׁ שׂ ת
Greek	Α Β Γ Δ Ε Ζ Η Θ Ι Κ Λ Μ Ν Ο Π Ρ Σ Τ Υ Φ Χ Ψ Ω
Arabic	ا ب ت ث ج ح خ د ذ ر ز س ش ص ض ط ظ ع غ ف ق ك ل م ن ه و ي
Runic	ᚠ ᚢ ᚦ ᚩ ᚱ ᚳ ᚷ ᚹ ᚻ ᚾ ᛁ ᛄ ᛇ ᛋ ᛏ ᛒ ᛖ ᛗ ᛚ ᛝ ᛟ ᛞ ᚪ ᚫ ᚣ ᛠ
Russian	А Б В Г Д Е Ё Ж З И Й К Л М Н О П Р С Т У Ф Х Ц Ч Ш Щ Ъ Ы Ь Э Ю Я

Exercises

1. Compare this section with Lesson 4, part D.
   a. The Hebrew alphabet is related to which alphabet that you studied in Lesson 4?
   b. The alphabet you named in *a* above is the ultimate source of (1) what four alphabets mentioned in Lesson 4? (2) what four alphabets (other than Greek) mentioned in this lesson?
2. Of what interest is the runic alphabet to English-speaking people of today?
3. Explain the relationship of the Russian alphabet to the Cyrillic and Roman alphabets.

D. 12 points
1. a. Phoenician
   b. (1) Greek, Etruscan, Roman, English
   (2) Arabic, Aramaic, Russian, Cyrillic
2. The runic alphabet was used by people whose descendants would later develop the English language.
3. The Russian alphabet is a modified form of the Cyrillic alphabet. The Russian alphabet was adapted to correspond more closely to the Roman alphabet.

Lesson 6—72 points (A–B)

LESSON 6

1	2	3	4	5
alley	amateur	Beatitudes	admonition	achievement
brethren	authority	Calvary	appearance	adjournment
briefest	aviator	Christendom	attendance	anniversary
canceled	circular	complexion	conference	annually
embargoes	commence	condemnation	confidence	carriage
employees	decent	confusion	credence	commitment
engineering	definite	discussion	credential	consideration
enrolled	director	fashionable	credible	desiring
graduating	employer	indebtedness	creed	development
hoarse	familiar	opinion	emergency	diary
hungrier	finance	possession	faithfully	lunar
listening	infinite	resurrection	fidelity	management
liveliest	initial	sacrifice	ignorance	meridian
pulleys	initiative	sacrilege	monitor	perennial
quizzes	mediator	sanctification	monument	pilgrimage
shepherds	medieval	sanctuary	nuisance	solar
straightened	particular	separation	ordinance	Colossians Col.
tariff	passenger	session	penitence	Isaiah Isa.
threaten	superior	suggestion	residence	Jeremiah Jer.
vacancies	treasurer	worldliness	summon	Thessalonians Thess.

A. UNEARTHING THE ROOTS

initi	beginning, start	***fid***	trust
medi	middle	***cred***	believe
fini	end, limit	***monit***	remind, warn
		ann	year
sacr	holy	***di***	day
sanct	holy	***sol***	sun
beat	bless	***lun***	moon
		sider, sir	star

21

See page 116 for test sentences.

1. The word element that contains the primary meaning of a word is the ____.
2. Write the correct terms.
   a. Any word element attached to a root.
   b. An element attached to the end of a root.
   c. An element attached to the beginning of a root.
3. Write the Lesson 1 words that have these English roots.
   a. quiz c. roll
   b. straight d. threat
4. Write the Lesson 1 words that have these Latin roots.
   a. gin b. vac

L2: initi, medi, fini

Note: The letters in brackets are the foreign root.

5. A beginning letter is an ____*.
6. The word c___*, meaning "begin," contains the *initi* root, even though it is hard to recognize.
7. People of the 1300s lived in ____* times.
8. Something ____* has no limits.
9. To "finish (a large purchase) by providing money for it" is to ____* it.

L3: sacr, sanct, beat

10. A Christian should present himself as "a living ____*, holy, acceptable unto God" (Romans 12:1).
11. Write the word that means "act of profaning something holy." Also write the *-ious* form of this word, being sure to spell it correctly.
12. The word ____* can mean either "holy place" or "place of protection."
13. "For this is the will of God, even your [sanct]*" (1 Thessalonians 4:3).
14. The nine "blessings" in Matthew 5 are called the ____*.

L4: fid, cred, monit

15. "In quietness and in [fid]* shall be your strength" (Isaiah 30:15).
16. The spelling of the *fid* root changed when it passed through the French language. This is evident in the word f___*.
17. Answer with three different words. We should follow the [cred]* of giving [cred]* to a person who proves himself [cred]*.
18. Write Lesson 4 words with the *monit* root and these affixes.
    a. *ad-* b. *-ment* c. *-or*

L5: ann, di, sol, lun, sider–sir

19. Most crops must be planted ____* (every year). Crops that are ____* (living through the year) do not require yearly planting.
20. A book for writing daily happenings may be called a d___* or a j___.
21. The second answer to exercise 20 contains *jour*, the French form of the *di* root. Write a Lesson 5 word that also contains *jour*. Then write another word with the same root that means "trip."
22. Write the answers. A word in parentheses indicates a root with that meaning.
    a. (sun) + ar = ____*
    b. (moon) + ar = ____*
    c. de + (star) + ing = ____*
23. Before making major decisions, ancient kings had their astrologers observe the positions of the stars. Careful thought about a decision is known today as ____*.

A. 39 points

1. root
2. a. affix
   b. suffix
   c. prefix
3. a. quizzes
   b. straightened
   c. enrolled
   d. threaten
4. a. engineering
   b. vacancies
5. initial
6. commence
7. medieval
8. infinite
9. finance
10. sacrifice
11. sacrilege, sacrilegious
12. sanctuary
13. sanctification
14. Beatitudes
15. confidence
16. faithfully
17. creed, credence, credible
18. a. admonition
    b. monument
    c. monitor
19. annually, perennial
20. diary, journal
21. adjournment, journey
22. a. solar
    b. lunar
    c. desiring
23. consideration

B. AFFIXING AFFIXES

Numbers in brackets are lesson numbers.

1. In each phrase, write correctly the word that should be a plural or possessive form.
   a. The aviator skill. c. Some old diary.
   b. A set of pulley. d. Two oral quiz.
2. Write the past form of each verb.
   a. listen c. commence
   b. cancel d. enroll
3. Write two forms of comparison for each.
   a. brief c. hungry
   b. hoarse d. lively
4. a. What English suffix is the equivalent of *-or* or *-ar*? [2]
   b. In which spelling word does this suffix have the French form *-eur*? [2]
5. Use the correct suffixes to form words that mean "one who
   a. mediates." [2] c. directs." [2]
   b. employs." [2] d. tells lies."
6. When *-ar* is used to form ____, it means "pertaining to or characteristic of." [2]

Inflectional Suffixes	
-s, -es	plural
-'s	possession
-s, -es	singular present
-ed, -ing	past and progressive
-er, -est	forms of comparison
Noun-forming Suffixes	
-or, -ar, -er	one who *or* that which
-ion, -ation, -ance, -ence, -ment	state of, quality or condition of, act of

7. Attach *-ar* to form adjectives from these.
   a. circle [2] c. particle [2]
   b. family [2] d. single
8. Form spelling words by combining each word with the correct noun-forming suffix.
   a. separate [3] d. ignore [4]
   b. suggest [3] e. confer [4]
   c. appear [4] f. commit [5]

Six-week review lessons have no part C.

D. LANGUAGE LINEAGE

1. The different versions of the Lord's Prayer illustrate what truth about all languages?
2. Describe two miracles related to language.
3. How is the origin of writing different from the origin of speech?
4. a. Name four systems of writing.
   b. Tell which system is the simplest to use, and why it is the simplest.
5. Name four alphabets that were forerunners of the Modern English alphabet.
6. What old alphabet was used by ancestors of the earliest English-speaking people?

B. 33 points
1. a. aviator's
   b. pulleys
   c. diaries
   d. quizzes
2. a. listened
   b. canceled
   c. commenced
   d. enrolled
3. a. briefer, briefest
   b. hoarser, hoarsest
   c. hungrier, hungriest
   d. livelier, liveliest
4. a. *-er*
   b. amateur
5. a. mediator
   b. employer
   c. director
   d. liar
6. adjectives
7. a. circular
   b. familiar
   c. particular
   d. singular
8. a. separation
   b. suggestion
   c. appearance
   d. ignorance
   e. conference
   f. commitment

D. 20 points
1. All languages change.
2. (Any two.) Man is able to make forty or more speech sounds. He can combine those sounds into words that have meaning. He can use words to express his thoughts. Man's language was confused by God at Babel.
3. Man's speech was created in a mature form, but writing appears to have developed gradually.
4. a. pictographic, ideographic, syllabic, alphabetic
   b. alphabetic; Only a small number of symbols are needed to write any word.
5. Phoenician, Greek, Etruscan, Roman
6. runic alphabet

LESSON 7

NEW WORDS

1. aboard
2. accordingly
3. accumulate
4. administration
5. admiration
6. approximately
7. arising
8. assignment
9. association
10. assortment
11. assumed
12. attitude
13. clamor
14. confession
15. controlled
16. faint
17. parallel
18. proclaim
19. professional
20. professor

REVIEW WORDS

21. abroad
22. appreciate
23. canceled
24. earnest
25. hungrier

A. UNEARTHING THE ROOTS

ROOT	MEANING	EXAMPLE
clam	cry out	clamor
fess	speak, admit	confess

clam

1. The ____* in the room was so great that conversation was almost impossible.
2. The spelling of the Latin root *clam* changed to *claim* when it passed through the ____ language. (See the etymology of *proclaim* in the Speller Dictionary.)
3. "Most men will ____* every one his own goodness: but a faithful man who can find?" (Proverbs 20:6).
4. Choose from these words: *acclaim, disclaimer, exclamatory, proclamation, reclaim.*
   a. If a sentence is declarative, it simply makes a statement; but if it is ____, the sentence "cries out."
   b. The people gave Herod great ____, declaring that he was a god and not a man (Acts 12:21–23).
   c. Abraham Lincoln issued a ____ declaring freedom for the slaves in the Confederate States.
   d. The Dutch work hard to ____ land from the sea.
   e. The advertisement included a ____ saying that the pills were not guaranteed to work for everyone.

fess

5. "For with the heart man believeth unto righteousness; and with the mouth ____* is made unto salvation" (Romans 10:10).
6. The ____* gave his lecture in a ____* way.
7. Other forms of *fess* are *fab, fam,* and *fat*. Choose from these words for the sentences below: *fable, famous, fatal, ineffable.*
   a. Many people were talking about the ____ event.
   b. A ____ is an imaginary story that is told and retold.
   c. The driver's mistake resulted in a ____ accident. (This word originally had the idea of "decreed by fate.")
   d. Heaven is a place of ____ (unspeakable) glory.

Lesson 7—55 points (A–C)

A. 15 points
1. clamor
2. French
3. proclaim
4. a. exclamatory
   b. acclaim
   c. proclamation
   d. reclaim
   e. disclaimer
5. confession
6. professor, professional
7. a. famous
   b. fable
   c. fatal
   d. ineffable

Test Sentences

1. *association*	An *association* bought our land.
2. *clamor*	Every morning the kittens *clamor* to be fed.
3. *professor*	A *professor* could answer the question.
4. *aboard*	Happily everyone climbed *aboard* the train.
5. *canceled*	School was *canceled* because of snow.
6. *assortment*	Grandma had an *assortment* of fruit.
7. *confession*	David's *confession* won our respect.
8. *admiration*	Job had a deep *admiration* for God.
9. *abroad*	Last year the Martins traveled *abroad.*
10. *earnest*	God answered Elijah's *earnest* prayer.
11. *accordingly*	It was rainy; *accordingly*, we played inside.
12. *hungrier*	The calves grew *hungrier* every minute.

B. AFFIXING AFFIXES

Prefixes change the meanings of roots or even make the meanings completely opposite.

done—redone (means "done again")

done—undone (means "not done")

1. Write the spelling words that contain these elements.
   a. ad + min   b. ad + mir

To simplify pronunciation, the end of a prefix is often changed to make it similar to the beginning of a root. This change is called *assimilation*.

ad + ply = apply (*not* adply)

in + port = import (*not* inport)

2. Write the spelling words that contain these elements.
   a. ad + sort   c. ad + cor
   b. ad + sum   d. ad + cum

PREFIX	MEANING	EXAMPLE
ad-	at, to, toward	advance

   e. ad + preti   g. ad + soci
   f. ad + prox   h. ad + sign
3. Look at the five words listed in Part A, exercise 4. Which word contains an assimilated form of *ad-* and a form of the *clam* root?
4. The English equivalent of the Latin *ad-* is *a-*. Attach *a-* to these words.
   a. board   d. cross
   b. rising   e. flame
   c. light   f. sleep
5. Use *-ion* or *-ation* to write words with these meanings.
   a. Act of admiring.
   b. Act of confessing.
   c. Act of associating.
   d. Act of appreciating.

C. SOUND, STRUCTURE, AND MEANING

1. Write the spelling words in which you hear these sounds.
   a. /sh/ spelled *ss* before *-ion* (2)
   b. /l/ spelled *ll* and then *l*
   c. /īn/ spelled *ign*
2. Two spelling words are past forms ending with *led*.
   a. Which word has a double *l* because the last syllable is accented?
   b. Which word has a single *l* because the last syllable is not accented?
3. Which REVIEW WORD is a comparative form of a word that ends with *y*?
4. Which word may mean "one who claims to hold a certain belief" or "an instructor in a college"? How many sets of double letters are in this word?
5. Certain words in dictionaries have usage labels such as *Archaic*. Which NEW WORD has the archaic meaning "to become weary and discouraged"?
6. Write the spelling word that belongs with each pair.
   a. announce, declare
   b. leadership, management
   c. collection, mixture
7. Which spelling words are antonyms of these? (Words must be the same part of speech to be a true antonyms.)
   a. despise   d. halfhearted
   b. exactly   e. contempt
   c. revive   f. silence

25

B. 21 points
1. a. administration
   b. admiration
2. a. assortment
   b. assumed
   c. accordingly
   d. accumulate
   e. appreciate
   f. approximately
   g. association
   h. assignment
3. acclaim
4. a. aboard
   b. arising
   c. alight
   d. across
   e. aflame
   f. asleep
5. a. admiration
   b. confession
   c. association
   d. appreciation

C. 19 points
1. a. confession, professional
   b. parallel
   c. assignment
2. a. controlled
   b. canceled
3. hungrier
4. professor; one
5. faint
6. a. proclaim
   b. administration
   c. assortment
7. a. appreciate
   b. approximately
   c. faint
   d. earnest
   e. admiration
   f. clamor (*also accept* proclaim)

13.	*assumed*	Jerry *assumed* responsibility for the work.
14.	*controlled*	We carefully *controlled* our experiment.
15.	*appreciate*	All teachers *appreciate* smiles.
16.	*accumulate*	Do not desire to *accumulate* riches.
17.	*faint*	If you feel *faint*, lie down.
18.	*attitude*	Your *attitude* speaks louder than words.
19.	*administration*	The tyrant's *administration* was cruel.
20.	*approximately*	We parked *approximately* in the center.
21.	*parallel*	No *parallel* lines cross each other.
22.	*arising*	Few were *arising* at six o'clock.
23.	*proclaim*	Faithful ministers *proclaim* the Gospel.
24.	*assignment*	Our first *assignment* was an essay.
25.	*professional*	A health *professional* may help.

D. LANGUAGE LINEAGE

Semantic Study: GENERALIZATION

Semantics is the study of word meanings, and especially of how word meanings develop and change. You have probably noticed that in old writings, words are sometimes used in ways that would seem strange today. Probably the most familiar example of this is words used in the King James Bible. The reason that certain words no longer fit in a given context is that they have gone through semantic change.

The type of semantic change that you will study in this lesson is known as *generalization*. This is the process through which a word with a narrow, specific meaning becomes broader and more general in meaning. For example, the word *lady* as used long ago referred only to a woman of high social rank, such as one in a king's household. *Lady* is used for "queen" in Isaiah 47:5, 7. Today the word still applies particularly to a woman of nobility, but it is also used commonly in referring to any woman.

Below are several more words whose meanings have changed through generalization.

GENERALIZATION

Word	*Earlier meaning*	*Modern meaning*
cupboard	shelf for storing cups	any small closet with shelves
decimate	kill one out of every ten	kill or destroy a large portion
injury	violation of one's rights	any harm or damage
picture	painting	any visual representation on a flat surface, as a painting, drawing, or photograph
wretch	person in exile	any person in great misery

Exercises

1. Why do some words no longer have the meanings that they had long ago?
2. What is meant by the process of generalization?
3. Why is the word *ladies* more suitable than *women* in Judges 5:28, 29?
4. Explain the reasons for the earlier meanings of *cupboard* and *decimate*. Use a dictionary if you need help.

D. 10 points

1. Such words have gone through semantic change.
2. Generalization is the process by which a word with a narrow, specific meaning becomes broader and more general in meaning.
3. These were women of high social rank. (Sisera was an army captain.)
4. A cupboard was a "cup board" long ago. *Deci* in *decimate* refers to a tenth.

LESSON 8

NEW WORDS

1. benediction
2. contradiction
3. controversy
4. correspond
5. devise
6. indicate
7. indict
8. inquiries
9. liquid
10. obedience
11. oppose
12. procession
13. production
14. pronunciation
15. proposed
16. questionnaire
17. request
18. requirements
19. requisition
20. response

REVIEW WORDS

21. advertisement ad
22. contrary
23. dessert
24. examination exam
25. observation

A. UNEARTHING THE ROOTS

ROOT	MEANING	EXAMPLE
dic, dict	say	dictate
quer, quest	ask, seek	request
spond, spons	pledge, answer	respond

dic, dict

1. To say exactly what or which one is to ____*.
2. For which New Word is *blessing* a synonym and *cursing* an antonym?
3. In which spelling word is *dict* pronounced /dīt/?
4. "Consider him that endured such ____* of sinners against himself" (Hebrews 12:3).
5. What word with the *dict* root names a common reference book that gives the definitions of words?

quer, quest

6. The following analogy is read, "*Request* is to *requisition* as *question* is to what?" Answer with a New Word.
   request : requisition :: question : ____*
7. Write the three New Words in which the *quer, quest* root is spelled *quir* or *quis*.
8. "Always in every prayer of mine for you all making ____* with joy" (Philippians 1:4).
9. Choose from these words: *acquire, conquer, query.*
   a. We must seek to ____ bad habits.
   b. To ____ true wisdom, we should ask for it from God.
   c. The Pharisees came to Jesus with a ____ about paying taxes.

spond, spons

10. When Jesus' enemies tried to trap Him with a trick question, He always gave an excellent ____*.
11. Saul's words did not ____* with the sounds that Samuel was hearing (1 Samuel 15:13, 14).
12. Choose from these words: *despondent, responsible, sponsor.*
    a. A ____ person can give answers about a task assigned to him.
    b. A ____ is someone who pledges to support a person or cause.
    c. If you give up hope about a pledge, you may become ____.

Lesson 8—55 points (A–C)

A. 18 points
1. indicate
2. benediction
3. indict
4. contradiction
5. dictionary
6. questionnaire
7. inquiries, requirements, requisition
8. request
9. a. conquer
   b. acquire
   c. query
10. response
11. correspond
12. a. responsible
    b. sponsor
    c. despondent

See page 36 for test sentences.

B. AFFIXING AFFIXES

PREFIX	MEANING	EXAMPLE
contra-	against	contradict
ob-	against	obstruct
pro-	for, forth, forward	proceed

1. Write the spelling word that has *contra-* and means "act of speaking against."
2. Which word has the general meaning "inclined to be against"?
3. Another spelling of *contra-* is *contro-*. Write the NEW WORD that has this spelling.
4. Which spelling word contains *ob-* and the Latin root *serv* (to watch)?
5. One NEW WORD means "act of listening to" (ob + audi + ence). However, the vowel in the root is changed to *e*. Write this word.
6. In which NEW WORD did *ob-* become *op-* through assimilation?
7. Use assimilation to spell words by joining *ob-* to the following roots.
   a. cur b. fend c. press
8. Write spelling words with the prefix *pro-* to match these definitions.
   a. A manner of speaking forth words.
   b. A group of persons going forward.
   c. Set forth for consideration.
   d. An act of giving forth or yielding.
9. Make other words by joining *pro-* with these roots. All the words you write have the idea of "forth" or "forward."
   a. ject d. gress
   b. mote e. clam (claim)
   c. pel f. trude

C. SOUND, STRUCTURE, AND MEANING

1. Write the spelling words in which you hear these sounds.
   a. /n/ spelled *nn*
   b. /p/ spelled *pp*
   c. final /əns/ spelled *ence*
2. Write the word that ends with /īz/. Remember: /īz/ may be spelled *ise* or *ize*, but never *ice*.
3. Write *device* or *devise* for each sentence.
   a. A clock is a ____ for keeping time.
   b. Darius tried hard to ____ a way to save Daniel from the lions.
4. *Math* is a shortened form of *mathematics*. Write the full words for these shortened forms.
   a. ad c. exam
   b. bike d. phone
5. Make an open compound by combining *production* with *mass*.
6. Write spelling words with these meanings.
   a. Things required; necessities.
   b. Act of pronouncing a blessing.
   c. The condition of being required.
7. Write *desert* or *dessert* for each sentence.
   a. We have ____ after the main course.
   b. God will never ____ His children.
8. *Indict* is a homophone of *indite,* which means "write." Write *indicted* or *indited* for each sentence.
   a. Menno Simons was ____ for his beliefs.
   b. He ____ a poem about his conversion.

B. 19 points
1. contradiction
2. contrary
3. controversy
4. observation
5. obedience
6. oppose
7. a. occur
   b. offend
   c. oppress
8. a. pronunciation
   b. procession
   c. proposed
   d. production
9. a. project
   b. promote
   c. propel
   d. progress
   e. proclaim
   f. protrude

C. 18 points
1. a. questionnaire
   b. oppose
   c. obedience
2. devise
3. a. device
   b. devise
4. a. advertisement
   b. bicycle
   c. examination
   d. telephone
5. mass production
6. a. requirements
   b. benediction
   c. requisition
7. a. dessert
   b. desert
8. a. indicted
   b. indited

Test Sentences

1. *liquid*	Any *liquid* can be poured.
2. *requirements*	Obey God's *requirements* gladly.
3. *observation*	Nature *observation* is rewarding.
4. *benediction*	A prayer of *benediction* was given.
5. *obedience*	True *obedience* comes from the heart.
6. *contradiction*	There is no *contradiction* in the Bible.
7. *inquiries*	Teachers answer many *inquiries* daily.
8. *oppose*	We must firmly *oppose* evil.
9. *controversy*	The *controversy* ended peacefully.
10. *procession*	The *procession* went to the cemetery.
11. *request*	King Solomon made a wise *request*.
12. *correspond*	Sarah and Judy *correspond* by mail.

D. LANGUAGE LINEAGE

LANGUAGE FAMILIES

Languages are like families. They have immediate family members as well as other relatives, both near and distant. Like human families, language families also have their own peculiar traits. By noting the similarities and dissimilarities, linguists have divided the languages of the world into families.

The accuracy of these divisions is somewhat uncertain, however, especially as it relates to the original or "parent" languages. We know that in the beginning, God gave man only one language. But how many and which languages originated at Babel, and how similar they were to each other, we do not know. We do know that those languages have gradually changed and divided. People speaking the same language became separated, and as they settled in isolated areas, their language slowly changed until each group had a related yet distinctly different language.

Below is a graph showing approximate percentages of the world's population that use the more common language families. English belongs to the Indo-European family. From the chart beside the graph, can you guess which languages belong to the same family?

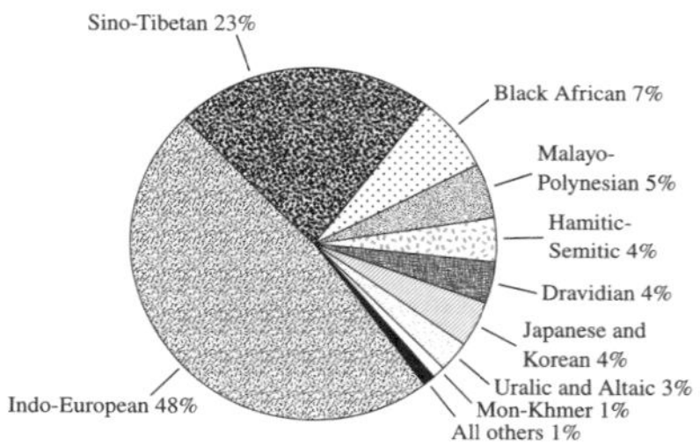

ENGLISH	father	mother	day	night
SPANISH	padre	madre	día	noche
ITALIAN	padre	madre	giorno	notte
FRENCH	père	mère	jour	nuit
GERMAN	Vater	Mutter	Tag	Nacht
SWEDISH	fader	moder	dag	natt
FINNISH	isä	äiti	päivä	yö
ESTONIAN	isa	ema	päev	öö
HEBREW	ab	em	yom	layela
ARABIC	ab	omm	yom	leil

Exercises

1. In what two ways are languages like families?
2. Why is the accuracy of language divisions somewhat uncertain?
3. Besides the miracle at Babel, what is another reason for the different languages of today?
4. The words on the chart can be grouped into three different language families.
   a. How many other languages are in the same family as English? Which other languages have strong similarities in these basic words?
   b. What language is in the same family as Estonian? as Hebrew?

13. *production* Their milk *production* has increased.
14. *dessert* Mother made a lemon *dessert* for supper.
15. *response* The eager *response* cheered the teacher.
16. *devise* Can you *devise* a better plan?
17. *pronunciation* Proper *pronunciation* is good.
18. *requisition* Queen Esther made *requisition* for the Jews.
19. *indicate* Please *indicate* your choice of color.
20. *proposed* Father *proposed* a plan to us.
21. *contrary* Spot is our most *contrary* cow.
22. *indict* False witnesses tried to *indict* Jesus.
23. *questionnaire* Fill out this *questionnaire*.

For numbers 24 and 25, write the words *and* their clipped forms.

24. *advertisement* *ad* Leo saw an *advertisement* for a dog.
25. *examination* *exam* Jerry's last *examination* seemed hard.

D. 11 points

1. Languages have immediate family relations as well as distant relatives. Language families have their own peculiar traits.
2. It is not known how many and which languages originated at Babel, nor how similar those languages were to each other.
3. People speaking the same language became separated, and their language gradually changed until each group had developed a different language of its own.
4. a. five
   b. Finnish; Arabic

Teacher: The first six languages on the chart are in the Indo-European family; Finnish and Estonian are in the Ural-Altaic family; and Hebrew and Arabic are in the Hamitic–Semitic family.

LESSON 9

NEW WORDS

1. abnormal
2. abscess
3. absolute
4. accomplish
5. advise
6. apparent
7. desperate
8. despise
9. disappointment
10. discount
11. dismissal
12. evidence
13. expectation
14. inspect
15. interview
16. renown
17. spectator
18. visible
19. vision
20. visual

REVIEW WORDS

21. amateur
22. appearance
23. Beatitudes
24. principal
25. respectable

A. UNEARTHING THE ROOTS

ROOT	MEANING	EXAMPLE
spec	look at	inspect
vid, vis	see	vision
par	appear	apparent

spec

1. To ____* something is to look at it closely.
2. A ____* is one who looks at something that is happening.
3. If we are in ____* of something, we are looking out in anticipation of it.
4. A ____* person is someone that we can look up to.
5. Write the New Word in which *spec* became *spis* when it passed through French.
6. Choose from these words: *circumspectly, spectacle, suspect.*
   a. To ____ someone is to look at him in a distrustful way.
   b. "See then that ye walk ____" (Ephesians 5:15).
   c. "We are made a ____ unto the world" (1 Corinthians 4:9).

vid, vis

7. You have ____* when light from ____* objects enters your ____* organs (your eyes).
8. Faith is "the [vid]* of things not seen" (Hebrews 11:1). This is a paradox because faith operates without seeing.
9. Use these words: *advice, advise, adviser.*
   A good ____ will ____ his friend with good ____.
10. An alternate spelling of *vid* is *view*. Write the New Word that has this spelling.
11. Another form of *vid* is *vey*. Combine this form with the prefix *sur-* to form a word that means "look over."

par

12. If something is an ____* mistake, it has the ____* of being a mistake.
13. Choose from these words: *apparition, disappear, transparent.*
    a. Because we can see through glass, we say it is ____.
    b. The ____ that the disciples saw was Jesus walking on the sea.
    c. After the resurrection, Jesus would appear or ____ at will.

Lesson 9—67 points (A–C)

A. 22 points
1. inspect
2. spectator
3. expectation
4. respectable
5. despise
6. a. suspect
   b. circumspectly
   c. spectacle
7. vision, visible, visual
8. evidence
9. adviser, advise, advice
10. interview
11. survey
12. apparent, appearance
13. a. transparent
    b. apparition
    c. disappear

Test Sentences

1. *evidence*	His accusers found no *evidence* of evil.
2. *despise*	Jesus did not *despise* children.
3. *renown*	Moses was a leader of great *renown*.
4. *abnormal*	The spot was *abnormal* in color.
5. *dismissal*	After *dismissal*, Ruth walked home.
6. *visible*	Many stars become *visible* at night.
7. *abscess*	A painful wound may have an *abscess*.
8. *amateur*	Dale is an *amateur* wood carver.
9. *apparent*	It became *apparent* that we were lost.
10. *respectable*	Our homes should look *respectable*.
11. *spectator*	Lois was a *spectator* at the barn raising.
12. *absolute*	God's Word is *absolute* and unchanging.

B. AFFIXING AFFIXES

PREFIX	MEANING	EXAMPLE
ab-	away, from	abstain
dis-	away, apart	dismiss

1. Write spelling words beginning with *ab-* to match these definitions.
   a. Having no limits.
   b. Different from usual.
   c. Infected area. (The word originally referred to body fluids flowing to the area.)
2. Write more words with the prefix *ab-* by joining these elements.
   a. ab + hor   d. abs + tract
   b. ab + rupt   e. ab + use
   c. ab + duct   f. ab + sorb
3. Write spelling words beginning with *dis-* for these definitions.
   a. A sending away.
   b. To reckon away (part of a price).
4. The prefix *dis-*, like *un-*, may simply mean "not." Join *dis-* to the following words.
   a. like   d. appointment
   b. agree   e. loyalty
   c. trust   f. obedient
5. Write the spelling words that have *ad-* and other elements as shown. Some prefixes are assimilated.
   a. ad + par   d. ad + vis
   b. ad + pear   e. ad + com + pli
   c. dis + ad + point
6. Which Review Word has
   a. the plural suffix *-s*?
   b. the French form of *-or*?
   c. the adjective suffix *-al*?

C. SOUND, STRUCTURE, AND MEANING

1. Write the spelling words in which you hear these sounds.
   a. /yo͞o/ spelled *iew*
   b. /tûr/, /cho͝or/, or /chər/ spelled *teur*
   c. /īz/ spelled *ise* (2)
2. Write *visible, vision,* or *visual* for the blanks in this sentence.
   The boy's ____ handicap was not ____, but it seriously impaired his ____.
3. Write the spelling words that complete these analogies.
   a. Hearing : listener :: seeing : ____
   b. Town : mayor :: school : ____
   c. Load : lighten :: price : ____
   d. Honor : respect :: fame : ____
   e. Exodus : Ten Commandments :: Matthew : ____
4. Write *principal* or *principle* for these.
   a. The ____ of sowing and reaping is taught in Galatians 6:7.
   b. The interest paid on the ____ amounted to more than $100.
5. Which words have these meanings?
   a. To examine carefully.
   b. Unusual; irregular.
   c. A sending away.
   d. Supporting proof.
6. a. Divide *desperate* into syllables. (Use the Speller Dictionary for help.)
   b. The middle letters spell (par, per).

31

B. 25 points
1. a. absolute
   b. abnormal
   c. abscess
2. a. abhor
   b. abrupt
   c. abduct
   d. abstract
   e. abuse
   f. absorb
3. a. dismissal
   b. discount
4. a. dislike
   b. disagree
   c. distrust
   d. disappointment
   e. disloyalty
   f. disobedient
5. a. apparent
   b. appearance
   c. disappointment
   d. advise
   e. accomplish
6. a. Beatitudes
   b. amateur
   c. principal

C. 20 points
1. a. interview
   b. amateur
   c. advise, despise
2. visual, visible, vision
3. a. spectator
   b. principal
   c. discount
   d. renown
   e. Beatitudes
4. a. principle
   b. principal
5. a. inspect
   b. abnormal
   c. dismissal
   d. evidence
6. des/per/ate; per

13.	*expectation*	We await Christ's return with *expectation*.
14.	*appearance*	My *appearance* excited the birds.
15.	*accomplish*	Linda could usually *accomplish* her goals.
16.	*vision*	A blind man has no *vision*.
17.	*principal*	The school *principal* is Brother Yoder.
18.	*disappointment*	Samson was a *disappointment*.
19.	*Beatitudes*	Jesus gave the *Beatitudes* on a mountain.
20.	*discount*	Gary bought his shoes at a *discount*.
21.	*visual*	A giraffe's *visual* ability is amazing.
22.	*advise*	What would you *advise* me to do?
23.	*inspect*	Mr. Smith will *inspect* our building.
24.	*desperate*	He made a *desperate* attempt to escape.
25.	*interview*	The board will *interview* the teachers.

D. LANGUAGE LINEAGE

ENGLISH AND ITS RELATIVES

English is a member of the Indo-European language family. This is the largest of all language families. As the name suggests, its roots are found in the areas of India and Europe. Some of its branches have died out, but others have multiplied and became a wide array of different languages.

The diagram below shows the more widely known members in the Indo-European family of languages. There are also some less widely known members in the family, which are not shown.

Languages that are closely related are close together on the tree. The Frisian language is the one most closely related to English. Here is John 3:16 as it appears in Frisian.

> "Hwent sa ljeaf hat God de wrâld hawn, dat Er syn ienichstberne Soan jown hat, dat in elts dy't yn him leaut, net fordjerre, mar it ivige libben hawwe mei."

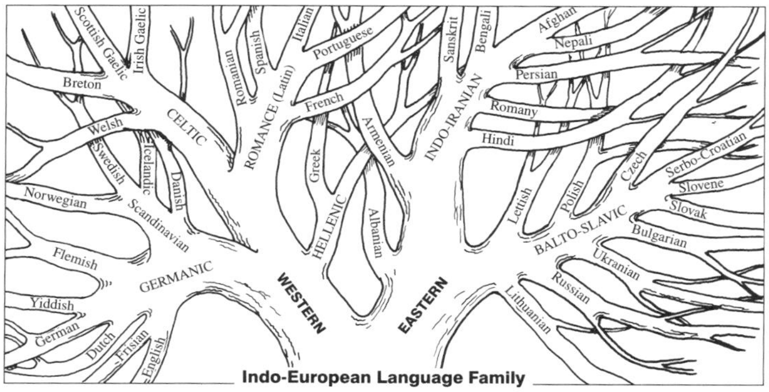

Indo-European Language Family

Exercises

1. What is the largest of all language families? How did this family receive its name?
2. Name the language that is the closest relative of English. Do you think you could easily converse with a speaker of this language? Explain.
3. Write the English form of these Frisian words.
   a. wrâld c. Soan
   b. dat d. net
4. Use the "family tree" to answer these questions.
   a. Besides Frisian, what are four other languages that are closely related to English?
   b. Which five languages developed from Latin?
   c. Which two languages in the eastern division are not closely related to any other languages? (Both start with *A*.)

D. 22 points
1. the Indo-European family; Its roots are found in the areas of India and Europe.
2. Frisian; no; The Frisian version of John 3:16 shows that there is considerable difference between the languages.
3. a. world
   b. that
   c. Son
   d. not
4. a. Dutch, German, Yiddish, Flemish
   b. Romanian, Spanish, Italian, Portuguese, French
   c. Armenian, Albanian

LESSON 10

NEW WORDS

1. acknowledge
2. advantageous
3. antecedent
4. anteroom
5. broadcast
6. conscience
7. conscientious
8. conscious
9. docile
10. doctrine
11. document
12. farewell
13. frequent
14. high school
15. kindergarten
16. moral
17. northwestern
18. prejudice
19. prevail
20. welfare

REVIEW WORDS

21. acquaint
22. everlasting
23. knowledge
24. overlook
25. separation

A. UNEARTHING THE ROOTS

ROOT	MEANING	EXAMPLE
sci	know	science
doc	teach	doctrine

sci

1. A person's (conscious, conscience) makes him feel guilty when he is (conscious, conscience) of having done wrong.
2. If a person heeds his ____* concerning how well he does his work, he is a ____* worker.
3. Use *un-*, *semi-*, *-ly*, and *-ness* with *conscious* to form words that fit in these sentences.
   a. Awareness of things inside or outside the mind is ____.
   b. When we dream at night, we are ____ (partly conscious).
   c. If a person has no awareness of anything, he is either asleep, ____, or dead.
   d. The boy was ____ trying to improve his handwriting.
4. Choose from these words: *omniscient, prescient, science.*
   a. Paul instructed Timothy to avoid "oppositions of ____ falsely so called" (1 Timothy 6:20).
   b. God is both ____ (knowing everything) and ____ (knowing beforehand).

doc

5. To be ____* means to be teachable.
6. The "doctors of the law" in Christ's day were men who (a) healed the Law; (b) taught the Law.
7. "Till I come, give attendance to reading, to exhortation, to ____* [teaching]" (1 Timothy 4:13).
8. Write the New Word that originally meant "lesson" but today means "written record that gives proof."
9. To indoctrinate someone means to (a) make him teachable; (b) make him a teacher; (c) teach him thoroughly.
10. A doctorate is (a) a degree from a university; (b) a license to teach; (c) a license to practice medicine.

33

Lesson 10—53 points (A–C)

A. 17 points
1. conscience, conscious
2. conscience, conscientious
3. a. consciousness
   b. semiconscious
   c. unconscious
   d. consciously
4. a. science
   b. omniscient, prescient
5. docile
6. b
7. doctrine
8. document
9. c
10. a

See page 42 for test sentences.

B. AFFIXING AFFIXES

PREFIX	MEANING	EXAMPLE
ante-	before	antecedent
pre-	before	premature

1. a. The word ____* has the idea of going before (ante + ced).
   b. This term is often used for a (noun, pronoun).
2. In one word, the Latin phrase *ab ante* ("from before") eventually became the spelling *advanta* in English. Write the New Word that contains this spelling.
3. Which New Word names a chamber in the front part of a building?
4. Give the answers.
   a. If Isaiah antedated Jeremiah, which prophet lived first?
   b. Antediluvian events occurred (before, after) the Flood of Noah's time.
   c. The abbreviation A.M. stands for the Latin phrase *ante meridiem* and refers to time in the (forenoon, afternoon).
5. Write spelling words beginning with *pre-* as suggested by these phrases.
   a. Judging before all the facts are known.
   b. Overcome by being stronger or more abundant.
6. Join *pre-* with the following words to make words that match the definitions below.
   caution occupation
   dawn position
   a. Happening before daybreak.
   b. Care taken beforehand so as to avoid harm or danger.
   c. The state of being absorbed by something that was in the mind beforehand.
   d. A common word coming before a noun.

B. 13 points
1. a. antecedent
   b. noun
2. advantageous
3. anteroom
4. a. Isaiah
   b. before
   c. forenoon
5. a. prejudice
   b. prevail
6. a. predawn
   b. precaution
   c. preoccupation
   d. preposition

C. SOUND, STRUCTURE, AND MEANING

1. Write the spelling words in which you hear these sounds.
   a. /shəs/ spelled *scious*
   b. /n/ spelled *kn* (2)
   c. /jəs/ spelled *geous*
   d. final /in/ spelled *ine*
   e. /kw/ spelled *cqu*
2. Do not confuse *moral, morale,* and *mortal.* Write the correct word for each sentence.
   a. Ahab received a ____ wound in a battle against Syria.
   b. The ten faithless spies did great harm to Israel's ____
   c. Stealing is a ____ offense.
3. Write the New Word that is an open compound. Then write the two closed compounds made from *fare* and *well.*
4. Write the spelling words that are antonyms of these.
   a. union c. headstrong
   b. rare d. notice
5. Write *advantage* and *advantageous*, dividing them into syllables. Show which syllable is accented in each word.
6. Write the compound word that contains
   a. cast. c. look.
   b. last. d. west.
7. Which word comes from two German words that mean "children" and "garden"?

C. 23 points
1. a. conscious
   b. acknowledge, knowledge
   c. advantageous
   d. doctrine
   e. acquaint
2. a. mortal
   b. morale
   c. moral
3. high school; farewell, welfare
4. a. separation
   b. frequent
   c. docile
   d. overlook
5. ad/van′/tage, ad/van/ta′/geous
6. a. broadcast
   b. everlasting
   c. overlook
   d. northwestern
7. kindergarten

Test Sentences

1.	*moral*	Stealing is breaking a *moral* law.
2.	*conscientious*	Joseph was very *conscientious*.
3.	*prevail*	Goliath could not *prevail* over David.
4.	*broadcast*	We must not *broadcast* a secret.
5.	*kindergarten*	She taught *kindergarten* at home.
6.	*document*	The *document* was signed by the mayor.
7.	*prejudice*	Jesus had neither *prejudice* nor pride.
8.	*acknowledge*	We *acknowledge* our weakness before God.
9.	*northwestern*	Oregon is a *northwestern* state.
10.	*high school*	Many students in *high school* study algebra.
11.	*advantageous*	Typing is an *advantageous* skill.
12.	*acquaint*	Did you *acquaint* yourselves with them?

D. LANGUAGE LINEAGE

DIALECTS

Not all speakers of a given language pronounce all their words alike. For example, the word *better* is pronounced (bet′ər) by people in some parts of the country; and in other parts the people say (bet′ə) or (bed′ə). For *process*, people in the United States generally say (pros′es), and those in Canada say (prō′ses). All these persons are speaking English, but each speaker uses a different *dialect* of English.

A dialect is the "flavor" that a certain group of people gives to a standard language. Dialects are generally more noticeable in speech than in writing because they mainly affect pronunciation. But since dialect also affects vocabulary, it can be observed in writing as well. For example, what Americans call a *biscuit* the British call a *scone*. The British use *biscuit* for what Americans call a *cookie* or a *cracker*.

Every person uses one dialect or another of a standard language. If there is only a small difference between two dialects, the speakers will have little difficulty understanding each other. But some dialects are so different that the speakers may as well be using two different languages. Such was the case in Germany at one time, when a speaker of High German from the South had great difficulty understanding a speaker of Low German from the North.

You have already learned that related languages developed from a single language. It seems that dialectal differences were the first stage in this development. The dialect of Latin that was used in France, for example, developed into the French language; the dialect used in Italy developed into Italian; and likewise for Spanish, Romanian, and Portuguese. New languages are not developing as rapidly today as they did long ago. Because of modern communications, the language of vast geographical areas is much more stable and more uniform today than was possible in times past.

Exercises

1. What is a dialect?
2. What two areas of language are chiefly affected by dialect?
3. Why must we not look down on a person just because his dialect is different from ours?
4. What part did dialects have in the development of new languages?

13. *welfare*	The *welfare* of each other is our goal.
14. *antecedent*	Which is the *antecedent* of this pronoun?
15. *knowledge*	God's *knowledge* is past finding out.
16. *anteroom*	Susan left her coat in the *anteroom*.
17. *frequent*	Washing dishes is a *frequent* task.
18. *docile*	Old Bess is a very *docile* horse.
19. *separation*	We must practice *separation* from the world.
20. *conscience*	Our *conscience* pricks us at times.
21. *overlook*	We should *overlook* minor faults.
22. *doctrine*	All true *doctrine* agrees with the Word.
23. *conscious*	She was *conscious*, though badly hurt.
24. *farewell*	Simon bade his guests *farewell*.
25. *everlasting*	Jesus gives *everlasting* life.

D. 8 points

1. A dialect is the "flavor" that a certain group of people gives to a standard language. It is a localized form of the language.
2. pronunciation and vocabulary
3. (Sample answers.) Every person uses one dialect or another of a standard language. Our dialect probably sounds as unusual to the other person as his dialect sounds to us.
4. It seems that different dialects gradually developed into different but related languages.

LESSON 11

NEW WORDS

1. biannual
2. biennial
3. biscuit
4. centipede
5. century
6. communion
7. decimal
8. dual
9. duplicate
10. millipede
11. multiplicity
12. octave
13. quartet
14. quintuple
15. semiconscious
16. septet
17. sextet
18. triplet
19. triune
20. unique

REVIEW WORDS

21. admonition
22. finance
23. proclaim
24. sacrifice
25. vacancies

A. UNEARTHING THE ROOTS

ROOT	MEANING	ROOT	MEANING
uni	one	*sept*	seven
duo	two	*oct*	eight
bi	two, twice	*novem*	nine
tri	three	*dec*	ten(th)
quad	four	*cent*	hundred(th)
quart	fourth	*mill*	thousand(th)
quin	five	*semi*	half
sex	six	*multi*	many

uni, duo, bi, tri

1. Write New Words to match these definitions.
   a. One and only.
   b. Twice per year.
   c. Living two years.
   d. One of two; a copy.
   e. Having two; double.
   f. One of three.
   g. Three in one.
2. Write the New Word that names a food and originally meant "twice cooked."

quad, quart, quin, sex

3. Write New Words to match these definitions.
   a. Group of four.
   b. Multiply by five.
   c. Group of six.
4. What is one-fourth of a gallon? One-fourth of a dollar?

sept, oct, novem, dec

5. Write New Words to match these definitions.
   a. A group of seven.
   b. Pertaining to ten or a tenth.
   c. A group of eight notes.
6. Name the months on our calendar that were the seventh, eighth, ninth, and tenth months on the old Roman calendar.

cent, mill, semi, multi

7. Write New Words to match these definitions.
   a. A period of one hundred years.
   b. A creature supposed to have one hundred feet.
   c. A creature supposed to have one thousand feet.
   d. Only partly aware of things ("half knowing").
   e. The condition of being very many.
8. Write the New Word in which the letters *uni* come not from the *uni* root but from the Latin word for *common*.

Lesson 11—64 points (A–C)

A. 26 points

1. a. unique
   b. biannual
   c. biennial
   d. duplicate
   e. dual
   f. triplet
   g. triune
2. biscuit
3. a. quartet
   b. quintuple
   c. sextet
4. quart, quarter
5. a. septet
   b. decimal
   c. octave
6. September, October, November, December
7. a. century
   b. centipede
   c. millipede
   d. semiconscious
   e. multiplicity
8. communion

Test Sentences

1. *dual*	Our tractor has *dual* wheels.
2. *admonition*	Ed's *admonition* humbled Sue.
3. *biennial*	Hollyhocks are *biennial* flowers.
4. *finance*	The company will *finance* cars for buyers.
5. *duplicate*	May I have a *duplicate* copy?
6. *proclaim*	We will *proclaim* a fast.
7. *biannual*	The *biannual* report was read.
8. *unique*	Penguins are *unique* birds.
9. *millipede*	How many legs does a *millipede* have?
10. *septet*	Seven people would make a *septet*.
11. *biscuit*	Would you like a *biscuit* with jam?
12. *triune*	God is a *triune* being.

B. AFFIXING AFFIXES

1. The Latin roots *bi* and *tri* are used as the English prefixes *bi-* and *tri-*. Join these prefixes with the words in parentheses to build words that fit in the sentences.
   a. A three-wheeled vehicle that children ride is a (cycle).
   b. Something involving both poles of the earth is (polar).
   c. A (partisan) agreement involves two parties.
   d. A figure with three corners is a (angle).
   e. A mollusk with two shells hinged together is a (valve).
   f. A tooth with three points is a (cuspid).
2. The roots *semi* and *multi* have also become English prefixes. Join *semi-* and *multi-* with the words in parentheses to build words that fit in the sentences.
   a. Wood is a (purpose) building material.
   b. We are (conscious) when we sleep.
   c. A (lingual) person should not have much trouble with language barriers.
   d. Some substances are neither liquid nor solid, but (solid).
   e. Silicon is a (conductor) used in electronic devices.
   f. We should not use a (syllable) word when a simple word is sufficient.
3. Make words by joining these roots and suffixes.

a. biannual + ly	d. sacrifice + ial
b. triune + ity	e. duplicate + or
c. finance + ial	f. unique + ness

4. What spelling change did you make in several words that you wrote for exercise 3?
5. Write the REVIEW WORD that has
   a. the prefix *ad-* and the suffix *-ion*.
   b. the suffixes *-cy* and *-es*.

C. SOUND, STRUCTURE, AND MEANING

1. Write the spelling words in which you hear these sounds.
   a. /s/ spelled *c* and /ch/ spelled *t*
   b. /kit/ spelled *cuit*
   c. /klām/ spelled *claim*
2. Write the NEW WORD with final /ēk/ spelled *ique*. Then write the following words, using the same spelling of /ēk/.

a. ant/ēk/	c. obl/ēk/
b. techn/ēk/	d. phys/ēk/

3. Which words have these definitions?
   a. A group of seven singers.
   b. The distance from low *do* to high *do*.
   c. A group of four singers.
   d. Three notes sung in the time of two.
4. Distinguish carefully between *biannual* and *biennial*. For each underlined phrase, write the correct word to replace it.
   a. We are harvesting our every two years crop of apples.
   b. Real estate taxes are commonly paid on a twice-a-year basis.
5. Write the capitalized form of *communion*. What is another name for this ordinance? (See the Speller Dictionary.)
6. How many pronunciations does the Speller Dictionary show for *quintuple*?

37

B. 21 points
1. a. tricycle
   b. bipolar
   c. bipartisan
   d. triangle
   e. bivalve
   f. tricuspid
2. a. multipurpose
   b. semiconscious
   c. multilingual
   d. semisolid
   e. semiconductor
   f. multisyllable
3. a. biannually
   b. triunity
   c. financial
   d. sacrificial
   e. duplicator
   f. uniqueness
4. Final *e* was dropped.
5. a. admonition
   b. vacancies

C. 17 points
1. a. century
   b. biscuit
   c. proclaim
2. unique
   a. antique
   b. technique
   c. oblique
   d. physique
3. a. septet
   b. octave
   c. quartet
   d. triplet
4. a. biennial
   b. biannual
5. Communion; Lord's Supper
6. four

13. *multiplicity*	She had a *multiplicity* of schemes.
14. *centipede*	Can a *centipede* crawl backward?
15. *sacrifice*	Abel offered a *sacrifice* to God.
16. *octave*	From low "do" to high "do" is one *octave*.
17. *century*	Nylon was unknown a *century* ago.
18. *vacancies*	Three *vacancies* remained in the motel.
19. *quartet*	The *quartet* of girls sang two songs.
20. *communion*	Our *Communion* is close.
21. *triplet*	Point to the *triplet* in this song.
22. *quintuple*	Please *quintuple* the recipe.
23. *decimal*	Move the *decimal* one place.
24. *semiconscious*	Mary was *semiconscious*.
25. *sextet*	A mixed *sextet* sang for Uncle Ben.

D. LANGUAGE LINEAGE

Semantic Study: SPECIALIZATION

The semantic change known as *specialization* is the opposite of generalization. It is the process through which a word with a broad meaning becomes more narrow and specific in meaning.

The King James Bible contains a number of words whose meanings have became specialized. One of the best examples is the word *corn*. When the King James Bible was produced, this word had the general meaning of "grain." Today, *corn* refers to maize in the United States, wheat in England, and oats in Scotland and Ireland.

Another example is the word *meat*, which is a synonym of *food* as used in the King James Bible. When *meat* as we know it is intended, the word *flesh* is used. There seems to be no difference between *food* and *meat* in the King James Bible.

Below are several more words whose meanings have changed through specialization.

SPECIALIZATION

Word	*Earlier meaning*	*Modern meaning*
cattle	any livestock	livestock of the same family as oxen
deer	any animal	a certain kind of wild animal
disease	any discomfort	an illness
doom	judgment in general	a ruinous fate
liquor	any liquid or juice	a type of alcoholic drink
verb	any word	a class of words that express action or being

Exercises

1. What is meant by generalization? by specialization?
2. Copy 1 Corinthians 8:13, replacing the words *meat* and *flesh* with the words we would use today.
3. Genesis 13:7 mentions the "cattle" of Abram and Lot. According to Genesis 12:16, what four kinds of livestock were included in this term?
4. Numbers 6:3 says that one who took the Nazarite vow was not to drink "any liquor of grapes." Does *liquor* refer only to fermented wine in this verse? Explain.

D. 13 points
1. Generalization is the process through which a word with a narrow, specific meaning becomes broader and more general in meaning. Specialization is the process through which a word with a broad meaning becomes more narrow and specific in meaning.
2. "Wherefore, if [food] make my brother to offend, I will eat no [meat] while the world standeth, lest I make my brother to offend."
3. sheep, oxen, asses, camels
4. no; *liquor* means "juice" in this verse. One who took the Nazarite vow was not allowed to drink even unfermented grape juice.

Lesson 12—82 points (A–B)

LESSON 12

7	8	9	10	11
aboard	benediction	abnormal	acknowledge	biannual
accordingly	contradiction	abscess	advantageous	biennial
accumulate	controversy	absolute	antecedent	biscuit
administration	correspond	accomplish	anteroom	centipede
admiration	devise	advise	broadcast	century
approximately	indicate	apparent	conscience	communion
arising	indict	desperate	conscientious	decimal
assignment	inquiries	despise	conscious	dual
association	liquid	disappointment	docile	duplicate
assortment	obedience	discount	doctrine	millipede
assumed	oppose	dismissal	document	multiplicity
attitude	procession	evidence	farewell	octave
clamor	production	expectation	frequent	quartet
confession	pronunciation	inspect	high school	quintuple
controlled	proposed	interview	kindergarten	semiconscious
faint	questionnaire	renown	moral	septet
parallel	request	spectator	northwestern	sextet
proclaim	requirements	visible	prejudice	triplet
professional	requisition	vision	prevail	triune
professor	response	visual	welfare	unique

A. UNEARTHING THE ROOTS

clam	cry out	***uni***	one	***sept***	seven
fess	speak, admit	***duo***	two	***oct***	eight
dic, dict	say	***bi***	two, twice	***novem***	nine
quer, quest	ask, seek	***tri***	three	***dec***	ten(th)
spond, spons	pledge, answer	***quad***	four	***cent***	hundred(th)
spec	look at	***quart***	fourth	***mill***	thousand(th)
vid, vis	see	***quin***	five	***semi***	half
par	appear	***sex***	six	***multi***	many
		sci	know	***doc***	teach

See page 117 for test sentences.

L7: clam, fess

1. Paul instructed us to put away bitterness, wrath, anger, ____*, and evil speaking.
2. Christians are baptized upon the ____* of their faith.
3. Write the word that illustrates the *claim* spelling of the *clam* root.
4. A [fess]* is a [fess]* instructor at a college or university.

L8: dic–dict, quer–quest, spond–spons

5. Write the New Word that means "act of saying (something) against."
6. Complete these analogies.
   a. factor : benefactor :: diction : ____*
   b. reference : refer :: indictment : ____*
7. Write the words with these spellings of the *quer, quest* root.
   a. quest (2) b. quir c. quis
8. Three of the answers to exercise 7 have the prefix ____.
9. The [spons]* of Sapphira did not [spond]* with the truth as Peter knew it.

L9: spec, vid–vis, par

10. Write New Words with the *spec* root (or its variations) for these definitions.
    a. To look at carefully; examine.
    b. One who looks at something.
    c. To look down on.
    d. The act of looking out at (something in the future).
11. When the doctor found [vid]* of a serious [vis]* defect, he decided to [vis]* surgery to correct the problem.
12. Write the New Word in which the *vid, vis* root is spelled *view*.
13. No hogs were [vis]*, but the tracks made it [par]* that they had been in the garden.

L10: sci, doc

14. A [sci]* person is [sci]* of the importance of heeding his [sci]*.
15. A ____* horse is tame and teachable.
16. Write the spelling word that originally meant "that which is taught" and now means "written record that gives proof."
17. Sound ____* is sound teaching.

L11: uni, duo, bi, tri, quad, quart, quin, sex

18. Write the answers. A word in parentheses indicates a root with that meaning.
    a. (one) + /ēk/ = ____*
    b. (two) + al = ____*
    c. (two) + (year) + al = ____* (2)
    d. (three) + (one) = ____*
    e. (four) + et = ____*
    f. (five) + tuple = ____*
    g. (six) + tet = ____*

L11: sept, oct, novem, dec, cent, mill, semi, multi

19. Write the answers as above.
    a. (seven) + et = ____*
    b. (eight) + ave = ____*
    c. (hundred) + (foot) = ____*
    d. (thousand) + (foot) = ____*
    e. (half) + con + (know) + ous = ____*
    f. (many) + plic + ity = ____*
20. Which months on our calendar were the seventh, eighth, ninth, and tenth months on the old Roman calendar?

A. 49 points
1. clamor
2. confession
3. proclaim
4. professor, professional
5. contradiction
6. a. benediction
   b. indict
7. a. questionnaire, request
   b. requirements
   c. requisition
8. re-
9. response, correspond
10. a. inspect
    b. spectator
    c. despise
    d. expectation
11. evidence, visual, advise
12. interview
13. visible, apparent
14. conscientious, conscious, conscience
15. docile
16. document
17. doctrine
18. a. unique
    b. dual
    c. biannual, biennial
    d. triune
    e. quartet
    f. quintuple
    g. sextet
19. a. septet
    b. octave
    c. centipede
    d. millipede
    e. semiconscious
    f. multiplicity
20. September, October, November, December

B. AFFIXING AFFIXES

ad-	at, to, toward
contra-, ob-	against
pro-	for, forth, forward
ab-	away, from
dis-	away, apart
ante-, pre-	before

1. Write the spelling words that begin with *ad-* and contain these roots.
   a. mir [7] b. minis [7] c. vis [9]
2. Write spelling words that have assimilated forms of *ad-* and these roots.
   a. sum [7]
   b. cum [7]
   c. soc [7]
   d. prox [7]
   e. par [9]
3. Attach *a-* (the English form of *ad-*) to form Lesson 7 words.
   a. board b. rising
4. Write Lesson 8 words beginning with *ob-* or *contra-* to match these definitions.
   a. To go against; resist.
   b. The act of speaking against.
   c. Holding an opinion that goes against others; strong disagreement.
5. Write words beginning with *pro-* for these definitions.
   a. To cry forth; declare. [7]
   b. A group going forward. [8]
   c. A manner of speaking forth words. [8]
6. List the three Lesson 9 words that begin with *ab-* and the three that begin with *dis-*.
7. Write Lesson 10 words that begin with *ante-* or *pre-* as suggested by these definitions.
   a. Coming or happening before.
   b. Judging before investigating.
   c. A waiting room at the entrance.
8. Form Lesson 11 words by changing the first word in each set to a prefix and combining it with the second word.
   a. (two) + annual
   b. (half) + conscious
9. Write the spelling words that are noun forms of these.
   a. confess [7]
   b. assign [7]
   c. assort [7]
   d. inquire [8]
   e. produce [8]
   f. expect [9]

D. LANGUAGE LINEAGE

1. Has the meaning of each word changed through *generalization* or *specialization*?
   a. **person.** *Former:* An actor in a play. *Modern:* Any human being.
   b. **starve.** *Former:* To die. *Modern:* To die of hunger.
2. Besides the languages that began at Babel, how have other new languages developed?
3. About half of the world's people speak languages in the _____ language family.
4. How is a dialect different from a standard language?

41

B. 33 points
1. a. admiration
   b. administration
   c. advise
2. a. assumed
   b. accumulate
   c. association
   d. approximately
   e. apparent
3. a. aboard
   b. arising
4. a. oppose
   b. contradiction
   c. controversy
5. a. proclaim
   b. procession
   c. pronunciation
6. abnormal, abscess, absolute; disappointment, discount, dismissal
7. a. antecedent
   b. prejudice
   c. anteroom
8. a. biannual
   b. semiconscious
9. a. confession
   b. assignment
   c. assortment
   d. inquiries
   e. production
   f. expectation

D. 7 points
1. a. generalization
   b. specialization
2. People speaking the same language became separated and developed new languages.
3. Indo-European
4. A standard language is a language used over a wide area; a dialect is the form of that language used in a certain small area. Also, a standard language usually has a written form but a dialect is chiefly a spoken form of the language.

LESSON 13

NEW WORDS

1. activity
2. actor
3. agency
4. agenda
5. agitate
6. defense
7. gracious
8. license
9. marvelous
10. mischievous
11. mobile
12. motivate
13. movement
14. mysterious
15. poisonous
16. prairie
17. promotion
18. thorough
19. verbose
20. virtuous

REVIEW WORDS

21. confidence
22. grease
23. initial
24. mediator
25. religious

A. UNEARTHING THE ROOTS

ROOT	MEANING	EXAMPLE
mov, mob, mot	move	mobile
ag, act	do, set in motion	agitate

mov, mob, mot

1. Write a New Word for each definition.
   a. Easy to be moved.
   b. The act or process of moving.
   c. The act of moving something ahead.
   d. To move someone to do something.
2. Choose from these words: *immovable, mismove, remove.*
   a. A wrong move is a ____.
   b. "If thou be willing, ____ this cup from me" (Luke 22:42).
   c. Something ____ cannot be moved.
3. Choose from these words: *automobile, immobile, mobilize.*
   a. To ____ an army is to get it moving.
   b. The ____ moves by itself; no horse is needed.
   c. A broken bone must be kept ____ so that it heals properly.
4. Choose from these words: *demote, motor, remote.*
   a. Something ____ has been moved far away.
   b. A ____ causes machinery parts to move.
   c. To ____ a person is to move him to a lower rank.

ag, act

5. An ____* is one who does something in a play.
6. A travel ____* is an organization that does what is needed to make travel arrangements.
7. This [act]* is not on the day's [ag]*.
8. To ____* something is to set it in motion like the water in a washing machine.
9. Choose from these words: *actually, agile, reaction, transaction.*
   a. Every action causes an equal and opposite ____.
   b. Do you ____ understand this scientific principle?
   c. A good secretary keeps a record of every business ____.
   d. A monkey is a very ____ creature.

Lesson 13—66 points (A–C)

A. 22 points
1. a. mobile
   b. movement
   c. promotion
   d. motivate
2. a. mismove
   b. remove
   c. immovable
3. a. mobilize
   b. automobile
   c. immobile
4. a. remote
   b. motor
   c. demote
5. actor
6. agency
7. activity, agenda
8. agitate
9. a. reaction
   b. actually
   c. transaction
   d. agile

Test Sentences

1. *marvelous*	What a *marvelous* God we serve!
2. *promotion*	David accepted his *promotion* to be king.
3. *religious*	Saul was very *religious* before his conversion.
4. *activity*	The kitchen was a beehive of *activity.*
5. *mischievous*	Mark flashed a *mischievous* grin.
6. *thorough*	Thomas did a *thorough* job of weeding.
7. *actor*	An *actor* works on a stage.
8. *mobile*	A trailer is called a *mobile* home.
9. *verbose*	Some writing is *verbose* and meaningless.
10. *agency*	The travel *agency* sent a letter today.
11. *motivate*	Your enthusiasm can *motivate* others.
12. *virtuous*	Solomon described a *virtuous* woman.

B. AFFIXING AFFIXES

Adjective-forming Suffixes		
SUFFIX	MEANING	EXAMPLE
-ous	full of, having	virtuous
-ose	full of, abounding in	verbose

1. Compare the meanings of *-ous* and *-ose*.
   a. Which suffix indicates a greater degree of the quality possessed?
   b. A ____* person is one who practices religion. But if he goes to extremes, he may be called "religiose."
2. Write the spelling words with the suffix *-ous* that are derived from these words.
   a. virtue d. mystery
   b. grace e. marvel
   c. poison
3. Write the spelling word in which final *f* was changed to *v* before adding *-ous*.
4. Attach *-ous* to these words, making spelling changes as needed.
   a. covet c. courage
   b. fury d. sacrilege
5. Which New Word ends with *-ose*? This suffix is not nearly as common as *-ous*.
6. Add *-ose* to form words with the meanings given.
   a. mor___: Dismal; gloomy.
   b. varic___: Swollen, as veins.
   c. plum___: Resembling plumes; feathery.
7. Write two more words by attaching *-ose* to the words below. Use the letter in parentheses to link the root and the suffix.
   a. coma (t) b. grand (i)
8. In chemistry, the suffix *-ose* may indicate the name of a sugar, as in *fructose* (fruit sugar). Complete these words with *-ose* to form the names of other sugars.
   a. sucr___ b. malt___

C. SOUND, STRUCTURE, AND MEANING

1. Write the spelling words in which you hear these sounds.
   a. /o͞ov/ spelled *ove*
   b. final /ər/ spelled *or* (2)
   c. final /shəl/ spelled *tial*
   d. final /shəs/ spelled *cious*
2. Write the four words that end with /s/ spelled *se*. Which one has final /s/ spelled *ce*?
3. Write *agency* and *agent*. Observe that there is no *t* in the first word.
4. Write *though, through,* or *thorough* for these sentences.
   a. We gave the room a ____ cleaning.
   b. When you begin something, follow it ____ until it is finished.
   c. Even ____ it was raining, the sun was shining.
5. Which spelling words are synonyms of these words?
   a. wordy d. advancement
   b. grassland e. conscientious
   c. excite f. amazing
6. Divide *mischievous* into syllables. Does this word have three syllables or four? Which syllable is accented?

43

B. 20 points
1. a. -ose
   b. religious
2. a. virtuous
   b. gracious
   c. poisonous
   d. mysterious
   e. marvelous
3. mischievous
4. a. covetous
   b. furious
   c. courageous
   d. sacrilegious
5. verbose
6. a. morose
   b. varicose
   c. plumose
7. a. comatose
   b. grandiose
8. a. sucrose
   b. maltose

C. 24 points
1. a. movement
   b. actor, mediator
   c. initial
   d. gracious
2. defense, license, verbose, grease; confidence
3. agency, agent
4. a. thorough
   b. through
   c. though
5. a. verbose
   b. prairie
   c. agitate
   d. promotion
   e. religious
   f. marvelous
6. mis/chie/vous; three; first syllable

13. *agenda* What is on your *agenda* for today?
14. *movement* Allen saw a *movement* in the bushes.
15. *confidence* Jonathan had *confidence* in David.
16. *agitate* Do not *agitate* the dog unnecessarily.
17. *mysterious* What made that *mysterious* footprint?
18. *grease* The bacon *grease* sputtered in the pan.
19. *defense* Paul made his *defense* to King Agrippa.
20. *poisonous* Turpentine is *poisonous* if swallowed.
21. *initial* Write only your first *initial* here.
22. *gracious* Aunt Jane is a very *gracious* hostess.
23. *prairie* The rolling *prairie* has few trees.
24. *mediator* Two estranged friends needed a *mediator.*
25. *license* The bakery's *license* must be renewed.

D. LANGUAGE LINEAGE

THE CELTIC PERIOD

In the history of England, the time from about 700 B.C. to A.D. 450 is known as the Celtic period. During this time the British Isles were inhabited by Celtic tribes who had come from central Europe. Some of these tribes were called *Brythons* or *Britons*; the term *Britain* is derived from that name.

In A.D. 43, the Romans conquered the Celts and made Britannia (as the island was called) a province of the Roman Empire. The island was under Roman rule for about three and one-half centuries, and there was general peace and prosperity during that period.

But about A.D. 400, the Romans began to leave Britannia to help defend the Roman Empire against barbarian invasions. In their absence, the Angles, Saxons, and Jutes from the northern mainland of Europe began to invade the islands. They brought their Germanic language with them and adopted only a few words from the native Celts.

As the Anglo-Saxon tribes pushed in, they drove back the Celts in much the some way that the white men later drove back the Indians of America. Many of the Celts moved north and west into what is now Scotland and Wales. (See the map on page 50.) The descendants of these and other Celts developed the modern Celtic languages—Welsh, Irish Gaelic, Scottish Gaelic, and Breton.

The Anglo-Saxon invaders called their new territory "Engle-land," from which the name *England* is derived. The language they spoke was "Engle-isc," the earliest form of the English language.

The Celtic Period

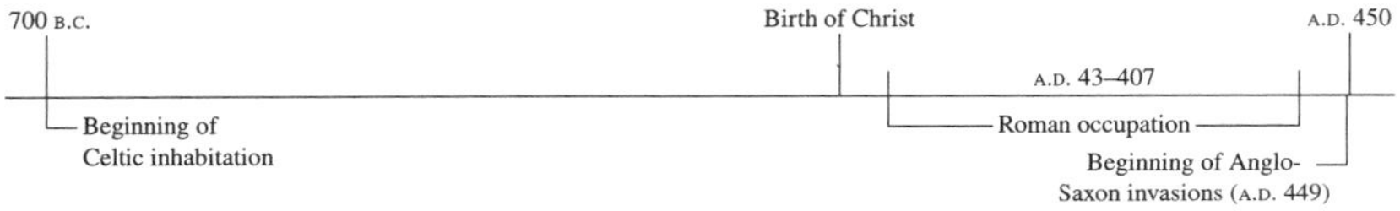

Exercises

1. Write the modern English words that are derived from these.
   a. Brython *or* Briton
   b. Engle-land
   c. Engle-isc
2. In what two ways was the Roman occupation of Britain a benefit to the Celtic people?
3. Why are the Gaelic and Welsh languages not very much like the English language? (See the diagram in Lesson 9.)
4. In what two ways was the Anglo-Saxon invasion of Britain like the white man's invasion of America?

D. 13 points
1. a Britain
   b. England
   c. English
2. The Roman occupation brought a time of peace and prosperity to the Celts. The Romans kept other invaders out; as soon as they left, the Anglo-Saxons began coming in.
3. The Gaelic and Welsh languages are of the Celtic branch; English is of the Germanic branch.
4. In both cases the native people were driven back by the invaders. In both cases the invaders introduced their own languages and adopted only a few words from the native languages.

LESSON 14

NEW WORDS

1. affected
2. affectionate
3. artificial
4. available
5. believable
6. beneficial
7. certificate
8. changeable
9. comfortable
10. cooperate
11. effective
12. facility
13. favorably
14. feasible
15. miserable
16. operation
17. perfectly
18. possibility
19. sensible
20. specified

REVIEW WORDS

21. development
22. factories
23. fashionable
24. production
25. professor

A. UNEARTHING THE ROOTS

ROOT	MEANING	EXAMPLE
fac, fic	make, do	manufacture
oper	work	operate

fac, fic

1. Write the New Word in which the *fac* root is spelled *fac*.
2. Establishments for making things by mass production are called ____*.
3. The *fac* root appears as *fect* in a number of spelling words. Write words containing this spelling to match these definitions.
   a. Done with the desired result; successful.
   b. Done with warm feelings; loving.
   c. In a manner done thoroughly and flawlessly.
   d. Acted upon, influenced; also, pretended.
4. An alternate spelling of *fac* is *fash*. Which spelling word contains this form?
5. In which spelling word is the *fac* root spelled *feas*?
6. Write New Words with the *fic* form of the root to match these.
   a. A document used to make something certain.
   b. Made by art; manmade.
   c. Doing good to; advantageous.
7. In some words, *fic* became *fy*. Write the New Word that ended with *fy* before *-ed* was added. Also write the *-fication* form of this word.
8. Add *-ation* to these words, changing *fy* to *fic* in each one.
   a. justify c. glorify
   b. sanctify d. magnify

oper

9. An act or process of working is an ____*.
10. To work together with a common purpose is to ____*.
11. Choose from these words: *inoperative, opera, optimum.*
    a. At the most favorable stage; ideal.
    b. Drama in which lines are sung rather than spoken.
    c. Not working; not functioning.

45

Lesson 14—65 points (A–C)

A. 22 points
1. facility
2. factories
3. a. effective
   b. affectionate
   c. perfectly
   d. affected
4. fashionable
5. feasible
6. a. certificate
   b. artificial
   c. beneficial
7. specified, specification
8. a. justification
   b. sanctification
   c. glorification
   d. magnification
9. operation
10. cooperate
11. a. optimum
    b. opera
    c. inoperative

See page 54 for test sentences.

B. AFFIXING AFFIXES

1. Write spelling words with the suffix *-able* to match these definitions.
   a. Tending to produce misery.
   b. Capable of being obtained.
   c. Belonging to the current style.
   d. Tending to provide comfort.
   e. Capable of being believed.

2. Attach *-able* to each word.
   a. teach c. value
   b. agree d. depend

3. Final *e* is usually dropped when *-able* is attached. But if a word ends with /s/ spelled *ce* or /j/ spelled *ge*, the final *e* is retained to "protect the soft *c* (or *g*)." Which New Word illustrates this pattern?

4. Attach *-able* to these words.
   a. trace c. manage
   b. notice d. recharge

Adjective-forming Suffixes

SUFFIX	MEANING	EXAMPLE
-able	capable of *or*	changeable
-ible	tending to	possible

5. Write the spelling words that contain these Latin roots and the suffix *-ible*.
   a. fac (feas) b. sens

6. Which New Word has the suffixes *-ible* and *-ity*?

7. Final *e* is not needed to "protect the soft *c* (or *g*)" when *-ible* is attached to a root. Join *-ible* with these roots.
   a. force b. submerge

8. For words that end with *-ate*, final *te* is sometimes dropped and the *a* becomes part of *-able* (as *irritate—irritable*). Use this pattern to attach *-able* to these words.
   a. appreciate b. venerate

C. SOUND, STRUCTURE, AND MEANING

1. Write the spelling words in which you hear these sounds.
   a. /fish/ spelled *fici* (2)
   b. /lē/ spelled *lie*
   c. /vər/ spelled *vor*
   d. /ō/ immediately followed by /o/

2. Write the plural form of *facility, possibility*, and *factory*.

3. Write New Words that are antonyms for these words.
   a. invariable d. futile
   b. foolhardy e. harmful
   c. unloving f. impractical

4. Write the *-ing* form of *specified*.

5. Write the spelling word that begins with *pro-* and ends with
   a. *-or*. b. *-ion*.

6. Do not confuse *affected—effected* and *facility—faculty*. Write the correct words for these sentences.
   a. A school is an educational ____.
   b. The teaching staff is the ____.
   c. Judas greeted Jesus with an ____ display of warmth and esteem.
   d. Most major improvements are not ____ in one day.

7. What part of speech is *certificate* when the last syllable is pronounced /kāt/?

46

B. 21 points
1. a. miserable
   b. available
   c. fashionable
   d. comfortable
   e. believable
2. a. teachable
   b. agreeable
   c. valuable
   d. dependable
3. changeable
4. a. traceable
   b. noticeable
   c. manageable
   d. rechargeable
5. a. feasible
   b. sensible
6. possibility
7. a. forcible
   b. submergible
8. a. appreciable
   b. venerable

C. 22 points
1. a. artificial, beneficial
   b. believable
   c. favorably
   d. cooperate
2. facilities, possibilities, factories
3. a. changeable
   b. sensible
   c. affectionate
   d. effective
   e. beneficial
   f. feasible or sensible
4. specifying
5. a. professor
   b. production
6. a. facility
   b. faculty
   c. affected
   d. effected
7. verb

Test Sentences

1. *specified*	Mother *specified* the length of drapes.
2. *possibility*	There is a *possibility* of failure.
3. *affected*	Naaman was *affected* by leprosy.
4. *sensible*	Bodies need a *sensible* amount of rest.
5. *affectionate*	Frisky is an *affectionate* puppy.
6. *development*	The housing *development* was built.
7. *cooperate*	You must *cooperate* with the dentist.
8. *effective*	Is this an *effective* fly spray?
9. *comfortable*	Our home is small but *comfortable*.
10. *facility*	Is there a cooking *facility* in the park?
11. *artificial*	My cousin has an *artificial* leg.
12. *operation*	Addition is an *operation* in math.

D. LANGUAGE LINEAGE

EARLY LATIN INFLUENCES

On an average page in a modern dictionary, more than half of the entry words come from the Latin language. But English is basically a Germanic language, whereas Latin is of the branch from which the modern Romance languages developed. How so many Latin words found their way into the English language makes an interesting study.

The first influence of Latin on the English language may be called the continental influence. While the Anglo-Saxons were still on the continent of Europe, they had already borrowed a number of Latin words from the Romans. Most of the Anglo-Saxons never came under actual Roman dominion, but they did have considerable contact with Roman soldiers and Roman traders. In this way a number of military and commercial terms came into the English language. *Camp, wall, street, mile, cheap, pound,* and *mint* are some of the modern words based on Latin terms borrowed during this period.

The second influence of Latin on English came through the Roman occupation of Britain. During that time the Celts adopted more than six hundred Latin words from the Romans. But because the Anglo-Saxons drove out the Celts rather than settling among them, very few Latin elements came into the English language through the Celts. About the only ones that did so are combining elements used in place names: *-caster* or *-chester*, as in *Lancaster* and *Winchester*; *-port*, as in *Stockport*; *-mont*, as in *Edmonton*; and *-wich* or *-wick,* as in *Greenwich* and *Warwick*. Therefore, of all the early Latin influences on English, the influence through Celtic transmission was the slightest of all.

About 150 years after the Anglo-Saxons first settled in Britain, a third Latin influence began to affect the English language. It came through the work of Roman Catholic missionaries who labored among the Anglo-Saxons. The Roman Catholic influence on English is discussed more fully in Lesson 16.

Exercises

1. What were the three early Latin influences that affected the English language?
2. Describe the kind of words that the Anglo-Saxons borrowed from Latin before they came to Britain, and tell how this borrowing came about.
3. If you were to study a modern Celtic language such as Welsh, would you expect to find any words of Latin origin in it? Why or why not?
4. In what kind of English words does one find almost the only Latin elements that were adopted through Celtic transmission?

47

13. *factories* We visited two glass *factories.*
14. *available* How much space is *available* to us?
15. *favorably* Did he respond *favorably* to our invitation?
16. *perfectly* A sphere is *perfectly* round.
17. *believable* This story hardly sounds *believable.*
18. *feasible* Your answer seems *feasible* to me.
19. *fashionable* The Bible forbids *fashionable* clothing.
20. *beneficial* Sunshine is *beneficial* to our health.
21. *miserable* Satan is a *miserable* taskmaster.
22. *production* Egg *production* is slowly increasing.
23. *certificate* He needed a *certificate* of identification.
24. *professor* Mr. Brown is a college *professor.*
25. *changeable* What is more *changeable* than wind?

D. 11 points
1. the continental influence, the influence through Celtic transmission, and the Roman Catholic influence
2. Before the Anglo-Saxons came to Britain, they borrowed a number of military and commercial terms from Latin. This came about through their contact with Roman soldiers and Roman traders.
3. Yes. The Celts adopted more than six hundred Latin words during the period of Roman occupation.
4. in place names

LESSON 15

NEW WORDS

1. actually
2. approval
3. attraction
4. compel
5. contractor
6. contracts
7. criminal
8. crystal
9. detract
10. essential
11. historical
12. impelling
13. impulsive
14. knight
15. personal
16. repellent
17. repulsive
18. spiritual
19. subtrahend
20. technical

REVIEW WORDS

21. acknowledge
22. controlled
23. dispatch
24. ordinance
25. parallel

A. UNEARTHING THE ROOTS

ROOT	MEANING	EXAMPLE
tract, trah	pull, draw, drag	tractor
pel, puls	drive, push	compel

tract, trah

1. Write spelling words that could replace the underlined words.
   a. The builder drew up agreements with the landowners.
   b. The appeal of this world must not draw away our attention from heavenly things.
2. In arithmetic, the ____* in a subtraction problem is the number by which the minuend is reduced or "drawn down."
3. Choose from these words: *extract, protract, traction, tractor.*
   a. A "puller" of farm implements.
   b. To pull out; remove.
   c. Drawing power, as of tires.
   d. Lengthen in time; prolong.

pel, puls

4. Write spelling words that could replace the underlined words.
   a. The hordes of mosquitoes made it urgent that we use a chemical that drives insects away.
   b. "Go out into the highways and hedges, and [constrain] them to come in" (Luke 14:23).
   c. The boy's rash and thoughtless manner was offensive to those who took more time to think before they acted.
5. Use the root *pel* to form words with these meanings.
   a. To drive forward (*pro-*).
   b. To drive back (*re-*).
   c. To drive away (*dis-*).
   d. To drive out (*ex-*).
6. Choose from these words: *compulsion, expulsion, propulsion, pulsation.*
   a. Each ____ of the heart pumps blood through the body.
   b. There is little merit in giving alms under ____.
   c. The ____ of unrepentant sinners from the church is necessary to keep the church pure.
   d. A rocket is driven by jet ____.

48

Lesson 15—67 points (A–C)

A. 22 points
1. a. contractor, contracts
   b. attraction, detract
2. subtrahend
3. a. tractor
   b. extract
   c. traction
   d. protract
4. a. impelling, repellent
   b. compel
   c. impulsive, repulsive
5. a. propel
   b. repel
   c. dispel
   d. expel
6. a. pulsation
   b. compulsion
   c. expulsion
   d. propulsion

Test Sentences

1. *detract*	Sloppy writing will *detract* from the message.
2. *acknowledge*	Everyone should *acknowledge* God.
3. *essential*	Fuel is *essential* to a fire.
4. *repulsive*	Lukewarmness is *repulsive* to God.
5. *actually*	The larger dog was *actually* younger.
6. *spiritual*	God's Word is our *spiritual* bread.
7. *historical*	The city has great *historical* value.
8. *subtrahend*	The *subtrahend* is smaller than the minuend.
9. *approval*	Your father's *approval* is important.
10. *impelling*	An inner force was *impelling* Lynn to go on.
11. *technical*	Engineering requires *technical* skill.
12. *attraction*	Niagara Falls is a known *attraction.*

B. AFFIXING AFFIXES

The suffix *-al* is used to form adjectives, but sometimes the adjective is more expressive than the noun it describes. Then the adjective may completely replace the noun. For example, *animal* means "living" or "breathing" in Latin. In English, we simply say "an animal" instead of "an animal creature."

1. Write the spelling words ending with *-al* that have these roots.
   a. crime b. tech c. essent
2. The suffix *-al* has become an English suffix. Attach that suffix to these words.
   a. refuse d. approve
   b. person e. function
   c. margin f. accident
3. In which two spelling words does the letter *u* join *-al* to the root? Which two end with both *-ic* and *-al*?

Adjective- and Noun-forming Suffixes

SUFFIX	MEANING	EXAMPLE
-al	pertaining to; act or condition of	personal approval

4. Write the New Word that means "transparent mineral." Observe that *-al* is not a suffix in this word.
5. Which spelling words have these affixes?
   a. de- c. -ion
   b. dis- d. -ance
6. Write the spelling word in which final *l* was doubled when *-ent* was attached.
7. Add *-ality* or *-uality* to each word.
   a. form c. sense
   b. act d. nation

C. SOUND, STRUCTURE, AND MEANING

1. Write the spelling words in which you hear these sounds.
   a. /o͞ov/ spelled *ov*
   b. /k/ spelled *ch*
   c. /l/ spelled *ll* and then *l*
   d. /n/ spelled *kn* (2)
2. Add *-ed* and *-ing* to *impel* and *control*. The final *l* (is, is not) doubled in these words.
3. Write the spelling word that belongs with each group.
   a. lord, vassal, serf, squire
   b. minuend, difference, remainder
   c. physical, emotional, mental
4. Which two New Words are synonyms that mean "disagreeable; disgusting"?
5. Write *personal* or *personnel* for each of these sentences.
   a. *He, she,* and *it* are ____ pronouns.
   b. The project was hindered by a lack of finances and ____.
   c. A busybody asks ____ questions about other people's affairs.
6. Write the New Word that is a synonym for *malefactor*, and name the two parts of speech that it may be. (See the Speller Dictionary.)
7. In what nation may people still be called knights today?

B. 23 points
1. a. criminal
   b. technical
   c. essential
2. a. refusal
   b. personal
   c. marginal
   d. approval
   e. functional
   f. accidental
3. actually, spiritual; historical, technical
4. crystal
5. a. detract
   b. dispatch
   c. attraction
   d. ordinance
6. repellent
7. a. formality
   b. actuality
   c. sensuality
   d. nationality

C. 22 points
1. a. approval
   b. technical
   c. parallel
   d. knight, acknowledge
2. impelled, impelling; controlled, controlling; is
3. a. knight
   b. subtrahend
   c. spiritual
4. repellent, repulsive
5. a. personal
   b. personnel
   c. personal
6. criminal; adjective, noun
7. England

13. *impulsive* Foolish, *impulsive* buyers lose money.
14. *controlled* The weather is *controlled* by God.
15. *compel* God does not *compel* anyone to serve Him.
16. *knight* Long ago, a *knight* lived in a castle.
17. *dispatch* Did the king *dispatch* a messenger?
18. *contractor* The *contractor* gave us an estimate.
19. *personal* Our *personal* appearance tells about us.
20. *ordinance* Jesus taught the *ordinance* of Feet Washing.
21. *criminal* The guilty *criminal* was sentenced.
22. *repellent* This mosquito *repellent* works well.
23. *parallel* Many streets have *parallel* parking.
24. *crystal* Put the flowers into a *crystal* vase.
25. *contracts* A muscle *contracts* when we use it.

D. LANGUAGE LINEAGE

THE OLD ENGLISH PERIOD

The map below shows how Anglo-Saxons from Denmark and northern Germany invaded Britain and drove out the Celts. The language used by the invaders is today known as Old English, or it may also be called Anglo-Saxon. The Old English period lasted from about A.D. 450 to 1100.

But Old English was very different from the English we use today. If someone spoke to us in Old English, we would find it almost impossible to understand him. The Lord's Prayer in Old English (Lesson 1) is a good illustration of this. The specific form of English in that example is West Saxon, a dialect of Old English that was spoken in the southwestern part of England.

Old English was a highly localized language. There were nearly two hundred dialects, and these were often so dissimilar that people living only fifteen miles apart had great difficulty conversing with each other. It was largely through early English literature, including translations of the Bible, that English gradually developed into a stable, uniform language.

Anglo-Saxon Invasions

Exercises

1. Make a list of the following facts.
   a. The two areas from which the Anglo-Saxons came.
   b. The two areas to which the Celts fled.
   c. The two names given to the earliest form of English.
   d. The years spanned by the Old English period.
2. What is meant by the statement that "Old English was a highly localized language"?
3. How was stability and uniformity brought into the English language?

D. 11 points

1. a. Denmark and northern Germany
   b. Scotland and Wales
   c. Old English and Anglo-Saxon
   d. about A.D. 450–1100
2. Each locality had its own dialect of Old English. Many of these dialects were so dissimilar that the different speakers could hardly understand each other.
3. This came about largely through early English literature, including translations of the Bible.

LESSON 16

NEW WORDS

1. absolutely
2. assistant
3. bankruptcy
4. continuous
5. correspondent
6. dissolve
7. erupt
8. excellent
9. exorbitant
10. immigrant
11. impatient
12. intelligent
13. interrupt
14. liable
15. ligament
16. maintenance
17. obligation
18. obtained
19. resolve
20. solution

REVIEW WORDS

21. ceiling
22. contradiction
23. indicate
24. league
25. requirements

A. UNEARTHING THE ROOTS

ROOT	MEANING	EXAMPLE
lig	bind	ligament
ten, tin, tain	hold	retain
solv, solu	loosen, free	dissolve
rupt	burst, break	erupt

lig

1. A(n) ____* binds one bone to another.
2. A(n) ____* is something we are bound to do.
3. Two other forms of *lig* are *leag* and *li.*
   a. One who is legally bound to pay for damages is ____* for the damages.
   b. When people make a(n) ____*, they bind themselves together with an agreement.

ten, tin, tain

4. Father [tain]* a new fitting, and the [ten]* man used it to stop the [tin]* dripping.
5. Choose from these words: *contain, contents, retain, tenant.*
   a. One who holds a lease on a house is a ____.
   b. Things that packages ____ are called their ____.
   c. To hold something in your memory is to ____ it.

solv, solu

6. It was Lincoln's ____* to find a ____* to the nation's discord.
7. Lincoln did not want to see the Union ____* unless it was ____* impossible to prevent it.
8. Some religious officials claim the power to [ab + solv] a person from his sins, but only God can do this.

rupt

9. A volcano is said to ____* when lava bursts forth from it.
10. To break in between two persons who are talking is to ____* them.
11. Long ago bankers sat on benches to conduct their business. If a banker loaned out so much money that he could not pay his debts, his creditors would break his bench to symbolize the failure of his business. Today the state of being "bench-broken" is called ____*.

Lesson 16—63 points (A–C)

A. 19 points

1. ligament
2. obligation
3. a. liable
   b. league
4. obtained, maintenance, continuous
5. a. tenant
   b. contain, contents
   c. retain
6. resolve, solution
7. dissolve, absolutely
8. absolve
9. erupt
10. interrupt
11. bankruptcy

See page 60 for test sentences.

B. AFFIXING AFFIXES

Like *-al*, the suffixes *-ant* and *-ent* are used to form adjectives that often develop into nouns.

Adjective- and Noun-forming Suffixes		
SUFFIX	MEANING	EXAMPLE
-ent	in the process or act of	persistent
-ant	one who *or* that which	servant

1. Write the spelling word that means both "helping" (as in "a *helping* teacher") and "helper."
2. The *-ant* or *-ent* suffix is the Latin equivalent of the English suffix *-ing*. Write both the *-ing* and the *-ant* or *-ent* forms of these, noting their similarity in meaning.
   a. excel b. differ c. repent
3. Write spelling words ending with *-ant* or *-ent* to match these definitions.
   a. Being quick to learn.
   b. One who settles in a foreign country.
   c. Being much too high, as a price.
   d. Being unwilling to endure trouble.
   e. One who writes letters.

Words ending with *-ant* usually have an *-ance* form, and words ending with *-ent* usually have an *-ence* form.

4. Write the *-ance* or *-ence* forms of these.
   a. impatient c. important
   b. assistant d. excellent
5. Write the spelling words that contain these elements.
   a. dis + solv d. contra + dic
   b. lig + ment e. ab + solu
   c. inter + rupt f. re + quir
6. Combine these words and affixes.
   a. indicate + ion d. continue + ous
   b. liable + ity e. oblige + ation
   c. erupt + ion f. dis + solution

C. SOUND, STRUCTURE, AND MEANING

1. Write the spelling words in which you hear these sounds.
   a. final /shənt/ spelled *tient*
   b. /yo͞o əs/ spelled *uous*
   c. final /g/ spelled *gue*
   d. /ē/ spelled *ei* after *c*
2. In one New Word, /gz/ is spelled *x*. Write this word, observing that there is no *h* after the *x*.
3. Write spelling words for these phrases.
   a. The state of having more debts than assets.
   b. What a volcano may do.
   c. Legally responsible for an accident.
   d. Gotten; gained; acquired.
   e. An answer to a problem or puzzle.
   f. To commit oneself; decide; determine.
4. If a person is an *immigrant*, he is also an *emigrant*. Why?
5. Three of the Review Words have Latin roots that pertain to speaking. Write the words for these definitions.
   a. The act of speaking against.
   b. To point out.
   c. Necessities.

Test Sentences

1.	*immigrant*	Carlos was an *immigrant* from Mexico.
2.	*bankruptcy*	The business filed for *bankruptcy.*
3.	*excellent*	Mrs. Yoder is an *excellent* seamstress.
4.	*liable*	Which party was *liable* for the accident?
5.	*continuous*	Loving others is a *continuous* debt.
6.	*obligation*	Our first *obligation* is to obey God.
7.	*ligament*	A torn *ligament* can be very painful.
8.	*absolutely*	The cave was *absolutely* dark.
9.	*exorbitant*	Farms sold for *exorbitant* prices.
10.	*assistant*	The teacher's *assistant* checked our papers.
11.	*solution*	Seawater is a *solution* of salt.
12.	*maintenance*	Ask the *maintenance* man to fix it.

B. 28 points
1. assistant
2. a. excelling, excellent
   b. differing, different
   c. repenting, repentant
3. a. intelligent
   b. immigrant
   c. exorbitant
   d. impatient
   e. correspondent
4. a. impatience
   b. assistance
   c. importance
   d. excellence
5. a. dissolve
   b. ligament
   c. interrupt
   d. contradiction
   e. absolutely
   f. requirements
6. a. indication
   b. liability
   c. eruption
   d. continuous
   e. obligation
   f. dissolution

C. 16 points
1. a. impatient
   b. continuous
   c. league
   d. ceiling
2. exorbitant
3. a. bankruptcy
   b. erupt
   c. liable
   d. obtained
   e. solution
   f. resolve
4. When an immigrant moves into a country, he first leaves some other country.
5. a. contradiction
   b. indicate
   c. requirements

D. LANGUAGE LINEAGE

ROMAN CATHOLIC INFLUENCES

The Anglo-Saxons were known as barbarians to the Latin-speaking people of what had been the Roman Empire. Pope Gregory the Great thought these people should be evangelized, and he sent a man by the name of Augustine to work as a missionary among them. Thus it was that Augustine and about forty monks arrived in Britain in A.D. 597 to begin the work of "Christianizing" the Anglo-Saxons.

These missionaries established churches, schools, and monasteries in England. They taught the Latin alphabet to the people, even though some of them could write with the runic alphabet, because the runes were associated with heathen worship. The missionaries also introduced classical learning—the Greek and Latin literature that had been produced by the civilizations of Greece and Rome.

All these things had a great influence on the language of the Anglo-Saxons. Dozens of religious terms became part of Old English—words such as *altar, angel, deacon, disciple, hymn, priest,* and *psalm*. Other words had to do with education—*school, master* (for "teacher"), *verse*, and *notary* (for "scribe"). There were also many new words that had to do with everyday life—names of foods such as *beet, pear, radish,* and *oyster;* names of clothing and household articles such as *cap, chest, sock, mat,* and *silk*; and other terms such as *anchor, fever, elephant, circle, giant,* and *talent*. The work of the Roman Catholic missionaries brought about the greatest of the three Latin influences that affected Old English.

The Anglo-Saxons were considered to be "Christianized" by A.D. 700—only about a hundred years after Augustine had first arrived in England. Scores of new words were added to Old English during that century, and now the horizons of the English language were much broader than they had ever been before.

Exercises

1. Tell what group was sent to England to "Christianize" the Anglo-Saxons, when they arrived, and how long it took to accomplish their work.
2. Why did the missionaries teach the Latin alphabet to the people rather than using the runic alphabet?
3. Describe four kinds of Latin words that were added to Old English during the 600s.
4. Name the Latin influence that had the greatest effect on Old English. Then name the two other Latin influences that affected the English language in its earliest stages. (Review Lesson 14.)

D. 12 points
1. Augustine and about forty monks were sent, they arrived in A.D. 597, and their work took about one hundred years.
2. The runic alphabet was associated with heathen worship.
3. religious terms, words pertaining to education, names of foods, names of clothing and household articles
4. the Roman Catholic influence; the continental influence and the influence through Celtic transmission

13.	*correspondent*	He is a newspaper *correspondent.*
14.	*resolve*	Daniel's firm *resolve* kept him from sin.
15.	*interrupt*	It is impolite to *interrupt* others.
16.	*dissolve*	Sugar can *dissolve* in water.
17.	*league*	The Gibeonites desired a *league* with Israel.
18.	*requirements*	The state's *requirements* are for our good.
19.	*impatient*	The *impatient* horse pawed the ground.
20.	*contradiction*	"I did not!" is a *contradiction.*
21.	*obtained*	Enoch *obtained* favor with God.
22.	*erupt*	When will that volcano *erupt* again?
23.	*intelligent*	Man is an *intelligent* being.
24.	*ceiling*	Our kitchen *ceiling* has been lowered.
25.	*indicate*	Orange signs *indicate* road construction.

LESSON 17

NEW WORDS

1. appetite
2. application
3. applied
4. attendant
5. auxiliary
6. complicated
7. compressor
8. conquer
9. curious
10. extension
11. flexible
12. guardian
13. inflection
14. intention
15. librarian
16. pressure
17. reflected
18. reflexes
19. republican
20. seize

REVIEW WORDS

21. antecedent
22. complexion
23. congress
24. expression
25. tongue

A. UNEARTHING THE ROOTS

ROOT	MEANING	EXAMPLE
tend, tens, tent	stretch	extend
flex, flect	bend	flexible
plic, plex	fold	complex
press	press	compress

tend, tens, tent

1. An act of stretching out (*ex-*) is a(n) ____*.
2. The ____* at the service station had the ____* of serving each customer in a courteous, professional manner.
3. Add final *e* to one form of the *tend* root to make a word that means "tightly stretched."
4. Choose from these words: *tendril, tensile, tent.*
   a. "It is [God] . . . that stretcheth out the heavens as a curtain, and spreadeth them out as a ____ to dwell in" (Isaiah 40:22).
   b. Each ____ on the vine stretched out and clung to a support.
   c. The ____ strength of a rope is its ability to resist breaking when it is stretched.

flex, flect

5. Something ____* bends easily.
6. Light is "bent back" when it is ____* by a mirror.
7. Because of your ____*, your hand jerks away from a hot stove and your eye blinks when something flies toward it.
8. A(n) ____* is the "bending" of a word to fit a certain use.
9. You have flexor and extensor muscles in your arm. You would expect to use ____ muscles when you bend your elbow.

plic, plex

10. Something ____* may be folded together in an elaborate way.
11. The boy ____* for the job by filling out a(n) ____*.
12. Your ____* is the appearance of the skin on your face.

press

13. pact : compactor :: press : ____*
14. Great emotional ____* will affect the ____* on a person's face.
15. Write words with the *press* root and these meanings.
    a. Press back (*re-*).
    b. Press down (*de-*).
    c. Press in (*im-*).

Lesson 17—61 points (A–C)

A. 22 points
1. extension
2. attendant, intention
3. tense
4. a. tent
   b. tendril
   c. tensile
5. flexible
6. reflected
7. reflexes
8. inflection
9. flexor
10. complicated
11. applied, application
12. complexion
13. compressor
14. pressure, expression
15. a. repress
    b. depress
    c. impress

Test Sentences

1. *conquer*	Satan will never *conquer* the church.
2. *librarian*	Ask the *librarian* to reserve the book.
3. *antecedent*	Thinking right is *antecedent* to doing right.
4. *pressure*	Water *pressure* increases with depth.
5. *curious*	After our accident, *curious* people came.
6. *seize*	The border police will *seize* illegal goods.
7. *appetite*	Many people have no *appetite* for olives.
8. *congress*	A country's *congress* can pass new laws.
9. *extension*	We asked for an *extension* of time.
10. *application*	Nelson filled out an *application.*
11. *reflected*	Titus's image was *reflected* in the water.
12. *complexion*	A Jew has a dark *complexion.*

B. AFFIXING AFFIXES

The suffix *-an* is another affix used to form adjectives that readily become nouns.

1. Write the spelling word that means both "associated with a republic" and "one who favors a republic."
2. Attach *-an* or *-ian* to each word. In the words you write, *-an* or *-ian* has a meaning much like that of *-er* or *-or* ("one who").
   a. guard c. library
   b. history d. electric
3. Use these Latin roots and the suffix *-an* to form words with the meanings indicated.
   a. *pag*: Heathen; idolatrous.
   b. *hum*: Pertaining to man.
   c. *urb*: Pertaining to the city.
   d. *medi*: Pertaining to the middle.
   e. *veter:* Pertaining to old age.

Adjective- and Noun-forming Suffixes

SUFFIX	MEANING	EXAMPLE
-an	belonging to *or* associated with	Roman
-ian	one who specializes in	musician

Many proper adjectives with *-an* or *-ian* become proper nouns whose suffixes indicate "inhabitant of" or "follower of."

4. Attach *-an* or *-ian* to these.
   a. Christ d. America
   b. Africa e. Mohammed
   c. Canada f. Italy
5. Write spelling words with these suffixes to match the definitions that follow.
   a. *-ible*: Capable of flexing.
   b. *-ant*: Accompanying; following.
   c. *-ary*: Helping; assisting.
   d. *-ite*: Desire for food.

C. SOUND, STRUCTURE, AND MEANING

1. Write the spelling words in which you hear these sounds.
   a. initial /g/ spelled *gu*
   b. /gz/ spelled *x*
   c. /ng/ spelled *n* before /g/
   d. final /ng/ spelled *ngue*
2. In which New Word is /ng/ spelled *n* and /kər/ spelled *quer*?
3. Write two spelling words for each.
   a. /s/ spelled *ss*
   b. /sh/ spelled *ss*
4. Which word has /ēz/ spelled *eize*? Write a homophone that means "large bodies of water," observing that in both words the *e* comes first.
5. Join *pressure* with *cabin, gauge,* and *cooker* to form open compounds with these meanings.
   a. A device for measuring pressure.
   b. A utensil for cooking under pressure.
   c. A pressurized airplane compartment.
6. Write the spelling words that are synonyms for these.
   a. language c. inquisitive
   b. pliant d. preceding
7. Capitalize a New Word and join it with *Party* to form an open compound that names a political group.

B. 20 points
1. republican
2. a. guardian
   b. historian
   c. librarian
   d. electrician
3. a. pagan
   b. human
   c. urban
   d. median
   e. veteran
4. a. Christian
   b. African
   c. Canadian
   d. American
   e. Mohammedan
   f. Italian
5. a. flexible
   b. attendant
   c. auxiliary
   d. appetite

C. 19 points
1. a. guardian
   b. auxiliary
   c. congress
   d. tongue
2. conquer
3. a compressor, congress
   b. pressure, expression
4. seize, seas
5. a. pressure gauge
   b. pressure cooker
   c. pressure cabin
6. a. tongue
   b. flexible
   c. curious
   d. antecedent
7. Republican Party

13. *applied*	Barbara *applied* oil to the squeaky hinges.
14. *flexible*	A garden hose is *flexible* and soft.
15. *expression*	The king saw Nehemiah's *expression.*
16. *attendant*	The station *attendant* checked our oil.
17. *guardian*	Mordecai was Esther's *guardian.*
18. *auxiliary*	"Will" is an *auxiliary* verb.
19. *inflection*	Our voice *inflection* helps to show our meaning.
20. *reflexes*	Your muscle *reflexes* are automatic.
21. *complicated*	Digestion of food is a *complicated* process.
22. *intention*	His *intention* was not to deny Christ.
23. *republican*	America has a *republican* government.
24. *compressor*	The air *compressor* would not work.
25. *tongue*	An anteater's *tongue* is long and thin.

D. LANGUAGE LINEAGE

Semantic Study: ELEVATION AND DEGENERATION

Elevation is the semantic change through which the meaning of a word becomes more pleasing and favorable than before. The meanings of the words on this chart have changed through elevation.

ELEVATION

Word	*Earlier meaning*	*Modern meaning*
affection	tendency of mind; inclination	a warm feeling
careful	full of care; anxious	thorough and diligent
constable	chief groom of a stable	a government official
emulation	selfish envy and ambition	a desire to excel
minister	a servant; slave	a church or civil leader

A word goes through *degeneration* when its meaning becomes less pleasant and favorable. The meanings of the words on the next chart have changed through degeneration.

DEGENERATION

Word	*Earlier meaning*	*Modern meaning*
forward	eager; earnest	bold; without proper reserve
heresy	a division; faction	a false doctrine
usury	interest on borrowed money	extremely high interest
villain	a farmer	a criminal
wench	a servant girl	an immoral woman

The degree of favorableness in the meaning of a word is part of its *connotation*. When a word goes through elevation, it takes on a better connotation. When a word goes through degeneration, it takes on a poorer connotation.

Exercises

1. In each verse, the King James Version has a word whose meaning has changed as described above. Copy the word, and write a word or phrase that could be used to replace it.
   a. Philippians 4:6 c. Galatians 2:10 e. 1 Corinthians 11:19
   b. 2 Samuel 17:17 d. Galatians 5:24 f. Matthew 20:26
2. These verses have words that could be replaced by the words shown in parentheses. Write the word whose meaning has changed, and tell whether it has gone through elevation or degeneration.
   a. 1 Corinthians 1:28 (lowly) c. Nehemiah 13:26 (foreign)
   b. Matthew 9:26 (report) d. Matthew 25:27 (interest)

D. 10 points
1. a. careful; anxious
   b. wench; servant girl
   c. forward; eager
   d. affections; inclinations
   e. heresies; divisions
   f. minister; servant
2. a. base; degeneration
   b. fame; elevation
   c. outlandish; degeneration
   d. usury; degeneration

Lesson 18—82 points (A–B)

LESSON 18

13	14	15	16	17
activity	affected	actually	absolutely	appetite
actor	affectionate	approval	assistant	application
agency	artificial	attraction	bankruptcy	applied
agenda	available	compel	continuous	attendant
agitate	believable	contractor	correspondent	auxiliary
defense	beneficial	contracts	dissolve	complicated
gracious	certificate	criminal	erupt	compressor
license	changeable	crystal	excellent	conquer
marvelous	comfortable	detract	exorbitant	curious
mischievous	cooperate	essential	immigrant	extension
mobile	effective	historical	impatient	flexible
motivate	facility	impelling	intelligent	guardian
movement	favorably	impulsive	interrupt	inflection
mysterious	feasible	knight	liable	intention
poisonous	miserable	personal	ligament	librarian
prairie	operation	repellent	maintenance	pressure
promotion	perfectly	repulsive	obligation	reflected
thorough	possibility	spiritual	obtained	reflexes
verbose	sensible	subtrahend	resolve	republican
virtuous	specified	technical	solution	seize

A. UNEARTHING THE ROOTS

mov, mob, mot	move	***lig***	bind
ag, act	do, set in motion	***ten, tin, tain***	hold
fac, fic	make, do	***solv, solu***	loosen, free
oper	work	***rupt***	burst, break
tract, trah	pull, draw, drag	***tend, tens, tent***	stretch
pel, puls	drive, push	***flex, flect***	bend
		plic, plex	fold
		press	press

See page 118 for test sentences.

L13: mov–mob–mot, ag–act

1. Answer with words having different forms of the *mov* root.
   a. The action of moving is ____*.
   b. "Shame shall be the ____* of fools" (Proverbs 3:35).
   c. There are some differences between modular homes and ____* homes.
2. Hiking was one [act]* on the day's [ag]*.
3. resident : residency :: agent : ____*

L14: fac, fic, oper

4. Be sure to use the correct spelling of the *fac* root in each word.
   a. bene__ial   d. __ility
   b. af__tionate   e. __ible
   c. ef__tive
5. Which New Word is a past form in which *fac* was spelled *fy* before *-ed* was added?
6. The [cert + fic]* stated that the leather was genuine and not [art + fic]*.
7. The [oper]* was unsuccessful because the men would not [oper]* (work together).

L15: tract–trah, pel–puls

8. Write the words with these elements.
   a. de (away) + tract (pull)
   b. con (together) + tract (draw) + or
   c. im (in) + puls (push) + ive
   d. im (in) + pel (drive) + ing
9. In a subtraction problem, the minuend is "drawn down" by the amount of the ____*.
10. Write the two words that begin with *re-* and have similar meanings but different forms of the *pel* root.
11. "And whosoever shall [pel]* thee to go a mile, go with him twain" (Matthew 5:41).

L16: lig, ten–tin–tain, solv–solu, rupt

12. Write the words with these elements.
    a. ob (toward) + lig (bind)
    b. lig (bind) + ment
    c. ab (from) + solu (loosen)
    d. bank (bench) + rupt (break)
    e. inter (between) + rupt (break)
13. Be sure to use the correct spelling of the *ten* root in each word.
    a. main__ance   c. ob__ed
    b. con__uous
14. "I have heard of thee, that thou canst make interpretations, and [solv]* doubts" (Daniel 5:16).
15. To [solv]* a problem is to find a [solu]* for it.
16. A dormant volcano is [li]* to [rupt]* again sometime, even after years of inactivity.

L17: tend–tens–tent, flex–flect, plic–plex, press

17. Write the words with these meanings.
    a. The act of stretching out.
    b. Capable of bending.
    c. Elaborately folded together; complex.
    d. A device that presses together.
    e. Actions that are "bent back" by nerves.
18. The service station [tend]* checked the air [press]* in all the tires.
19. The publisher was impressed by the job [plic],* for it [flect]* good writing skill.
20. The [flect]* of your voice often shows the [tent]* of a statement that you make.

A. 48 points
1. a. movement
   b. promotion
   c. mobile
2. activity, agenda
3. agency
4. a. beneficial
   b. affectionate
   c. effective
   d. facility
   e. feasible
5. specified
6. certificate, artificial
7. operation, cooperate
8. a. detract
   b. contractor
   c. impulsive
   d. impelling
9. subtrahend
10. repellent, repulsive
11. compel
12. a. obligation
    b. ligament
    c. absolutely
    d. bankruptcy
    e. interrupt
13. a. maintenance
    b. continuous
    c. obtained
14. dissolve
15. resolve, solution
16. liable, erupt
17. a. extension
    b. flexible
    c. complicated
    d. compressor
    e. reflexes
18. attendant, pressure
19. application, reflected
20. inflection, intention

B. AFFIXING AFFIXES

Adjective- and Noun-forming Suffixes	
-ous, -ose	full of, having, abounding in
-able, -ible	capable of *or* tending to
-al	pertaining to; act or condition of
-ant, -ent	in the process or act of; one who *or* that which
-an, -ian	belonging to *or* associated with; one who specializes in

1. Form Lesson 13 words by adding *-ous.*
   a. marvel d. grace
   b. virtue e. poison
   c. mystery f. mischief
2. Write the word that ends with *-ose* and means "full of words." [13]
3. In chemistry, *-ose* often indicates the name of a ____. [13]
4. Write spelling words ending with *-able* or *-ible* that are derived from these words.
   a. sense [14] c. believe [14]
   b. avail [14] d. flex [17]
5. a. Add *-able* to *change.* [14]
   b. Final *e* in *change* is (dropped, retained).
6. Write Lesson 14 words with these parts.
   a. favor + able c. miser + able
   b. posse + ible d. fac (feas) + ible
7. Make spelling words by attaching *-al, -ant,* or *-ent* to these words.
   a. approve [15] c. excel [16]
   b. assist [16] d. correspond [16]
8. Attach *-an* or *-ian* to these.
   a. guard [17] c. library [17]
   b. republic [17] d. physic
9. When *-an* or *-ian* is attached to a proper noun, the result is often a proper noun that means "____ of or ____ of." [17]
10. Attach *-an* or *-ian* to these proper nouns.
    a. Egypt b. Luther
11. Make spelling words by attaching *dis-, ex-, im-,* or *pro-* to these words.
    a. motion [13] c. solve [16]
    b. patient [16] d. tension [17]

D. LANGUAGE LINEAGE

1. Name two modern languages that developed from the speech of the Celts.
2. About what fraction of all Modern English words are of Latin origin?
3. Why could not all speakers of Old English understand each other?
4. Name two things that the Roman Catholic missionaries did which had a definite influence on the English language.
5. Long ago *amateur* meant "one who loves an activity." Today it means "one who is unskilled in an activity." Has *amateur* gone through elevation or degeneration?

B. 34 points
1. a. marvelous
   b. virtuous
   c. mysterious
   d. gracious
   e. poisonous
   f. mischievous
2. verbose
3. sugar
4. a. sensible
   b. available
   c. believable
   d. flexible
5. a. changeable
   b. retained
6. a. favorably
   b. possibility
   c. miserable
   d. feasible
7. a. approval
   b. assistant
   c. excellent
   d. correspondent
8. a. guardian
   b. republican
   c. librarian
   d. physician
9. inhabitant, follower
10. a. Egyptian
    b. Lutheran
11. a. promotion
    b. impatient
    c. dissolve
    d. extension

D. 8 points
1. (Any two.) Welsh, Irish Gaelic, Scottish Gaelic, Breton
2. about half
3. There were many dialects of Old English, with great differences between some of them.
4. (Any two; other answers possible.) They established churches. They taught the Latin alphabet. They introduced classical learning.
5. degeneration

LESSON 19

NEW WORDS

1. compensation
2. dependent
3. edition
4. effort
5. eliminate
6. enormous
7. estate
8. exaggerated
9. excommunicate
10. exemption
11. exhibit
12. existing
13. expenditure
14. expenses
15. experiment
16. explanation
17. expose
18. extremely
19. premium
20. redemption

REVIEW WORDS

21. credible
22. enrolled
23. excellent
24. honestly
25. virtuous

A. UNEARTHING THE ROOTS

ROOT	MEANING	EXAMPLE
pend, pens	hang, weigh	suspend
empt, em	take, buy	redemption

pend, pens

1. A child who depends on his parents for support is called a ____*.
2. Three New Words with the *pend, pens* root have to do with paying money. The reason is that payments long ago were made by weighing out silver or gold with a hanging balance. Write these words; they begin with *com-* or *ex-*.
3. Choose from these words: *appendix, impending, pendant, pendulum, pension, suspense*.
   a. We may gasp and hold our breath when we are in great ____.
   b. A Foucault ____ hangs from a high support and swings slowly back and forth, showing the rotation of the earth.
   c. A section "hung to" the end of a book is called a(n) ____.
   d. A hanging ornament may be called a(n) ____.
   e. A certain amount of money "weighed out" each month to a retired person is called a(n) ____.
   f. Danger hanging directly overhead is ____ danger.
4. Both a suspension bridge and a suspended ceiling (hang from a higher support, rest on a lower support).

empt, em

5. An ____* from military service takes one out of the army.
6. a. The blood of Jesus has purchased the ____* of all men.
   b. What is the verb form of the word you wrote for *a*?
7. Something extra given as a reward is a ____*. (This word comes from *pre-* and *em*.)
8. Choose from these words: *pre-empt, prompt*.
   a. To ____ something is to take or buy it before another person has the chance.
   b. To be ____ is to act without delay. (This word comes from *pro-* and *empt*.)

Lesson 19—58 points (A–C)

A. 17 points
1. dependent
2. compensation, expenditure, expenses
3. a. suspense
   b. pendulum
   c. appendix
   d. pendant
   e. pension
   f. impending
4. hang from a higher support
5. exemption
6. a. redemption
   b. redeem
7. premium
8. a. pre-empt
   b. prompt

Test Sentences

1. *edition*	This is the third *edition* of our paper.
2. *explanation*	Please give an *explanation* to me.
3. *exhibit*	We enjoyed the museum's airplane *exhibit.*
4. *dependent*	A baby is totally *dependent* on others.
5. *experiment*	We will *experiment* with bean seeds.
6. *existing*	Only a few bald eagles are *existing* now.
7. *compensation*	Ray received *compensation* for his work.
8. *expenditure*	Buying a car is a big *expenditure.*
9. *premium*	Do you buy *premium* gasoline?
10. *effort*	With *effort,* Lois pulled the stubborn weed.
11. *credible*	He had a *credible* reason for being late.
12. *exemption*	The blind receive a tax *exemption.*

B. AFFIXING AFFIXES

PREFIX	MEANING	EXAMPLE
ex-, e-	away, out from	expel

1. Write spelling words beginning with *ex-* to match these definitions.
   a. To place outside; remove cover from.
   b. To put out for display.
   c. Inflated out of proportion; overstated.
   d. To put out of the church.
   e. To try out a hypothesis.
   f. To a degree farthest out; exceedingly.
2. Write the New Word that is a combination *ex-* and *fort* (a form of *forc*). Observe that assimilation has affected this spelling.
3. Write the New Words with the prefix *e-* and these roots.
   a. norm b. dit
4. Write the New Word with the prefix *e-* and the original meaning "cast out over the threshold" (*limen*).
5. You have studied the following roots in previous lessons. Write an English verb beginning with *ex-* that contains each one.
   a. clam (claim) c. pel
   b. tract d. press
6. Write the spelling words that have these affixes.
   a. -ible c. com-, ation
   b. en-, -ed d. ex-, -ing
7. Write the *-ion* or *-ation* forms of these words.
   a. edit c. exempt
   b. explain d. redeem
8. Write the New Word that has *pre-* and the root *em,* but only one *e*.

C. SOUND, STRUCTURE, AND MEANING

1. Write the spelling words in which you hear these sounds.
   a. /mē/ spelled *mi*
   b. /j/ spelled *gg*
2. Which two spelling words have *h* but no /h/ sound?
3. Join *real* with a New Word to form an open compound that means "tract of land, along with the buildings, trees, and minerals on it."
4. Write the spelling words that complete these analogies.
   a. gnat : tiny :: whale : ____*
   b. automobile : model :: book : ____*
   c. school : expel :: church : ____*
   d. Jezebel : idolatrous :: Hannah : ____*
   e. balloon : inflated :: story : ____*
5. Which spelling words are synonyms for these?
   a. wages c. salvation
   b. believable d. superior
6. An *enormity* is an outrageous crime.
   a. In the Speller Dictionary, what definition for *enormous* has a similar idea?
   b. How is this definition labeled?
7. Which syllable of *estate* is accented?
8. The *er* in *experiment* should be pronounced (/er/, /îr/).

61

B. 23 points
1. a. expose
   b. exhibit
   c. exaggerated
   d. excommunicate
   e. experiment
   f. extremely
2. effort
3. a. enormous
   b. edition
4. eliminate
5. a. exclaim
   b. extract
   c. expel
   d. express
6. a. credible
   b. enrolled (1)
   c. compensation (1)
   d. existing (1)
7. a. edition
   b. explanation
   c. exemption
   d. redemption
8. premium

C. 18 points
1. a. premium
   b. exaggerated
2. exhibit, honestly
3. real estate
4. a. enormous
   b. edition
   c. excommunicate
   d. virtuous
   e. exaggerated
5. a. compensation
   b. credible
   c. redemption
   d. excellent
6. a. very wicked; shocking; abominable
   b. Archaic
7. second syllable
8. /er/

13. *expose* — Do not *expose* yourself to unsound teaching.
14. *enrolled* — Twenty children *enrolled* in the class.
15. *eliminate* — We must try to *eliminate* bad habits.
16. *expenses* — His employer paid his business *expenses.*
17. *enormous* — Whales are *enormous* mammals.
18. *redemption* — Our *redemption* was bought by Jesus.
19. *extremely* — Dynamite is *extremely* dangerous.
20. *estate* — A deceased person's *estate* belongs to his heirs.
21. *excellent* — Moses was an *excellent* leader.
22. *exaggerated* — Goliath *exaggerated* his strength.
23. *honestly* — The apostle Paul lived *honestly* before men.
24. *excommunicate* — The church must *excommunicate* disobedient members.
25. *virtuous* — Dorcas was a *virtuous* woman.

D. LANGUAGE LINEAGE

FIRST BIBLE ACCOUNTS IN ENGLISH

The language of the Roman Catholic Church was Latin. The priests and the monks in England must have used the English language in teaching the doctrines of the church to the people; but the church services were always conducted in Latin, and the Bible was read only in Latin. All the religious knowledge that the common people had was what the church leaders taught them.

This began to change in about the year 680. Around that time a monk named Caedmon (kad′mən) began to write some of the accounts in the Latin Bible as Old English poetry. His works included stories from Genesis, Exodus, Daniel, and other books of the Bible. Caedmon did not do any actual translating of the Scriptures, but his work did allow the common people to obtain some knowledge of the Bible on their own.

Other writers were inspired by Caedmon's example, and soon they too were writing Bible accounts as Old English poetry. While only one of Caedmon's poems has survived to modern times, a number of these other writers' works are in existence today. Below are several lines from such a poem, along with a translation in a more modern form of English.

Ne beoth ge thy forhtran, theah the Faraon
brohte sweordwigendra side hergas, eorla
unrim! Him eallum wile mihtig drihten thurh
mine hand to daege thissum daedlean gyfan,
thaet hie lifigende leng ne moton aegnian
mid yrmthum Israhela cyn.

Be not ye frightened thereat, though Pharaoh
hath brought sword-wielders, vast troops,
men unnumbered! To them all will the mighty
Lord through my hand this very day a recom-
pense give, that they might not live long to
frighten with distress Israel's kin.

Exercises

1. In the 600s, the religious knowledge of the common people in England came almost entirely from the church leaders. Why was this so?
2. What were the first Bible accounts written in the English language? In your answer, include the name of the man who first wrote these accounts.
3. How were the first Bible accounts in English a benefit to the common people?
4. How was the work of Caedmon carried on by others?

D. 8 points
1. The church services were always conducted in Latin, and the Bible was read only in Latin.
2. They were accounts from the Latin Bible, which Caedmon wrote as Old English poetry.
3. They allowed the common people to obtain some knowledge of the Bible on their own.
4. Other writers were inspired by Caedmon's example, and soon they produced more Bible accounts in Old English.

LESSON 20

NEW WORDS

1. collateral
2. consequently
3. covenant
4. declaration
5. deduct
6. deference
7. deferred
8. denomination
9. difference
10. educational
11. executive
12. latitude
13. persecution
14. reduction
15. relation
16. sequence
17. submitted
18. substitute
19. subway
20. transferred

REVIEW WORDS

21. agitate
22. despise
23. doctrine
24. inspect
25. mobile

A. UNEARTHING THE ROOTS

ROOT	MEANING	EXAMPLE
duc	lead	conduct
sequ, secut	follow	sequence
fer, lat	bear, carry	transfer, relate
later	side	lateral

duc

1. The Bible is the most highly [duc]* book because it can "lead (men) out" of spiritual darkness.
2. To ____* is to "lead down" (take away or subtract).
3. The act of leading to a lower or smaller condition is ____*.
4. Combine each prefix with the *duc* root (spelled *duce*) to form verbs with the meanings given.
   a. *in-:* "To lead into"; persuade.
   b. *se-:* "To lead away"; entice.
   c. *into-:* "To lead toward"; present.
   d. *pro-:* "To lead forth"; bring about.

sequ, secut

5. Friday comes before Thursday in alphabetical ____*.
6. If something happens ____*, it follows an action that caused it.
7. An ____* is one who "follows out" or carries through business decisions. (Note that the *x* of *ex-* replaces the *s* of *secut.*)
8. Thousands of Christians have been followed and hunted down during times of religious ____*.

fer, lat

9. To show [fer]* to one's parents in areas of [fer]* is one way to "honour thy father and thy mother."
10. Another way of saying that a meeting has been postponed is to say that it has been ____*.
11. The broken transmission no longer ____* (carried across) the power from the engine to the wheels.
12. The root *lat* is related to *fer* because Latin *latus* is a past form of *ferre* (to carry). Write the New Word with *re-* and *lat.*

later

13. Property "placed alongside" a loan for security is ____*.
14. If a person has a wide enough space to work, he has ____* to work. (This word is derived not from a lesson root but from the Latin word *latus,* wide.)

63

Lesson 20—64 points (A–C)

A. 18 points
1. educational
2. deduct
3. reduction
4. a. induce
   b. seduce
   c. introduce
   d. produce
5. sequence
6. consequently
7. executive
8. persecution
9. deference, difference
10. deferred
11. transferred
12. relation
13. collateral
14. latitude

See page 72 for test sentences.

B. AFFIXING AFFIXES

PREFIX	MEANING	EXAMPLE
de-	down, away	detract
sub-	under	submerge

1. Write spelling words with the prefix *de-* to match these definitions.
   a. To take away (a number or an amount).
   b. To look down on.
   c. The act of yielding to the wishes of another.
   d. Delayed; put off.
   e. The name of a class; category.
2. Attach *de-* to each word.
   a. part c. valuate
   b. tour d. pressurize

An *intensifier* is a prefix that makes the meaning of a root more emphatic. The prefix *de-* is a common intensifier.

3. Write the NEW WORD with the prefix *de-*, the root *clar,* and the original meaning "act of making completely clear."
4. Write spelling words beginning with *sub-* to match these definitions.
   a. Came under the authority of.
   b. A train that travels under the street level.
5. Attach *sub-* to each word.
   a. soil c. conscious
   b. sonic d. division
6. Sometimes *sub-* means "instead." Write the word that means "put or do instead of."
7. Which two NEW WORDS end with *-al*?
8. Write spelling words with these affixes.
   a. -ile c. -ive
   b. trans- d. con-, -ly

C. SOUND, STRUCTURE, AND MEANING

1. Write the spelling words in which you hear these sounds.
   a. /kw/ spelled *qu* (2)
   b. /j/ spelled *d*
   c. /uv/ spelled *ov*
   d. final /trin/ spelled *trine*.
2. Write the past forms of these.
   a. submit c. transfer
   b. excel d. equip
3. Join *book* with a REVIEW WORD to form a closed compound that means "traveling library."
4. Which two NEW WORDS are verbs that are synonyms of *yielded*?
5. Write a NEW WORD to match each pair.
   a. subtract, decrease
   b. kinsman, relative
   c. freedom, leeway
6. Write spelling words that are antonyms for these.
   a. calm (verb) c. similarity
   b. enlargement d. stationary
7. Write the two REVIEW WORDS whose roots have to do with "looking." (See Lesson 9.)
8. *Defer* has two entries in the Speller Dictionary. Match the meanings below to the entries by writing 1 or 2.
   a. To obey; yield; comply.
   b. To put off; delay; postpone.

64

B. 23 points
1. a. deduct
   b. despise
   c. deference
   d. deferred
   e. denomination
2. a. depart
   b. detour
   c. devaluate
   d. depressurize
3. declaration
4. a. submitted
   b. subway
5. a. subsoil
   b. subsonic
   c. subconscious
   d. subdivision
6. substitute
7. collateral, educational
8. a. mobile
   b. transferred
   c. executive
   d. consequently

C. 23 points
1. a. consequently, sequence
   b. educational
   c. covenant
   d. doctrine
2. a. submitted
   b. excelled
   c. transferred
   d. equipped
3. bookmobile
4. deferred, submitted
5. a. deduct
   b. relation
   c. latitude
6. a. agitate
   b. reduction
   c. difference
   d. mobile
7. despise, inspect
8. a. 2
   b. 1

Test Sentences

1. *deferred*	We *deferred* our trip until next year.
2. *reduction*	A discount is a *reduction* in price.
3. *substitute*	Margarine is a *substitute* for butter.
4. *collateral*	Mr. Hansen used his car as *collateral* for a loan.
5. *agitate*	Bubbles form when we *agitate* soapy water.
6. *denomination*	Which *denomination* do we attend?
7. *relation*	Nancy is a blood *relation* of mine.
8. *consequently*	Anna fell and *consequently* broke her leg.
9. *inspect*	We wanted to *inspect* the pretty butterfly.
10. *difference*	Tell the *difference* between the two.
11. *sequence*	Number them in the proper *sequence*.
12. *covenant*	God made a *covenant* with Abraham.

D. LANGUAGE LINEAGE

OLD ENGLISH DIALECTS

The Angles, Saxons, and Jutes formed seven main kingdoms on the island of Britain. All these people spoke Germanic dialects that were different yet essentially similar. Their language is known today as Old English; but as you learned in Lesson 15, there were nearly two hundred dialects of the language. These dialects can be divided into four groups, each with certain basic similarities. The map below shows the general area where each group of dialects was spoken.

The dialects in the Northumbrian and the Mercian groups were spoken in the areas inhabited mostly by the Angles. The Kentish dialects were used in the small area where the Jutes lived, and the dialects of West Saxon were spoken by people of the Saxon tribe. Most of the Old English literature that we have today was written in West Saxon dialects.

As time passed, the kingdom of the West Saxons (Wessex) slowly gained power and influence over all the other kingdoms. By 829 King Egbert of Wessex had subdued the other kings and was starting to blend the seven kingdoms into one unified nation. Through these events, the dialects of Wessex became more uniform and grew in esteem. Eventually the speech of Wessex became something of a standard for the speech of the entire nation.

Dialectal Regions of Britain, c. A.D. 700

Exercises

1. Write the names of the four groups of Old English dialects in a column. Beside each, write the name of the tribe which spoke dialects of that group.
2. What two major rivers marked the boundaries of dialectal regions in Britain?
3. What reason is there to think that the Northumbrian, Mercian, and Kentish dialects were chiefly spoken rather than written?
4. Why did the speech of Wessex become more uniform and gain higher esteem in the 800s?

D. 14 points

1. Northumbrian—Angles
   Mercian—Angles
   Kentish—Jutes
   West Saxons—Saxons
2. Humber River and Thames River
3. Most of the Old English literature that we have today was written not in those dialects but in West Saxon dialects.
4. King Egbert of Wessex started to blend the seven Anglo-Saxon kingdoms into one unified nation.

13. *educational* A visit to the zoo is *educational.*
14. *transferred* Brian *transferred* to our school.
15. *declaration* They rejected his *declaration* of truth.
16. *executive* A business *executive* makes many decisions.
17. *submitted* Jesus *submitted* to His Father's will.
18. *deduct* Did you *deduct* any points from his score?
19. *latitude* Lines of *latitude* encircle a globe.
20. *subway* The Millers rode a *subway* in the city.
21. *deference* We must show *deference* to the elderly.
22. *mobile* A new *mobile* home was being set up.
23. *doctrine* The Sadducees taught a false *doctrine.*
24. *persecution* Paul suffered severe *persecution.*
25. *despise* God does not *despise* a humble heart.

LESSON 21

NEW WORDS

1. caution
2. circuit
3. circumference
4. circumstances
5. coarse
6. communication
7. compliance
8. confirming
9. contrition
10. conversation
11. conversion
12. converted
13. conviction
14. cooperation
15. coordinate
16. diverse
17. involved
18. revolution
19. rhubarb
20. wrought

REVIEW WORDS

21. circular
22. essential
23. possibility
24. visual
25. wrestle

A. UNEARTHING THE ROOTS

ROOT	MEANING	EXAMPLE
vert, vers	turn	reverse
volv, volu	roll	revolve
circum	around	circumference

vert, vers

1. Write a New Word for each meaning.
   a. The act of turning completely (*con-*).
   b. A speaking back and forth by turns.
   c. Turned completely; changed.
2. Items "turned away" (different) from each other are ____*.
3. Choose from these words: *avert, invert, subvert.*
   a. To turn upside down.
   b. To turn away from happening; prevent.
   c. To turn (a person) away from sound doctrine.
4. Choose from these words: *perverse, reverse, transverse.*
   a. To turn back; go in the opposite direction.
   b. Turned completely from the good and right.
   c. Turned crosswise.

volv, volu

5. Write a New Word for each meaning.
   a. Rolled (something) into; included.
   b. An act of rolling over; complete change.
6. Choose from these words: *convolution, evolution, volume.*
   a. According to the theory of ____, things in the world just happened to turn out as they are today.
   b. "In the ____ [roll or scroll] of the book it is written of me" (Hebrews 10:7).
   c. A ____ is something that is rolled together.

circum

7. Write a spelling word for each meaning.
   a. Factors around an event.
   b. A going around; circular route.
   c. The distance around a circle.
   d. Shaped like a circle.

Lesson 21—57 points (A–C)

A. 19 points
1. a. conversion
   b. conversation
   c. converted
2. diverse
3. a. invert
   b. avert
   c. subvert
4. a. reverse
   b. perverse
   c. transverse
5. a. involved
   b. revolution
6. a. evolution
   b. volume
   c. convolution
7. a. circumstances
   b. circuit
   c. circumference
   d. circular

Test Sentences

1. *contrition*	Psalm 51 shows David's *contrition.*
2. *diverse*	The world has many *diverse* languages.
3. *conversation*	The boys' *conversation* was about tractors.
4. *caution*	Handle explosives with great *caution.*
5. *conversion*	Saul's *conversion* was near Damascus.
6. *involved*	Our church is *involved* in a prison work.
7. *circuit*	Electricity travels in a *circuit.*
8. *converted*	He *converted* our oil furnace to gas.
9. *revolution*	The moon's *revolution* takes a month.
10. *circumference*	We measured its *circumference.*
11. *conviction*	Brother John talked with *conviction.*
12. *rhubarb*	Mother baked a *rhubarb* pie.

B. AFFIXING AFFIXES

PREFIX	MEANING	EXAMPLE
com-	with, together	compress

1. The prefix *com-* is derived from the Latin preposition *cum* (with). By assimilation, this prefix may also be spelled *con-, col-* and *cor-*. Write the spelling words that have *com-* and these roots.
   a. trit b. pli
2. Attach a form of *com-* to each word.
   a. pose d. respond
   b. lapse e. lateral
   c. tend f. sequence
3. Before vowels, *com-* is spelled *co-*. Write the two New Words that have this spelling.
4. Like *de-*, the prefix *com-* is often used as an intensifier. Write the spelling words that have *com-,* the following roots, and the original meanings after them.
   a. *firm*: Make thoroughly firm.
   b. *vic*: Conquer thoroughly.
5. Different meanings of *com-* can be seen in its combinations with *vers*.
   a. Which spelling word means "act of talking together by turns"?
   b. Which two words have the idea of "turning completely"?
6. In one spelling word beginning with *com*, these letters are not a prefix but are part of the Latin word for *common*. Which word is this?
7. Write the New Word in which *dis-* became *di-* before *vers*.
8. Which spelling words have these affixes?
   a. -ible, -ity b. re-, -ion
9. Write the derived forms indicated.
   a. coarse + ness b. circuit + ous

C. SOUND, STRUCTURE, AND MEANING

1. Write the spelling words in which you hear these sounds.
   a. /zhōō/ spelled *su*
   b. /kit/ spelled *cuit*
   c. initial /r/ spelled *rh*
   d. initial /r/ spelled *wr* (2)
2. Form open compounds by joining *circuit* and *visual* with the following words.
   a. aid b. short
3. Do not confuse *coarse* and *course.* Write the correct word for each sentence.
   a. The last ____ of bricks was laid.
   b. This sandpaper is so ____ that it leaves a rough surface.
4. Which spelling words have these meanings?
   a. The act of yielding; obedience.
   b. Very important; absolutely necessary.
   c. A firm religious belief.
   d. To cause to act harmoniously.
   e. Carefulness; wariness.
5. One New Word has the archaic meaning "worked, done, or made" (as in Numbers 23:23) and the modern meaning "shaped by hammering." Write this word.
6. Read the entry for *circumference* in the Speller Dictionary. Then write this word and a synonym that has a similar history but comes from Greek.

B. 21 points
1. a. contrition
   b. compliance
2. a. compose
   b. collapse
   c. contend
   d. correspond
   e. collateral
   f. consequence
3. cooperation, coordinate
4. a. confirming
   b. conviction
5. a. conversation
   b. conversion, converted
6. communication
7. diverse
8. a. possibility
   b. revolution
9. a. coarseness
   b. circuitous

C. 17 points
1. a. visual
   b. circuit
   c. rhubarb
   d. wrought, wrestle
2. a. visual aid
   b. short circuit
3. a. course
   b. coarse
4. a. compliance
   b. essential
   c. conviction
   d. coordinate
   e. caution
5. wrought
6. circumference, periphery

13. *circumstances* — Under no *circumstances* should we steal.
14. *cooperation* — This job requires *cooperation.*
15. *wrought* — The railing was made of *wrought* iron.
16. *coarse* — Cornmeal is a *coarse* flour.
17. *circular* — The earth travels in a *circular* path.
18. *visual* — Our eyes are *visual* organs.
19. *communication* — Prayer is *communication.*
20. *essential* — Water is *essential* to living things.
21. *possibility* — There is a *possibility* I may come.
22. *compliance* — We want willing *compliance* with the rules.
23. *wrestle* — Ralph found it hard to *wrestle* with the problem.
24. *coordinate* — Which will *coordinate* with yellow?
25. *confirming* — His honesty is *confirming* our trust.

D. LANGUAGE LINEAGE

CHARACTERISTICS OF OLD ENGLISH

Old English (or Anglo-Saxon) may be considered the foundation of Middle English and Modern English. It was during the Old English period that the basic structure and vocabulary of the language developed. About 15 percent of the Modern English vocabulary is of Anglo-Saxon origin, and most of these words are the common ones that we use in everyday speech.

Old English was a highly inflected language. There were many spelling changes and word endings to indicate gender, number, case, person, mood, and tense. The tables below illustrate some of the many Old English inflections.

As time passed, the language slowly became simpler. Most of the inflections were gradually lost, and today we have only the ones shown in part B of Lesson 1. This fact illustrates the general truth that languages tend to change from a complex form to a simpler form; they do not "evolve" from the simple to the complex. The most complex form of a language is its earliest form; and the longer a language is used, the simpler it tends to become.

Old English Noun Inflections (for *hunter*)

	Singular	*Plural*
Nominative case	the **hunta** came	the **huntan** came
Possessive case	the **huntan** arrows	the **huntena** arrows
Dative case	gave the **huntan** permission	gave the **huntum** permission
Objective case	for the **huntan**	for the **huntan**

Old English Verb Inflections (for *drive*)

	Present tense		Past tense	
	Singular	*Plural*	*Singular*	*Plural*
First person	I **drīfe**	we **drīfath**	I **drāf**	we **drifon**
Second person	thou **drīfst**	you **drīfath**	thou **drife**	you **drifon**
Third person	he **drīfth**	they **drīfath**	he **drāf**	they **drifon**

Exercises

1. a. What portion of today's English words come from Anglo-Saxon?
   b. What kind of words are they?
2. In a highly inflected language, different forms of words are used to show what six things?
3. As a language develops, does it generally become more simple or more complex?
4. Write the correct Modern English form of each underlined word.
   a. The three <u>huntena</u> dogs were soon chasing a fox.
   b. Most farmers <u>drifon</u> horses and wagons in the 1800s.
   c. Pedro <u>drīfth</u> a water buffalo to the rice fields every day.

D. 12 points
1. a. about 15 percent
   b. the common words used in everyday speech
2. gender, number, case, person, mood, tense
3. more simple
4. a. hunters'
   b. drove
   c. drives

LESSON 22

NEW WORDS

1. admission
2. committee
3. conceit
4. convenience
5. convention
6. enterprise
7. exceed
8. illustrate
9. inspired
10. intercede
11. interfere
12. interior
13. internal
14. investigate
15. precede
16. relieve
17. remittance
18. succeed
19. successfully
20. succession

REVIEW WORDS

21. dismissal
22. hygiene
23. missionary
24. reindeer
25. seize

A. UNEARTHING THE ROOTS

ROOT	MEANING	EXAMPLE
mit, miss	send, let go	mission
cede, ceed, cess	go, yield	proceed
ven, vent	come	convene

mit, miss

1. Write a spelling word for each meaning.
   a. A group of persons sent (assigned) to do a certain thing.
   b. Money that is sent.
   c. The act of letting one go in.
   d. One who is sent to preach the Gospel.
   e. The act of sending away.

2. Choose from these words: *omit, permit, submit, transmit.*
   a. To let go through; allow.
   b. To leave out; neglect.
   c. To send across; pass on.
   d. To let go under; yield.

cede, ceed, cess

3. Write a spelling word for each meaning.
   a. To go between; mediate.
   b. To go before.
   c. A going one after another.
   d. To go beyond (a limit); surpass.
   e. To go well; prosper.
   f. In a prosperous manner.

4. Choose from these words: *concede, recede, secede.*
   a. To go apart; withdraw.
   b. To go back; abate.
   c. To go along with; acknowledge.

ven, vent

5. Write a spelling word for each meaning.
   a. A coming together well; suitability.
   b. A coming together; meeting.

6. Choose from these: *circumvent, invent, intervene.*
   a. To come between.
   b. To come (or go) around; avoid.
   c. To cause to come into being; devise.

Lesson 22—64 points (A–C)

A. 23 points
1. a. committee
   b. remittance
   c. admission
   d. missionary
   e. dismissal
2. a. permit
   b. omit
   c. transmit
   d. submit
3. a. intercede
   b. precede
   c. succession
   d. exceed
   e. succeed
   f. successfully
4. a. secede
   b. recede
   c. concede
5. a. convenience
   b. convention
6. a. intervene
   b. circumvent
   c. invent

See page 78 for test sentences.

B. AFFIXING AFFIXES

PREFIX	MEANING	EXAMPLE
in-	in, into	inspire
inter-	between, within	intercede

1. Which spelling words beginning with *in-* have these definitions?
   a. To look into a matter.
   b. Breathed in; also, stirred with a feeling.
2. Form verbs by attaching *in-* to these roots.
   a. spect d. habit
   b. volv e. quir
   c. dulg f. clud
3. The prefix *in-* may become *il-, im-,* or *ir-* by assimilation. Join one of these forms to each word.
   a. pulse c. radiate
   b. lustrate d. migrant
4. Write spelling words beginning with *inter-* to match these definitions.
   a. To hinder by coming between.
   b. Pertaining to what is within. (2)
   c. To go between as a mediator.
5. Write words with *inter-* to fit in these sentences. The words in italics are clues.
   a. An ____ highway connects various *states* one to another.
   b. Many *nations* were represented in the ____ convention.
   c. Airplanes on ____ flights allow travel between different *continents.*
6. The French spelling of *inter-* is *enter-* or *entre-*. Write the New Word that illustrates this spelling.
7. Write the spelling words that are the *-ion, -ance,* or *-al* forms of these words.
   a. admit c. convene
   b. remit d. dismiss

C. SOUND, STRUCTURE, AND MEANING

1. Write the spelling words in which you hear these sounds.
   a. /m/, /t/, and /ē/ spelled with double letters
   b. /sē/ spelled *sei*
   c. final /ēn/ spelled *iene*
   d. final /ēv/ spelled *ieve*
2. Write the spelling word in which *e* comes before *i* because
   a. *ei* spells /ā/. b. *ei* follows *c*.
3. Write *proceed,* and then write two New Words that have the same spelling of /sēd/. *Note:* These are the only three English words with /sēd/ is spelled *ceed.*
4. The most common spelling of /sēd/ is *cede.* Which two New Words have this spelling?
5. Write the spelling words that could replace the underlined words.
   a. These fumes should not be inhaled.
   b. Jesus is at the Father's right hand to mediate for the believer.
   c. The new birth is necessary for entrance into God's kingdom.
   d. Shaking hands is a custom that has been practiced for centuries.
6. Write the New Words that are antonyms for *external* and *exterior.*

B. 24 points
1. a. investigate
   b. inspired
2. a. inspect
   b. involve
   c. indulge
   d. inhabit
   e. inquire
   f. include
3. a. impulse
   b. illustrate
   c. irradiate
   d. immigrant
4. a. interfere
   b. interior, internal
   c. intercede
5. a. interstate
   b. international
   c. intercontinental
6. enterprise
7. a. admission
   b. remittance
   c. convention
   d. dismissal

C. 17 points
1. a. committee
   b. seize
   c. hygiene
   d. relieve
2. a. reindeer
   b. conceit
3. proceed, exceed, succeed
4. intercede, precede
5. a. inspired
   b. intercede
   c. admission
   d. convention
6. internal, interior

Test Sentences

1. *interfere* — The weather could *interfere* with our plans.
2. *remittance* — Please send your *remittance* soon.
3. *succeed* — Joash could not *succeed* without God.
4. *convention* — This *convention* is held every year.
5. *interior* — The trailer's *interior* walls were brown.
6. *enterprise* — His new business *enterprise* failed.
7. *dismissal* — Before *dismissal,* they sang a song.
8. *missionary* — Lucy is a *missionary* in Africa.
9. *internal* — Our heart is an *internal* organ.
10. *exceed* — Drivers should not *exceed* the speed limit.
11. *admission* — The museum's *admission* charge is low.
12. *illustrate* — Many parables *illustrate* truth.

D. LANGUAGE LINEAGE

CHARACTERISTICS OF OLD ENGLISH

Old English writing such as the Lord's Prayer in Lesson 1 appears quite strange to a reader of Modern English. One reason is that it contains several Old English characters that are no longer in use today. These characters are discussed in Lesson 25.

A second reason for the strange appearance of Old English is that the spelling patterns are unfamiliar to us. A number of Old English words were pronounced very much as we pronounce them today; but because of their spelling, it is difficult for us to recognize those words.

In Old English, the /sh/ sound is spelled *sc*. Thus we find *scort* for *short* and *scip* for *ship*. The /k/ sound is spelled *c*: *cynn* for *kin* and *folc* for *folk.* The spelling of /kw/ is *cw: cwic* for *quick* and *cwēn* for *queen.* It appears that Old English spellings were determined almost entirely by the spoken sounds in words; there were very few words in which the spelling did not agree with the pronunciation. However, since pronunciations varied from one dialect to another, it was a definite problem to establish regular spellings.

Although some Old English words have not changed in pronunciation, there are a number that did change. One example is some words with the /ā/ sound, in which /ā/ has changed to /ō/. Thus *stān* has become *stone, hālig* is now *holy*, and *bāt* has changed to *boat.* Other words whose vowels have changed are *hūs* (house), *gōd* (good), *strang* (strong), and *cild* (child)—which was pronounced like *killed*.

As you can see, the basic form of many English words has stayed unchanged since the Old English period. But there have been so many changes in spelling and pronunciation that special study is necessary before a reader of Modern English can read Old English literature in its original form.

Exercises

1. For what three reasons does Old English writing appear strange to a reader of Modern English?
2. Why was it difficult to establish regular spellings in Old English times?
3. Write the modern spelling of each Old English word. You will need to drop the *-an* endings.
   a. scēap c. wascan e. cwellan
   b. sēcan d. cyng f. scrincan
4. Also write the modern spellings of these, whose pronunciations have changed according to the patterns described above.
   a. bān c. rād e. hōc
   b. ūt d. lang f. clūd

D. 20 points
1. Such literature contains Old English characters that are no longer used today. The words have unfamiliar spelling patterns. The pronunciations of some of the words have changed.
2. Spellings were determined almost entirely by the spoken sounds in words; and since pronunciations varied from one dialect to another, spellings would also have varied.
3. a. sheep
   b. seek
   c. wash
   d. king
   e. quell
   f. shrink
4. a. bone
   b. out
   c. road
   d. long
   e. hook
   f. cloud

13. *successfully*	They *successfully* completed their work.
14. *hygiene*	Daily *hygiene* includes brushing our teeth.
15. *inspired*	The Bible was *inspired* by God.
16. *committee*	The food *committee* planned the dinner.
17. *reindeer*	Herds of *reindeer* live in Lapland.
18. *investigate*	The police will *investigate* the burglary.
19. *succession*	He fired three shots in *succession.*
20. *conceit*	God despises *conceit* and flattery.
21. *precede*	Plowing must *precede* sowing.
22. *intercede*	Jesus will *intercede* with God for us.
23. *convenience*	Enclose an envelope for his *convenience*.
24. *relieve*	Drugs are used to *relieve* pain.
25. *seize*	An angry crowd tried to *seize* Jesus.

LESSON 23

NEW WORDS

1. aggressive
2. assistance
3. constitution
4. deposit
5. disagreeable
6. disapprove
7. disposition
8. gradually
9. graduate
10. impossible
11. institute
12. invalid
13. locality
14. negligent
15. negotiations
16. nonresistance
17. opponent
18. statute
19. transgressions
20. unnecessary

REVIEW WORDS

21. consideration
22. flexible
23. guardian
24. stationary
25. stationery

A. UNEARTHING THE ROOTS

ROOT	MEANING	EXAMPLE
pos, pon	put, place	position, opponent
loc	place (noun)	location
stat, stit, sist	set up, stand	statue, resist
grad, gress	walk, step	progress

pos, pon

1. Money that is "put down" (de + pos) to hold an item until you can later pay the balance is called a ____*.
2. To make quick ____* of a matter is to promptly "put it away" (dis + pos).
3. Your ____* is one who "puts himself against" you (ob + pon).
4. Choose from these words: *compose, depose, impose.*
   a. To ____ something is to put it where it is not welcome.
   b. To ____ a king is to put him down from his position.
   c. To ____ a song is to put it together.

loc

5. A specific place is a ____*.
6. Choose from these words: *allocation, dislocation, locomotion.*
   a. A condition of being out of place.
   b. A movement from one place to another.
   c. An assignment of items to certain places; distribution.

stat, stit, sist

7. Write a spelling word for each definition.
   a. The Christian practice of not standing against mistreatment.
   b. The act of standing by to give help.
   c. A law set up by authority; decree.
   d. A group of rules "set up together" to govern an organization.
   e. To set up; start; establish.
   f. Standing still; not moving.
   g. Writing materials (formerly sold at a stand).

grad, gress

8. Knowledge comes "in small steps at a time," or ____*.
9. We never ____* from (step out of) the school of experience.
10. "Acts of stepping across" into wrongdoing are ____*.
11. A(n) ____* person actively "steps toward" his goal.

Lesson 23—62 points (A–C)

A. 21 points
1. deposit
2. disposition
3. opponent
4. a. impose
   b. depose
   c. compose
5. locality
6. a. dislocation
   b. locomotion
   c. allocation
7. a. nonresistance
   b. assistance
   c. statute
   d. constitution
   e. institute
   f. stationary
   g. stationery
8. gradually
9. graduate
10. transgressions
11. aggressive

Test Sentences

1. *locality* — In which *locality* do you live?
2. *disapprove* — Christians *disapprove* of cheating.
3. *invalid* — Our class sang for an old *invalid* lady.
4. *opponent* — Larry's *opponent* won the checkers game.
5. *disposition* — Susan has a sunny *disposition.*
6. *negligent* — Lazy, *negligent* farmers reap poorly.
7. *transgressions* — Jesus forgave the woman's *transgressions.*
8. *aggressive* — Samson was *aggressive* and bold.
9. *gradually* — The joy *gradually* faded from his eyes.
10. *negotiations* — After many *negotiations*, a price was set.
11. *statute* — A common *statute* mile measures 5,280 feet.
12. *consideration* — After *consideration,* we moved.

B. AFFIXING AFFIXES

PREFIX	MEANING	EXAMPLE
ne-, neg-	opposite of *or* absence of	never, neglect
in-		insecure
dis-		disobey

1. The primary meaning of *ne-, neg-, in-*, and *dis-* is "not." Write the spelling words with those prefixes to match these definitions.
   a. Not careful; heedless.
   b. Not pleasant or friendly.
   c. Not having force or effect.
   d. To give the opposite of favor; condemn.
   e. A prevailing mood or tendency.
2. Attach *in-* or *dis-* to each word.
   a. appear c. efficient
   b. complete d. satisfied
3. The prefix *in-* also appears as *il-, im-* and *ir-* by assimilation. Write the New Word in which you see one of these forms.
4. Attach an assimilated form of *in-* to each word.
   a. mature c. regular
   b. legal d. patient
5. One New Word had the original meaning "conditions of not being idle and leisurely" (from *neg* not + *otium* ease, leisure). Today the word means "discussions held to seek an agreement." Write this word.
6. Write the two New Words with the negative prefixes *un-* and *non-*.
7. Write New Words that have these prefixes.
   a. *de-* with the meaning "down"
   b. *in-* with the meaning "in"
8. Write the spelling words that are derived forms of these.
   a. guard c. agree
   b. local d. gradual

C. SOUND, STRUCTURE, AND MEANING

1. Write the spelling words in which you hear these sounds.
   a. /shē/ spelled *ti*
   b. /j/ spelled *d* (2)
   c. /gär/ spelled *guar*
2. Which spelling word has two *g's*, one for /g/ and one for /j/?
3. Join a Review Word with *front* to form an open compound that means "nonmoving boundary between air masses."
4. Read Matthew 5:39. Which New Word names the principle taught in this verse?
5. Write spelling words that are synonyms for the following words.
   a. deliberation d. pliable
   b. militant e. aid
   c. careless f. sins
6. Do not confuse *statute, stature,* and *statue.* Write the correct word for each sentence.
   a. A Bible command may be called a precept, a ____, or an ordinance.
   b. Zacchaeus was a man of short ____.
   c. A ____ of Abraham Lincoln stood at the entrance of the park.
7. Find *invalid* in the Speller Dictionary. Tell whether the *first* or *second* entry word
   a. is pronounced (in′və lid).
   b. means "without force or effect."

B. 23 points
1. a. negligent
   b. disagreeable
   c. invalid
   d. disapprove
   e. disposition
2. a. disappear
   b. incomplete
   c. inefficient
   d. dissatisfied
3. impossible
4. a. immature
   b. illegal
   c. irregular
   d. impatient
5. negotiations
6. unnecessary, nonresistance
7. a. deposit
   b. institute
8. a. guardian
   b. locality
   c. disagreeable
   d. gradually

C. 18 points
1. a. negotiations
   b. gradually, graduate
   c. guardian
2. negligent
3. stationary front
4. nonresistance
5. a. consideration
   b. aggressive
   c. negligent
   d. flexible
   e. assistance
   f. transgressions
6. a. statute
   b. stature
   c. statue
7. a. first
   b. second

13. *assistance*	Do you need *assistance* with this?
14. *graduate*	Soon Michael will *graduate* from school.
15. *nonresistance*	God commands *nonresistance*.
16. *unnecessary*	During class, *unnecessary* talk is forbidden.
17. *constitution*	A healthy *constitution* resists illness.
18. *impossible*	Nothing is *impossible* with God.
19. *stationery*	Anna gave pink *stationery* to Linda.
20. *deposit*	Father made a *deposit* in the bank.
21. *flexible*	Rubber is a *flexible* material.
22. *stationary*	A moving object is not *stationary.*
23. *institute*	We attended an *institute* last weekend.
24. *disagreeable*	Camels are often *disagreeable.*
25. *guardian*	Our *guardian* angels watch over us.

D. LANGUAGE LINEAGE

Semantic Study: METAPHORICAL USAGE

Many words have literal meanings that refer primarily to certain objects. For example, *head, eye*, and *arm* refer primarily to certain parts of the body. But we also speak of the head of a pin, the eye of a needle, and the arm of a chair. These are called metaphorical usages because the things named are somewhat like a literal head, an eye, or an arm. The words provide a simple way of referring to things that would be difficult to name otherwise.

Head, eye, and *arm* have both literal and metaphorical meanings. But sometimes a word loses its literal meaning and comes to be used chiefly in the metaphorical sense. Finally the literal meaning may be forgotten altogether. Then the word is a *faded metaphor;* its meaning has changed entirely from the literal sense to the metaphorical sense.

One faded metaphor is *rehearse* (from *re-* again and *hercier* to harrow). This word was used first by farmers and later by anyone who prepared for something by doing an activity over and over. Today no one "rehearses" a field anymore, and the word means only "to practice in preparation for public performance."

Below are a few of the many faded metaphors in the English language.

FADED METAPHORS

Word	*Original meaning*	*Modern meaning*
delirium	*delirare,* get out of the furrow (*lira*) in plowing	temporary mental disturbance
eliminate	*eliminare*, cast out over the threshold (*limen*)	to do away with
tribulation	*tribulum*, threshing sledge	great affliction and distress

Exercises

1. Why do we speak of the "neck" of a bottle or the "leg" of a chair?
2. What is a faded metaphor?
3. Match these faded metaphors to the literal definitions below. Use the Speller Dictionary if you need help.

cancel	courteous	manage
contrition	discussion	possession

a. The act of sitting in power.
b. Fitting for a king's court.
c. The act of shaking something apart.
d. To mark out with small lattices.
e. To train horses.
f. The act of grinding thoroughly.

D. 10 points
1. The things named are somewhat like a literal neck and leg.
2. a word whose literal meaning has been replaced by a metaphorical meaning
3. a. possession
   b. courteous
   c. discussion
   d. cancel
   e. manage
   f. contrition

Lesson 24—93 points (A–B)

LESSON 24

19	20	21	22	23
compensation	collateral	caution	admission	aggressive
dependent	consequently	circuit	committee	assistance
edition	covenant	circumference	conceit	constitution
effort	declaration	circumstances	convenience	deposit
eliminate	deduct	coarse	convention	disagreeable
enormous	deference	communication	enterprise	disapprove
estate	deferred	compliance	exceed	disposition
exaggerated	denomination	confirming	illustrate	gradually
excommunicate	difference	contrition	inspired	graduate
exemption	educational	conversation	intercede	impossible
exhibit	executive	conversion	interfere	institute
existing	latitude	converted	interior	invalid
expenditure	persecution	conviction	internal	locality
expenses	reduction	cooperation	investigate	negligent
experiment	relation	coordinate	precede	negotiations
explanation	sequence	diverse	relieve	nonresistance
expose	submitted	involved	remittance	opponent
extremely	substitute	revolution	succeed	statute
premium	subway	rhubarb	successfully	transgressions
redemption	transferred	wrought	succession	unnecessary

A. UNEARTHING THE ROOTS

pend, pens	hang, weigh	***duc***	lead
empt, em	take, buy	***sequ, secut***	follow
mit, miss	send, let go	***fer, lat***	bear, carry
cede, ceed, cess	go, yield	***later***	side
ven, vent	come	***pos, pon***	put, place
vert, vers	turn	***loc***	place (noun)
volv, volu	roll	***stat, stit, sist***	set up, stand
circum	around	***grad, gress***	walk, step

See page 119 for test sentences.

L19: pend–pens, empt–em

1. Write spelling words with these elements.
   a. de + pend c. ex + empt
   b. com + pens d. pre + em
2. Write the two words beginning with *ex-* that have to do with paying out money.
3. detain : detention :: redeem : ____*
4. Choose from these: *append, spend, stipend.*
   a. To ____ is the same as to expend.
   b. To ____ is to hang one thing to another.
   c. To give a ____ is to pay a salary.

L20: duc, sequ–secut, fer–lat, later

5. Write spelling words with these elements.
   a. e + duc e. dis + fer
   b. de + duc f. re + lat
   c. ex + secu g. com + later
   d. con + sequ
6. Write spelling words with noun suffixes for these definitions.
   a. The act of leading to a lower level; decrease.
   b. The act of following to punish; oppression.
   c. A group of things following one another.
   d. The act of yielding to another.
7. Write the word that begins with *lat* and is not derived from the roots *lat* or *later* but from *latus* (wide).

L21: vert–vers, volv–volu, circum

8. Write spelling words with these elements.
   a. re + volu c. circum + fer
   b. con + vert (*not* vers)
9. a. The accident [volv]* a number of strange [circum]*.
   b. Our [con + vers]* covered a number of [dis + vers]* subjects.
   c. Five people experienced [vers]* when the evangelist made a [circ]* of the area.

L22: mit–miss, cede–ceed–cess, ven–vent

10. a. The delegates held a [con + ven]* lasting three days.
    b. The letters *m* and *n* [pre + cede]* the letters *s* and *t*.
    c. The [com + mit]* decided to charge an [ad + miss]* fee of $2.00.
    d. The present work of Jesus is to [cede]* for the saints.
    e. Please send the [re + mit]* at your earliest [con + ven]*
11. Which two spelling words have *sub-* (assimilated) and the *cess* form of *cede*?
12. Write the two spelling words in which the *cede* root is spelled *ceed*. Then use *pro-* to write the only other English word with this spelling of the *cede* root.

L23: pos–pon, loc, stat–sist, grad–gress

13. Write spelling words with these elements.
    a. de + pos d. re + sist
    b. dis + pos e. trans + gress
    c. loc + al
14. a. If an [ob + pon]* is [ad + gress]*, one may need [ad + sist]* to withstand him.
    b. The [grad]* went to a different [in + stit]* to continue his studies.
    c. Over the years, the company's original [con + stit]* was [grad]* changed.

A. 55 points
1. a. dependent
   b. compensation
   c. exemption
   d. premium
2. expenditure, expenses
3. redemption
4. a. spend
   b. append
   c. stipend
5. a. educational
   b. deduct
   c. executive
   d. consequently
   e. difference
   f. relation
   g. collateral
6. a. reduction
   b. persecution
   c. sequence
   d. deference
7. latitude
8. a. revolution
   b. converted
   c. circumference
9. a. involved, circumstances
   b. conversation, diverse
   c. conversion, circuit
10. a. convention
    b. precede
    c. committee, admission
    d. intercede
    e. remittance, convenience
11. successfully, succession
12. exceed, succeed, proceed
13. a. deposit
    b. disposition
    c. locality
    d. nonresistance
    e. transgressions
14. a. opponent, aggressive, assistance
    b. graduate, institute
    c. constitution, gradually

B. AFFIXING AFFIXES

ex-, e-	away, out from
de-	down, away
sub-	under
com-	with, together
in-	in, into
inter-	between, within
ne-, neg-, in-, dis-	opposite of *or* absence of

1. Write Lesson 19 words beginning with *ex-* or *e-* for these definitions.
   a. To act of paying out money.
   b. To place outside; remove cover from.
   c. Inflated out of proportion; overstated.
   d. To try out a hypothesis.
   e. The act of laying out plainly; clarification.
   f. To cast out; get rid of.
2. Write the Lesson 20 words that contain these elements.
   a. de + nom (to name)
   b. de + clar (to make clear)
3. Write the noun form of each word, using *-ance* or *-ence*. [16]
   a. negligent d. nonresistant
   b. assistant e. convenient
   c. different f. consequent
4. Make spelling words by adding *com-* to these, using assimilation as needed.
   a. __pensation [19]
   b. __lateral [20]
   c. __operation [21]
   d. __ordinate [21]
   e. __firming [21]
   f. __pliance [21]
5. Attach *in-*, *inter-* or *enter-* to these, using assimilation as needed.
   a. __volved [21] d. __fere [22]
   b. __cede [22] e. __prise [22]
   c. __lustrate [22] f. __spired [22]
6. Attach prefixes to make Lesson 23 words with opposite meanings.
   a. possible d. agreeable
   b. approve e. resistance
   c. valid f. necessary
7. Add noun suffixes to form spelling words.
   a. expend [19] d. converse [21]
   b. reduce [20] e. convert [21]
   c. defer [20] f. local [23]

D. LANGUAGE LINEAGE

1. In the 600s, why was there a special need for Bible accounts in English?
2. In what way was Old English more complex than Modern English?
3. Write the modern spellings of the Old English words *scip, stān, hūs*, and *cwic*.
4. Why was it difficult to establish uniform spellings in Old English times?
5. The meaning of *exorbitant* has changed from "out of track" to "extremely high." This is an example of a ____ ____.

B. 38 points
1. a. expenditure
   b. expose
   c. exaggerated
   d. experiment
   e. explanation
   f. eliminate
2. a. denomination
   b. declaration
3. a. negligence
   b. assistance
   c. difference
   d. nonresistance
   e. convenience
   f. consequence
4. a. compensation
   b. collateral
   c. cooperation
   d. coordinate
   e. confirming
   f. compliance
5. a. involved
   b. intercede
   c. illustrate
   d. interfere
   e. enterprise
   f. inspired
6. a. impossible
   b. disapprove
   c. invalid
   d. disagreeable
   e. nonresistance
   f. unnecessary
7. a. expenditure
   b. reduction
   c. deference
   d. conversation
   e. conversion
   f. locality

D. 11 points
1. There was no English translation of the Bible. (All Bible reading was done in Latin.)
2. Old English had many more inflections than Modern English has.
3. ship, stone, house, quick
4. Spelling depended on pronunciation, and pronunciation varied from one dialect to another.
5. faded metaphor

LESSON 25

NEW WORDS

1. associate
2. capitalization
3. carnality
4. commemorate
5. cordial
6. corporal
7. corporation
8. corps
9. corpse
10. corrupt
11. criticize
12. encourage
13. endeavor
14. identify
15. Incarnation
16. justify
17. manager
18. manual
19. manufacturer
20. merchandise

REVIEW WORDS

21. baptized
22. certificate
23. Christendom
24. consequently
25. extension

A. UNEARTHING THE ROOTS

ROOT	MEANING	EXAMPLE
cap	head	capital
cor, cord	heart	core
man	hand	manual
corp	body	corpse
carn	flesh	carnal

cap

1. Using a large letter at the head of a word or sentence is ____*.
2. Choose from these words: *cape, capital, captain.*
   a. The head city where government leaders meet.
   b. The head of a group of people.
   c. A head of land extending into a body of water.

cor, cord

3. God told Moses to ____* Joshua so that he would take heart.
4. Our ____* hosts gave us a hearty welcome.
5. If people's hearts are in unity, they have (concord, discord).

man

6. A ____* was originally one who made things by hand.
7. A store ____* is one who handles the business of the store.
8. With a ____* transmission, the driver shifts gears by hand.
9. Choose from these words: *manicure, manipulation, manuscript.*
   a. An act of handling skillfully or shrewdly.
   b. A document written by hand.
   c. A cosmetic treatment of the nails on one's hand.

corp

10. Write New Words with the *corp* root for these meanings.
    a. Pertaining to the body.
    b. A dead body.
    c. A body of trained persons acting together.
    d. A body of persons legally recognized as a unit.
11. Write the New Word in which initial *cor* is an assimilated form of the prefix *com-*. (It has the *rupt* root.)

carn

12. The ____* is Christ's assumption of a body of flesh.
13. The state of being controlled by desires of the flesh is ____*.
14. A (carnivorous, herbivorous) animal is one that eats flesh.

78

Lesson 25—61 points (A–C)

A. 21 points
1. capitalization
2. a. capital
   b. captain
   c. cape
3. encourage
4. cordial
5. concord
6. manufacturer
7. manager
8. manual
9. a. manipulation
   b. manuscript
   c. manicure
10. a. corporal
    b. corpse
    c. corps
    d. corporation
11. corrupt
12. Incarnation
13. carnality
14. carnivorous

Test Sentences

1. *corpse*	Jesus raised a *corpse* to life.
2. *manual*	Read the *manual* for directions.
3. *carnality*	Envy is a form of *carnality.*
4. *baptized*	Jesus was *baptized* in the Jordan River.
5. *corrupt*	Sodom was a very *corrupt* city.
6. *associate*	We usually *associate* salt with pepper.
7. *criticize*	The Pharisees did *criticize* Jesus.
8. *manufacturer*	This *manufacturer* makes paper products.
9. *capitalization*	Titles need *capitalization.*
10. *certificate*	His *certificate* hung on the wall.
11. *encourage*	We *encourage* proper reading habits.
12. *merchandise*	A store displays its *merchandise.*

B. AFFIXING AFFIXES

Verb-forming Suffixes		
SUFFIX	MEANING	EXAMPLE
-ate	do, make, become	motivate
-fy, -ify	make	justify
-ize, -ise	make into *or* bring about	equalize

1. Write the two New Words that are verbs ending with *-ate*.
2. Write the New Words formed by adding *-ion* after the *-ate* suffix in these words.
   a. Incarnate b. corporate

Some words ending with *-ate* can function as verbs, adjectives, or nouns. For example, when something is *duplicated*, the result may be called a *duplicate copy* or simply a *duplicate*.

3. Write the New Word ending with *-ate* that may be a verb, an adjective, or a noun.
4. The *-fy, -ify* suffix comes from the *fac, fic* root that you studied in Lesson 14. Write the *-fy* or *-ify* forms of these.
   a. just d. sanctity
   b. class e. glory
   c. identity f. unity
5. Attach *-ize* to these words.
   a. critic d. fertile
   b. real e. pressure
   c. civil f. social
6. Which spelling word has *-ize* and *-ation*? Which one has *-ify* and *-(c)ate*?
7. Write the New Word that ends with *-ise* and may function as a noun or verb.
8. The Review Word with the *-ize* suffix is a New Testament term that came from Greek rather than Latin. Write this word.
9. Which spelling word has *ex-* and *-ion*?

C. SOUND, STRUCTURE, AND MEANING

1. Write the spelling words in which you hear these sounds.
   a. /j/ or /dy/ spelled *di*
   b. /kûr/ spelled *cour*
   c. /īz/ or /īs/ spelled ise
   d. /dev/ spelled *deav*
2. Which New Word has a *ps* ending that is not pronounced?
3. Write the word that means "recognize as being a particular person or thing."
4. Write *corps* or *corpse* for each sentence.
   a. The ____ of scientists made an important discovery.
   b. If an Israelite touched a ____, he became ceremonially unclean.
   c. A ____ can usually accomplish more than one person working alone.
5. Write the spelling words that are synonyms for these.
   a. celebrate d. therefore
   b. handbook e. hearten
   c. pervert f. sensuality
6. Write the spelling word in which the *tian* of *Christian* is spelled *ten*.
7. a. Write the plural form of *corps*. (See the Speller Dictionary.)
   b. How is the plural form pronounced differently from the singular form?

B. 22 points
1. associate, commemorate
2. a. Incarnation
   b. corporation
3. associate
4. a. justify
   b. classify
   c. identify
   d. sanctify
   e. glorify
   f. unify
5. a. criticize
   b. realize
   c. civilize
   d. fertilize
   e. pressurize
   f. socialize
6. capitalization; certificate
7. merchandise
8. baptized
9. extension

C. 18 points
1. a. cordial
   b. encourage
   c. merchandise
   d. endeavor
2. corps
3. identify
4. a. corps
   b. corpse
   c. corps
5. a. commemorate
   b. manual
   c. corrupt
   d. consequently
   e. encourage
   f. carnality
6. Christendom
7. a. corps
   b. The final *s* of the plural is sounded.

13. *commemorate* — We *commemorate* the resurrection.
14. *identify* — Can you *identify* twenty different birds?
15. *Christendom* — All *Christendom* claims to believe the Bible.
16. *cordial* — The Yoders gave us all a *cordial* welcome.
17. *Incarnation* — Christ became a man through the *Incarnation.*
18. *consequently* — Lassie barked; *consequently,* John awoke.
19. *corporal* — Mr. Taylor was an army *corporal.*
20. *justify* — Good works alone do not *justify* us.
21. *endeavor* — We must *endeavor* to do our best.
22. *corporation* — A new *corporation* moved into town.
23. *manager* — Daniel is a sales *manager* for the company.
24. *extension* — We lengthened it with an *extension.*
25. *corps* — A group of trained soldiers is a *corps.*

D. LANGUAGE LINEAGE

OBSOLETE OLD ENGLISH CHARACTERS

Þ þ	Ð ð	Æ æ
thorn	edh *or* eth	ash

The Old English alphabet did not contain the letters *j, q, v,* and *z*. But it did have the three characters shown above, which are no longer used today.

The *thorn* was carried over from the runic alphabet. It was used for the /th/ sound as in *thin*. Thus we find such words as *wiþ* (with), *þū* (thou), and *þider* (thither) in Old English literature.

Sometimes the letter *y* is used as a makeshift replacement for the thorn. You have probably seen this done on signs such as "Ye Olde Shoppe." Here the first word is *The*, but the letter *Y* is used for *Þ*. As *th* was used more and more for the /th/ sound, the thorn gradually passed out of use.

The *edh* or *eth* (both forms are pronounced /eth/) represented the /th/ sound as in *there*. This letter appears in Old English words such as *ðā* (then) and *sūð* (south). As you can see, some unvoiced *th* sounds of Old English later became voiced (þū—thou), and some voiced *th* sounds became unvoiced (sūð—south). Eventually both the thorn and the edh were replaced by *th*.

The *ash* is a digraph formed by joining *a* and *e*. It appears in Old English words such as *þæt* (that), *æfter* (after), and *þær* (there). The ash represented the /a/ sound. It is still used sometimes as a ligature in certain names (Cæsar, Zacchæus), but the preferred practice today is to use *ae* (Caesar, Zacchaeus).

The Norman Conquest of 1066 introduced a strong French influence on the English language. It was largely because of this influence that the thorn, the edh, and the ash gradually fell into disuse. You will read about the Norman Conquest in Lesson 31.

Exercises

1. Name the Old English character used for each sound.
   a. /th/ b. /a/ c. /th/
2. Find the words below in the Old English version of the Lord's Prayer (Lesson 1), and give the modern spelling of each.
   a. þū
   b. eorðan
   c. dæg
   d. gelæd
   e. þīn, ðīn (These are two spellings of the same word.)
   f. Fæder
3. The pronunciation of the following words has changed little since Old English times. Write the modern spelling of each.
   a. bæc
   b. þus
   c. scēað
   d. þæt
   e. bæð
   f. þorn

D. 15 points
1. a. edh or eth
   b. ash
   c. thorn
2. a thou
   b. earth
   c. day
   d. lead
   e. thine
   f. Father
3. a. back
   b. thus
   c. sheath or sheathe
   d. that
   e. bath or bathe
   f. thorn

Lesson 26—55 points (A–C)

LESSON 26

NEW WORDS

1. affiliate
2. bargain
3. difficulty
4. dignity
5. emphasize
6. fiery
7. filial
8. fraternal
9. fraternity
10. hearty
11. humility
12. majority
13. maternal
14. matrimony
15. misery
16. paternal
17. patriarch
18. patriot
19. patron
20. remedy

REVIEW WORDS

21. difference
22. iniquity
23. physical
24. prophesy
25. tariff

A. UNEARTHING THE ROOTS

ROOT	MEANING	EXAMPLE
pater, patr	father	patriarch
mater, matr	mother	matron
frater, fratr	brother	fraternity
fili	son, child	filial

pater, patr

1. Your ____* grandparents are your father's parents.
2. Each of Jacob's twelve sons became a ____*, or the father of one of the twelve tribes of Israel.
3. A Christian should love his heavenly fatherland as a ____* loves his country.
4. As a father supports his children, so a ____* supports a store by helping its business.
5. Choose from these words: *paternoster, patrician, patrimony.*
   a. An inheritance from one's father is a ____.
   b. The Lord's Prayer is called the ____ because the first two words are "Our Father."
   c. In Greek and Roman society, an honored father of the upper class was a ___.

mater, matr

6. Your ____* grandparents are your mother's parents.
7. Though the root of ____* means "mother," this word now means "marriage."
8. A (matriarch, matron) is a woman who performs the duties of a mother at an institution such as a children's home.

frater, fratr

9. A brotherly friendship may be called a ____* relationship.
10. In a spiritual brotherhood there are stronger ties than in any social ____*.
11. A "brother" at a monastery is a (friar, prior).

fili

12. The ____* affection of children produces a strong bond with their parents.
13. To ____* a child is to adopt him. A more common meaning of this word is "associate (with)" or "unite (with)."

A. 15 points
1. paternal
2. patriarch
3. patriot
4. patron
5. a. patrimony
   b. paternoster
   c. patrician
6. maternal
7. matrimony
8. matron
9. fraternal
10. fraternity
11. friar
12. filial
13. affiliate

See page 90 for test sentences.

B. AFFIXING AFFIXES

1. Write the spelling words with the suffix *-y* to match these definitions. Observe that in some words *-y* has the additional meaning "one who or that which."
   a. The condition of being miserable.
   b. The state of being married.
   c. The quality of being difficult.
   d. Something that relieves or cures.

The suffix -*y* may form adjectives. It adds the meaning "full of; having."

2. Write adjectives ending with *-y* to match these definitions.
   a. Full of fire.*
   b. Full of feeling from the heart.*
   c. Full of curls.
   d. Having much wealth.

3. Write NEW WORDS that are *-ty* or *-ity* forms of these words.

Noun-forming Suffixes

SUFFIX	MEANING	EXAMPLE
-y, -ty, -ity	state of *or* condition of	misery, humility

a. humble   c. fraternal
b. major   d. dignified

4. Also attach *-ty* or *-ity* to these words.
   a. loyal   c. cruel
   b. secure   d. active

5. The word *inequity* means "condition of not being equal and fair." Write the REVIEW WORD which originally had that meaning but which now means "sin."

6. Write spelling words that are related forms of these.
   a. emphasis   d. different
   b. prophecy   e. affiliation
   c. remedial   f. physician

C. SOUND, STRUCTURE, AND MEANING

1. Write the spelling words in which you hear these sounds.
   a. /gən/ spelled *gain*
   b. /trē/ spelled *tri* (2)
   c. final /sī/ spelled *sy*

2. One Middle English spelling of *fire* is *fier*. Which NEW WORD gives evidence of this?

3. Which words are antonyms for these?
   a. pride   b. comfort

4. The words *father* and *mother* are counterparts because one refers to the one parent and the other refers to the other parent. Write the NEW WORDS that are counterparts of the following words.
   a. matron
   b. sorority (from *soror*, sister)
   c. paternal   d. matriarch

5. Write a form of *prophecy* or *prophesy* for each sentence.
   a. Micah ____ that Jesus would be born in Bethlehem.
   b. The ____ about Jesus' triumphal entry is found in Zechariah.
   c. In Matthew 24, Jesus was ____ about the destruction of Jerusalem.

6. Write the REVIEW WORD that names a kind of tax. According to its etymology, what two languages did this word come from?

82

B. 23 points
1. a. misery
   b. matrimony
   c. difficulty
   d. remedy
2. a. fiery
   b. hearty
   c. curly
   d. wealthy
3. a. humility
   b. majority
   c. fraternity
   d. dignity
4. a loyalty
   b. security
   c. cruelty
   d. activity
5. iniquity
6. a. emphasize
   b. prophesy
   c. remedy
   d. difference
   e. affiliate
   f. physical

C. 17 points
1. a. bargain
   b. patriarch, patriot
   c. prophesy
2. fiery
3. a. humility
   b. misery
4. a. patron
   b. fraternity
   c. maternal
   d. patriarch
5. a. prophesied
   b. prophecy
   c. prophesying
6. tariff; Italian, Arabic

Test Sentences

1.	*hearty*	Brother Ben gave me a *hearty* handshake.
2.	*fraternity*	The *fraternity* had twelve members.
3.	*affiliate*	Do *affiliate* with wholesome friends.
4.	*emphasize*	We need to *emphasize* brotherly love.
5.	*patriot*	Patrick Henry was an early American *patriot.*
6.	*humility*	Pride is the opposite of *humility.*
7.	*remedy*	Naaman found no *remedy* for leprosy in Syria.
8.	*bargain*	We struck a *bargain* with the trader.
9.	*majority*	The *majority* of animals are insects.
10.	*iniquity*	Dishonesty is an *iniquity* before God.
11.	*matrimony*	Holy *matrimony* was ordained by God.
12.	*patron*	The grocery store gave each *patron* a pen.

D. LANGUAGE LINEAGE

OLD ENGLISH PLACE NAMES

Before the Angles migrated to Britain, they had lived in a river valley in Holstein, Germany. This valley was shaped like a fishhook and was therefore called Angle (or Angul). *Angle* is an obsolete term for "fishhook"; today we may still refer to a fisherman as an angler. The words *England* and *English* come from the name of this hook-shaped valley in Germany.

Engle is the Old English plural of *Angle.* This is why *England* and *English* begin with *E* rather than *A*. England was so named because it was the "land of the Engle" (Angles), and the name "Englisc" (English) was given to the language of the Engle. It was not until about 1000, however, that these terms were in common use.

You learned in Lesson 14 that the Anglo-Saxon invaders adopted the names used by the Celts for various places. Some of the names contained Latin elements that had been introduced by the Romans who occupied Britain. These included endings such as *-caster* or *-chester* (from the Latin *castra*, camp), *-port* (from *portus*, harbor), and *-wich* or *-wick* (from *vīcus*, village). But some of the place names were native Celtic words.

The Celtic word *cumb* means "deep valley," and it is found in the names *Cumbria, Holcombe*, and *Winchcombe*. *Torr* is the Celtic word for "high rock; peak"; thus we find names such as *Torbay* and *Torhill*. *Brocc*, the Celtic word for "badger," is seen in *Brockholes* and *Brockhall*. These are all names of towns, cities, and counties in England, and some of them have been brought to America.

Many place names were devised by the Anglo-Saxons themselves. They used the name *Norfolk* for a county inhabited by the "north folk," and *Suffolk* for the county directly south of it, inhabited by the "south folk." The East Saxons lived in Essex, the Middle Saxons in Middlesex, and the Southern Saxons in Sussex. Lesson 27 gives more details about places that were named by the Anglo-Saxons.

Exercises

1. Explain how the tribe of the Angles received its name.
2. Why was the Angles' language called "English" rather than "Anglish"?
3. Write the meaning of the Latin or Celtic word from which each element is derived.
   a. -port d. -chester
   b. Brock- e. Tor-
   c. -combe f. -wich
4. Write the phrase from which each name is derived.
   a. Norfolk c. Middlesex
   b. Essex d. Suffolk

13. *maternal* Aunt Hilda is a loving, *maternal* woman.
14. *dignity* Begging was beneath the debtor's *dignity.*
15. *difficulty* Emily is having *difficulty* with reading.
16. *difference* What is the *difference* between the two?
17. *fiery* Who was cast into the *fiery* furnace?
18. *physical* Something *physical* can be seen or felt.
19. *misery* Sin has brought great *misery* to man.
20. *prophesy* Who will *prophesy* for the Lord?
21. *paternal* Only my *paternal* grandfather is still living.
22. *filial* We have *filial* ties to our parents.
23. *tariff* Tax on foreign goods is a *tariff.*
24. *patriarch* Abraham was a *patriarch* of old.
25. *fraternal* Jan and Ann are *fraternal* twins.

D. 14 points
1. In Germany the tribe had lived in a hook-shaped valley called Angle or Angul.
2. *Engle* is the Old English plural of *Angle*.
3. a. harbor
   b. badger
   c. deep valley
   d. camp
   e. high rock; peak
   f. village
4. a. north folk
   b. East Saxons
   c. Middle Saxons
   d. south folk

LESSON 27

NEW WORDS

1. bass
2. canary
3. canine
4. census

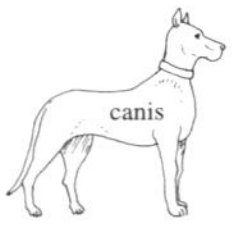

5. cereal
6. council
7. counsel
8. doubtless
9. equine

10. feline
11. feminine
12. infantile

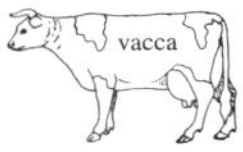

13. masculine
14. minor
15. reptile
16. rite

17. textile
18. vaccine
19. vein
20. versatile

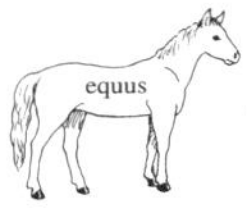

REVIEW WORDS

21. circumstances
22. covenant
23. domestic
24. indebtedness
25. involved

A. UNEARTHING THE ROOTS

ROOT	MEANING	EXAMPLE
can	dog	canine
fel	cat	feline
vacc	cow	vaccine
bos	ox, cow	bovine
equ	horse	equine
sus	hog	swine

can, fel

1. The ____* family of animals includes dogs and their relatives.
2. In World War II there was a unit called the K9 Corps. The "troops" in this unit were not men but ____. (Consider the sound of "K9.")
3. The ____* is a popular cage bird that originally came from the "Dog Islands."
4. A different form of the *can* root is *ken*. A place for keeping dogs is a (kendo, kennel).
5. The ____* family of animals includes cats and their relatives.
6. A felinophile is someone who is fond of (cats, dogs).

vacc, bos

7. People who have had cowpox, a mild disease, are immune to the deadly disease of smallpox. When doctors recognized this, they made the first ____* by using fluid from cowpox victims to prevent smallpox in healthy people.
8. The bovine family of animals includes ____ and their relatives.
9. *Bossy* is a common name for a (cow, horse).

equ, sus

10. The ____* family of animals includes horses and their relatives.
11. A man who belongs to the Equestrian Riding Club would probably own a ____.
12. For each group, write *bovine, canine, equine, feline,* or *swine.*
    a. foxes, wolves, coyotes
    b. hogs, wild boars, peccaries
    c. oxen, bison, water buffalo
    d. ponies, donkeys, zebras
    e. tigers, leopards, cheetahs

Lesson 27—57 points (A–C)

A. 16 points
1. canine
2. dogs
3. canary
4. kennel
5. feline
6. cats
7. vaccine
8. cows (cattle)
9. cow
10. equine
11. horse
12. a. canine
    b. swine
    c. bovine
    d. equine
    e. feline

Test Sentences

1. *equine*	Bridles and reins are *equine* gear.
2. *involved*	Our assignment *involved* much reading.
3. *feline*	Tigers are members of the *feline* family.
4. *bass*	Jonathan has a deep *bass* voice.
5. *rite*	Feet Washing is a *rite* commanded by Christ.
6. *canary*	The yellow *canary* sang sweetly.
7. *indebtedness*	We feel *indebtedness* to God.
8. *textile*	Cloth comes from the *textile* mills.
9. *feminine*	Roberta is the *feminine* form of Robert.
10. *canine*	Dogs and wolves belong to the *canine* family.
11. *covenant*	Israel broke her *covenant* to serve God.
12. *infantile*	The baby made gurgling, *infantile* sounds.

B. AFFIXING AFFIXES

Adjective-forming Suffixes		
SUFFIX	MEANING	EXAMPLE
-ile	of the quality *or* nature of	infantile
-ine		feminine

1. Write spelling words that are adjectives ending with *-ile* to match these definitions.
   a. Able to do various tasks well.
   b. Pertaining to or acting like a baby.
2. Some words ending with *-ile* are based on adjectives, but they function primarily as nouns. Write the spelling words ending with *-ile* that are nouns with these meanings.
   a. Cold-blooded creeping animal.
   b. Woven material; fabric.
3. Form adjectives by adding *-ile* to the roots *ag* and *doc*.
4. Use spelling words that end with *-ine* to rewrite the following phrases.
   Example: Qualities of a female.
   Answer: feminine qualities
   a. Agility of a cat.
   b. Interest in horses.
   c. Courage of a man.
   d. Tendencies of a dog.
5. Also rewrite these phrases, using adjectives with the roots in italics and the suffix *-ine*.
   a. Love of God (*div*).
   b. Leather that is real (*gen*).
   c. Creatures of the sea (*mar*).
   d. Solution containing salt (*sal*).
6. Write the spelling words with these roots.
   a. debt b. doubt c. Ceres

B. 17 points
1. a. versatile
   b. infantile
2. a. reptile
   b. textile
3. agile, docile
4. a. feline agility
   b. equine interest
   c. masculine courage
   d. canine tendencies
5. a. divine love
   b. genuine leather
   c. marine creatures
   d. saline solution
6. a. indebtedness
   b. doubtless
   c. cereal

C. SOUND, STRUCTURE, AND MEANING

1. Write the spelling words in which you hear these sounds.
   a. /îr/ spelled *er*
   b. /ā/ spelled *ei*
   c. /t/ spelled *bt* (2)
2. Write *counsel* or *council* for each.
   a. Absalom accepted poor ____.
   b. The Jewish ____ condemned Jesus.
   c. The men assembled to ____ together.
3. Write the correct homophones for these phrases.
   a. (1) A breakfast food.*
      (2) Pertaining to a series.
   b. (1) Smaller; less important.*
      (2) One who works in a mine.
   c. (1) Solemn ceremony.*
      (2) To put words on paper.
      (3) Proper; correct; true.
   d. (1) Blood vessel.*
      (2) Flat, finlike blade.
      (3) Proud; arrogant; conceited.
4. Write synonyms for these.
   a. included c. agreement
   b. womanly d. conditions
5. Which spelling word
   a. is pronounced (bas) or (bās)?
   b. sounds much like *senses*?
   c. describes animals that are not wild?

85

C. 24 points
1. a. cereal
   b. vein
   c. doubtless, indebtedness
2. a. counsel
   b. council
   c. counsel
3. a. (1) cereal
      (2) serial
   b. (1) minor
      (2) miner
   c. (1) rite
      (2) write
      (3) right
   d. (1) vein
      (2) vane
      (3) vain
4. a. involved
   b. feminine
   c. covenant
   d. circumstances
5. a. bass
   b. census
   c. domestic

13. *census*	A man came to collect *census* information.
14. *vaccine*	Polio *vaccine* has reduced that disease.
15. *masculine*	"He" and "his" are *masculine* pronouns.
16. *cereal*	We ate oatmeal *cereal* for breakfast.
17. *versatile*	Wood is a useful, *versatile* material.
18. *minor*	Do not let *minor* disagreements disturb you.
19. *council*	The village *council* met every month.
20. *vein*	A blood *vein* carries blood to the heart.
21. *reptile*	An alligator is a *reptile.*
22. *counsel*	Rehoboam asked the young men for *counsel.*
23. *domestic*	Dusting furniture is a *domestic* chore.
24. *circumstances*	Absalom lived in pleasant *circumstances.*
25. *doubtless*	I knew that, *doubtless,* I would be late.

D. LANGUAGE LINEAGE

OLD ENGLISH PLACE NAMES

You have probably noticed that many towns have names with similar endings. Some of the endings are simple to understand, such as *-town* in *Uniontown*. Other endings have meanings that are not clear. You saw in Lesson 26 that some of these endings are derived from Latin and Celtic words. But some are Old English forms that have not changed since the early days of England. The chart below lists a few of these.

Some of the place names shown below have been used in England for hundreds of years. But many towns have been named in more recent times by attaching the same endings to other names. For example, the city of Pittsburgh was named in the 1700s by attaching *-burgh* to the last name of William Pitt.

There are a few Modern English words that are derived from the same sources as the endings shown below. From the same source as *-ham* is *hamlet*, a word used for a small village; and from *-shire* we have *sheriff* (from the Old English words for "shire reeve"). And of course, the ending *-ton* (from Old English *tūn*) is of the same source as the modern word *town*.

PLACE NAMES—OLD ENGLISH ENDINGS

Ending	*Meaning*	*Examples*
-burg(h), -borough	fortified town	Lynchburg, Gainsborough
-ham	home or cluster of homes	Birmingham, Nottingham
-shire	county (in England)	Berkshire, Yorkshire
-ton	village or town	Lexington, Northampton

Exercises

1. List three sources of the endings that appear in many place names.
2. Just because a place name ends with *-ton*, we cannot assume that the name was used in Old English times. Why not?
3. Write *-ham, -shire,* and *-ton* in a column. Beside each ending, write one English word (a common noun) that comes from the same source as that ending.
4. Write a phrase that gives the meaning of each place name below.
   Example: Harrisburg   Answer: fortified town of Harris
   a. Louisburg   c. Worcestershire
   b. Markham   d. Charleston

D. 11 points
1. Latin words, Celtic words, Old English words
2. Many place names were formed in more recent times by attaching Old English endings such as *-ton* to other names.
3. -ham, hamlet
   -shire, sheriff
   -ton, town
4. a. fortified town of Louis
   b. home of Mark
   c. county of Worcester
   d. town of Charles

LESSON 28

NEW WORDS

1. attached
2. boundary
3. cassette
4. characters
5. chemistry
6. dinette
7. joyful
8. junior
9. juvenile
10. kitchenette
11. molecule
12. pamphlet
13. particularly
14. phrase
15. rejuvenate
16. ringlet
17. schedule
18. senator
19. senile
20. senior

REVIEW WORDS

21. adventure
22. booklet
23. chorus
24. paragraph
25. redemption

A. UNEARTHING THE ROOTS

ROOT	MEANING	EXAMPLE
sen	old	senior
juven	young	juvenile

sen

1. Uncle John is my ____* by twenty years.
2. In ancient Rome, the lawmaking body was a council of old men. But not every ____* in the United States Congress today is an old man.
3. We must never make fun of an elderly person who is ____*, even though he may repeat the same thing over and over.
4. Older people are commonly called _____* citizens.
5. "He made [Joseph] lord of his house, and ruler of all his substance: to bind his princes at his pleasure; and teach his _____ [elders] wisdom" (Psalm 105:21, 22).
6. Choose from these words: *senescent, senopia, sir.*
   a. The term ____ is used as a title of respect even when addressing a man who is not old.
   b. Myopia is nearsightedness. A condition called ____ may affect the eyes of an old person.
   c. A person who is ninety years old generally displays ____ characteristics.

juven

7. My younger brother Steven is my ____* by ten years.
8. To ____* something means literally to "make (it) young again."
9. It is ____* to think that play is more worthwhile than work.
10. A famous artist's juvenilia are the works that he produces in his (youth, middle age, old age).
11. *Young, youth,* and their derived forms are also related to the *juven* root. Write the missing words for the blanks below.
    a. "The elder shall serve the _____" (Genesis 25:23).
    b. "Even the _____ shall faint and be weary, and the _____ men shall utterly fall" (Isaiah 40:30).
    c. "Flee also _____ lusts" (2 Timothy 2:22).

Lesson 28—61 points (A–C)

A. 16 points
1. senior
2. senator
3. senile
4. senior
5. senators
6. a. sir
   b. senopia
   c. senescent
7. junior
8. rejuvenate
9. juvenile
10. youth
11. a. younger
    b. youths, young
    c. youthful

See page 96 for test sentences.

B. AFFIXING AFFIXES

1. Write the spelling words that have these meanings.
   a. Small ring.
   b. Small dining area.
   c. Small book.
   d. Small bit of matter.
   e. Small case.
   f. Small kitchen.
2. Which spelling word contains *part* and the suffixes *-ule, -ar,* and *-ly*?
3. Which word comes from a Latin word that means "small sheet (*scheda*) of papyrus"?
4. Form more words with diminutive suffixes by attaching these endings to the words that follow.
   a. *-ule*: globe, node
   b. *-let*: leaf, brook
   c. *-ette*: disk, statue
5. One New Word is a synonym for *leaflet*, but its root has nothing to do with writing materials. Rather, the word comes from *Pamphilus*, the name of a short poem. Write this word.

Diminutive Suffixes

SUFFIX	MEANING	EXAMPLE
-ule		globule
-let	small	booklet
-ette		kitchenette

The suffix *-ette* may be a feminine ending.

6. Use *-ette* to form words with these meanings.
   a. A woman farmer.
   b. A woman major.
7. Write the spelling words that have these roots and affixes.
   a. sen + ate + or
   b. ad + tach
   c. ad + ven
   d. bound + ary

B. 21 points
1. a. ringlet
   b. dinette
   c. booklet
   d. molecule
   e. cassette
   f. kitchenette
2. particularly
3. schedule
4. a. globule, nodule
   b. leaflet, brooklet
   c. diskette, statuette
5. pamphlet
6. a. farmerette
   b. majorette
7. a. senator
   b. attached
   c. adventure
   d. boundary

C. SOUND, STRUCTURE, AND MEANING

1. Write the spelling words in which you hear these sounds.
   a. /kar/ spelled *char*
   b. final /rē/ spelled *ry* (2)
   c. /f/ spelled *ph* (3)
2. Write the three words that end with /et/ spelled *ette*. Which syllable is accented in each word?
3. Write the full word represented by each beginning or ending abbreviation.
   a. John K. Wilson, Jr.
   b. Sen. Henry M. Jackson
   c. Ralph N. Thompson, Sr.
4. Which words have these meanings?
   a. Happy; glad.
   b. An organized group of singers; choir.
   c. Restore to youthful or new condition.
   d. Dividing line.
   e. To dare to undertake.
5. Write the spelling words associated with these phrases.
   a. Tape recorder.
   b. Curly hair.
   c. Salts and acids.
   d. Christ's sacrifice.
6. Write the New Word that means "youthful" or "childish." In what two ways may its last syllable be pronounced?

C. 24 points
1. a. characters
   b. boundary, chemistry
   c. pamphlet, phrase, paragraph
2. cassette, dinette, kitchenette; last syllable
3. a. Junior
   b. Senator
   c. Senior
4. a. joyful
   b. chorus
   c. rejuvenate
   d. boundary
   e. adventure
5. a. cassette
   b. ringlet
   c. chemistry
   d. redemption
6. juvenile; /nīl/ or /nəl/

Test Sentences

1. *chorus*	Outside, a *chorus* of birds was singing.
2. *junior*	Mr. Clark was only a *junior* officer.
3. *particularly*	Jason was not *particularly* fond of olives.
4. *attached*	A note was *attached* to the box.
5. *juvenile*	The book is too *juvenile* for teenagers.
6. *adventure*	Sleeping outside was a real *adventure.*
7. *kitchenette*	We ate in the tiny *kitchenette.*
8. *senile*	The elderly man seemed to be *senile* and ill.
9. *boundary*	The ball bounced over the *boundary* line.
10. *ringlet*	Jane touched a *ringlet* of the baby's hair.
11. *pamphlet*	I received a small *pamphlet* in the mail.
12. *cassette*	Barbara listened to a *cassette* tape.

D. LANGUAGE LINEAGE

DANISH INFLUENCES

From about A.D. 750 to 1000, England was repeatedly attacked by Scandinavian invaders (Vikings, or Northmen) who were from Denmark. These Norse invaders came in small robber bands at first, but later they arrived in large armies who came to conquer England and establish settlements. The Danes succeeded in gaining control of eastern England for a time. By about 1040, however, the English were again in power.

As the Danish settlers lived among the English natives, the English language gradually absorbed the language of the Danes. The people were probably able to communicate with each other to some degree, for both Old English and Old Norse are Germanic languages.

Many Danish words entered the English language. The Danish pronouns *they, their,* and *them* replaced the Old English *hie, her,* and *hem.* Many words with the /sk/ sound (rather than /sh/) also came in, such as *sky, skill, bask,* and *whisk*.

Often two words were used side by side until either the English or the Danish (Norse) term became more widely accepted. Thus the English words *shred, shell,* and *sheer* prevailed over the Norse *screde, skelle,* and *skere*. On the other hand, the Norse words *take, cut,* and *wing* replaced the Old English *niman, snīðan,* and *feþra*. But sometimes both words survived, and today we have related pairs such as *shirt—skirt, no—nay, hide—skin,* and *sick—ill.* (The first word in each pair is a native English word.)

Danish people even affected some word arrangements in English sentences. One is the omission of relative pronouns (*who, whom,* or *that*) in expressions such as "the man I saw." Another is the occurrence of a preposition at the end of a phrase, as in "what he was talking about." In this way the Danish language affected not only the vocabulary but also the basic structure of the English language. Thus the Danish influence was among the strongest forces that affected Old English.

Exercises

1. Give four names that can be applied to the men who invaded England from A.D. 750 to 1000.
2. Answer with *sh* or *sk*.
   a. During the years of Danish influence, the ___ pronunciation of *sc* or *sk* gradually prevailed in words such as *skil* (skill) and *wisken* (whisk).
   b. The ___ pronunciation of *sc* or *sk* gradually prevailed in words such as *screde* (shred) and *skelle* (shell).
3. When both an English word and a Danish word were used side by side, one of three things eventually happened. What were the three things?
4. Give two ways in which the Danish language affected the basic structure of English.

D. 11 points
1. Scandinavians, Vikings, Northmen (Norsemen), Danes
2. a. sk
   b. sh
3. The English word prevailed; the Danish word prevailed; or both words survived, resulting in pairs of related words.
4. the omission of relative pronouns, the occurrence of a preposition at the end of a phrase

13. *redemption* — Coupon *redemption* can save money.
14. *molecule* — A water *molecule* has hydrogen and oxygen.
15. *schedule* — Math class comes first on our *schedule.*
16. *characters* — Moses and Elijah are famous Bible *characters.*
17. *senator* — A state *senator* helps make new laws.
18. *phrase* — I remember only one *phrase* of the new song.
19. *chemistry* — In *chemistry* I learned about elements.
20. *senior* — Charles is a *senior* partner in that company.
21. *rejuvenate* — Rest can *rejuvenate* a tired body.
22. *dinette* — Their *dinette* set had a table and six chairs.
23. *booklet* — Our list of addresses is in a *booklet.*
24. *paragraph* — Read the first *paragraph* aloud.
25. *joyful* — An angel brought *joyful* news to Mary.

LESSON 29

NEW WORDS

1. agriculture
2. analyze
3. ancient
4. argument
5. atmosphere
6. category
7. congratulate
8. courteous
9. descent
10. judgment
11. mosquitoes
12. muscle
13. mystery
14. occurrence
15. ordinary
16. physician
17. proportion
18. sheriff
19. temperature
20. wherever

REVIEW WORDS

21. assistant
22. committee
23. cooperation
24. feasible
25. impulsive

A. UNEARTHING THE ROOTS

Latin Abbreviation	Meaning in Latin	Meaning in English
A.D.	anno domini	in the year of our Lord
A.M.	ante meridiem	before noon
P.M.	post meridiem	after noon
ad lib.	ad libitum	at pleasure
b.i.d.	bis in die	twice a day
c.	circa	about
cf.	confer	compare
D.V.	Deo volente	Lord willing
e.g.	exempli gratia	for example
et al.	et alii	and others
etc.	et cetera	and the rest (and so forth)
ff.	fecerunt	following
i.e.	id est	that is
lb.	libra	balance, pound
M.D.	Medicinae Doctor	Doctor of Medicine
no.	numero	number
p.r.n.	pro re nata	for the emergency (as needed)
P.S.	post scriptum	written afterwards
q.i.d.	quater in die	four times a day
q.v.	quod vide	which see
Rx (℞)	recipe	take (as directed)
vs.	versus	against
viz.	videlicet	one may see (namely)

In the box above are a number of Latin abbreviations that are useful to know. Write the correct one for each underlined word or phrase in the following sentences.

1. William Smith, Doctor of Medicine, prescribed two kinds of pills for me to take: one kind at 8:00 before noon and one kind as needed.
2. Today, the Lord willing, we will discuss the story of Ahab versus Naboth (about 855 B.C.) as recorded in 1 Kings 21 (which see).
3. The Messiah, that is, Jesus Christ, fulfilled many prophecies; for example, compare Matthew 26, Mark 14, and so forth, with Isaiah 53:3 and following.
4. Conrad Grebel and others (namely, George Blaurock and Felix Manz) received adult baptism in the year of our Lord 1525.

Lesson 29—56 points (A–C)

Teacher: Students are not required to memorize the meanings of the abbreviations listed. Remind them that only a few abbreviations, such as A.M., P.M., and M.D., are normally used in running text.

A. 16 points
1. M.D., Rx, A.M., p.r.n.
2. D.V., vs., c., q.v.
3. i.e., e.g., cf., etc., ff.
4. et al., viz., A.D.

Test Sentences

1. *mosquitoes*	Many *mosquitoes* buzzed around.
2. *ancient*	Pyramids are *ancient* Egyptian tombs.
3. *physician*	Luke was a *physician* in Bible times.
4. *feasible*	A round earth was *feasible* to Columbus.
5. *courteous*	Nabal was neither *courteous* nor kind.
6. *proportion*	Draw objects in proper *proportion.*
7. *agriculture*	David liked *agriculture.*
8. *descent*	The *descent* was breathtaking.
9. *assistant*	The dental *assistant* x-rayed Dale's teeth.
10. *sheriff*	A county *sheriff* enforces law and order.
11. *analyze*	Scientists *analyze* the needs of the soil.
12. *judgment*	Jethro's good *judgment* helped Moses.

B. AFFIXING AFFIXES

1. Write spelling words with noun-forming suffixes to match these definitions.
   a. One who specializes in treating physical ailments.
   b. The act of arguing.
   c. The act of cooperating.
   d. That which occurs.
2. Final *e* is usually retained to "protect the soft *g*" when attaching a suffix that begins with a consonant. Which New Word is an exception to this pattern? (The *e* may also be retained, but the form shown is the preferred spelling.)
3. Attach *-ment* to *acknowledge*, and drop the final *e* when you do so. The answers to exercises 2 and 3 are the only words commonly written for which the *e* of final *ge* is dropped when adding *-ment.*
4. Use adjective-forming suffixes to make spelling words with these meanings.
   a. Motivated by impulse; thoughtless.
   b. Capable of being done; practical.
   c. Full of courtesy; polite.
   d. Helping; assisting.
5. Write the word that contains the Latin root *ord* (order) and the suffix *-ary.*
6. Write New Words with diminutive suffixes to match these descriptions.
   a. Spanish for "small flies" (mosca + ito).
   b. Latin for "small mouse" (mus + ule).
7. Write the spelling words that have these prefixes. Some prefixes are changed through assimilation.
   a. in- c. ob- e. ana-
   b. de- d. pro- f. com- (2)

C. SOUND, STRUCTURE, AND MEANING

1. Write the spelling words in which you hear these sounds.
   a. /s/ spelled *sc* (2)
   b. /f/ spelled *ph* (2)
   c. final /f/ spelled *ff*
   d. /âr/ and final /ər/ both spelled *er*
2. The following nouns end with *o* preceded by a consonant. Form their plurals by adding *-es.*
   a. hero c. mosquito
   b. echo d. potato
3. Form the plurals of these musical terms by simply adding *s.*
   a. solo b. piano c. soprano
4. The following nouns end with *o* preceded by a vowel. Form their plurals by simply adding *-s.*
   a. ratio b. trio c. studio
5. Write *descent* or *decent* for each sentence.
   a. The beggar seldom had a ____ meal.
   b. The New Testament records Jesus' ____ from Abraham and David.
6. Write the spelling word that belongs with each group.
   a. secret, riddle, puzzle
   b. class, group, type
   c. farming, gardening, cultivation
   d. humidity, air pressure, wind speed
   e. long ago, pre-Flood, before Christ

13. *committee* The *committee* planned the menu.
14. *argument* The boys had an *argument.*
15. *muscle* God made *muscle* cells long and thin.
16. *temperature* Joel's *temperature* was rising.
17. *atmosphere* Gases make up our *atmosphere.*
18. *mystery* Gravity is still a *mystery* to man.
19. *wherever* Paul went *wherever* God led him.
20. *category* Each *category* of insects in interesting.
21. *occurrence* Rain is a daily *occurrence* there.
22. *impulsive* Peter made an *impulsive* promise.
23. *congratulate* We want to *congratulate* him.
24. *ordinary* Seventy years is an *ordinary* life span.
25. *cooperation* Good *cooperation* is needed.

B. 18 points
1. a. physician
   b. argument
   c. cooperation
   d. occurrence
2. judgment
3. acknowledgment
4. a impulsive
   b. feasible
   c. courteous
   d. assistant
5. ordinary
6. a. mosquitoes
   b. muscle
7. a. impulsive
   b. descent
   c. occurrence
   d. proportion
   e. analyze
   f. congratulate, committee (*also accept* cooperation)

C. 22 points
1. a. descent, muscle
   b. atmosphere, physician
   c. sheriff
   d. wherever
2. a. heroes
   b. echoes
   c. mosquitoes
   d. potatoes
3. a. solos
   b. pianos
   c. sopranos
4. a. ratios
   b. trios
   c. studios
5. a. decent
   b. descent
6. a. mystery
   b. category
   c. agriculture
   d. temperature (*also accept* atmosphere)
   e. ancient

D. LANGUAGE LINEAGE

Semantic Study: ABSTRACT AND CONCRETE MEANINGS

Through semantic change, a word may shift from a concrete meaning to an abstract meaning. That is, it may change from the name of an actual object to the name of something that has no substance—it is simply a quality or an idea. Some of the faded metaphors that you studied in Lesson 23 are examples of words whose meanings have changed from the concrete to the abstract.

Names of certain parts of the body have taken on abstract meanings. A *tongue* is an organ in the mouth, and it is also a language. The *heart* pumps blood, but to "take heart" means to take courage. Both the tongue and the heart are composed of *muscle,* but the ability of a group to make things happen may also be called its *muscle.* In each case, the name of something physical is applied to something that is symbolized by the physical thing.

The opposite may also happen. A word with an abstract meaning may be applied to an actual, physical object that is associated with that word. For example, we know what it is to be full of *curiosity*. But when a room is full of *curiosities*, it contains many things that make us curious. A *multitude* is simply a large number of anything—it may be objects, animals, or even ideas. But when we are told that a *multitude* filled an auditorium, we immediately picture a large crowd of people.

Many words have both concrete and abstract meanings, and they are likely to retain both meanings. But the faded metaphors of Lesson 23 show that one of the meanings of a word may be forgotten. Then the primary meaning of the word may change from the concrete to the abstract, or it may change from the abstract to the concrete.

Exercises

1. The following words are most commonly used with concrete meanings, but they also have abstract meanings. Write an abstract meaning for each, using the Speller Dictionary if you need help.
   a. carriage b. ceiling c. liquid d. shepherd
2. Give a concrete meaning for each of these abstract words. Use the Speller Dictionary if necessary.
   a. authority b. brief c. extension d. convenience
3. In the Speller Dictionary, read the etymology of each underlined word below. Then tell whether its meaning (as used in the sentence) has changed from *concrete to abstract* or from *abstract to concrete*. There are two of each kind.
   a. The abscess was caused by an infection.
   b. Father gave the visitors a cordial welcome.
   c. The twins were deeply attached to each other.
   d. Every pronoun must have an antecedent.

D. 12 points
1. a. A manner of carrying oneself; bearing.
   b. An upper limit, as on a price; maximum.
   c. Readily convertible into cash *or* Clear and flowing, as sounds.
   d. To care for, guide, or direct.
2. a. A person with superior knowledge about a subject; expert.
   b. A short document, usually about a legal matter or a news item.
   c. An additional outlet, as for a telephone.
   d. Something that saves work or affords comfort, as an electrical device.
3. a. abstract to concrete
   b. concrete to abstract
   c. concrete to abstract
   d. abstract to concrete

Lesson 30—81 points (A–B)

LESSON 30

25	26	27	28	29
associate	affiliate	bass	attached	agriculture
capitalization	bargain	canary	boundary	analyze
carnality	difficulty	canine	cassette	ancient
commemorate	dignity	census	characters	argument
cordial	emphasize	cereal	chemistry	atmosphere
corporal	fiery	council	dinette	category
corporation	filial	counsel	joyful	congratulate
corps	fraternal	doubtless	junior	courteous
corpse	fraternity	equine	juvenile	descent
corrupt	hearty	feline	kitchenette	judgment
criticize	humility	feminine	molecule	mosquitoes
encourage	majority	infantile	pamphlet	muscle
endeavor	maternal	masculine	particularly	mystery
identify	matrimony	minor	phrase	occurrence
Incarnation	misery	reptile	rejuvenate	ordinary
justify	paternal	rite	ringlet	physician
manager	patriarch	textile	schedule	proportion
manual	patriot	vaccine	senator	sheriff
manufacturer	patron	vein	senile	temperature
merchandise	remedy	versatile	senior	wherever

A. UNEARTHING THE ROOTS

can	dog	***cap***	head
fel	cat	***cor, cord***	heart
vacc	cow	***man***	hand
bos	ox, cow	***corp***	body
equ	horse	***carn***	flesh
sus	hog	***pater, patr***	father
sen	old	***mater, matr***	mother
juven	young	***frater, fratr***	brother
		fili	son, child

See page 120 for test sentences.

L25: cap, cor–cord, man, corp, carn

1. Write spelling words with these elements.
   a. cap + ize
   b. corp + ation
   c. cord + ial
   d. en + cor
   e. man + fac
   f. man + age
   g. in + carn
   h. carn + al
2. A [corp]* is a group of persons, but a [corp]* is a dead body.
3. The criminals were sentenced to [corp]* punishment and hard [man]* labor.
4. In which Lesson 25 word is initial *cor* an assimilated form of the prefix *com*-?

L26: pater–patr, mater–matr, frater–fratr, fili

5. Write the spelling words that are adjective forms pertaining to these.
   a. father
   b. mother
   c. brother
   d. son or child
6. Which word originally meant "ruling father" and now means "father of a tribe"?
7. Belonging to a [frater]* of [patr]s* would compel a Christian to [ad + fili]* too closely with unbelievers.

L27: can, fel, vacc, bos, equ, sus

8. Answer with spelling words whose roots have the meanings in parentheses.
   a. (dog) + ine
   b. (cat) + ine
   c. (horse) + ine
9. A [can]* is a bird, not a canine.
10. The word *bovine* on a bottle of medicine indicates that it should be used for (dogs, cats, cows, horses).
11. "And he went and joined himself to a citizen of that country; and he sent him into his fields to feed [sus]" (Luke 15:15).
12. A modern [vacc]* usually has nothing to do with cows.

L28: sen, juven

13. Complete these analogies.
   a. young : old :: __ile* : __ile*
   b. younger : older :: __ior* : __ior*
14. Write spelling words with these elements.
   a. sen + ate
   b. re + juven

L29: Latin Abbreviations

15. Write a Latin abbreviation for each word or phrase that follows a letter in parentheses.

It happened (a) in the year of our Lord 20—, on the fifth day of the twelfth month; (b) namely, December 5, (c) about 11:00 (d) before noon. I was splitting wood with a maul having a head that weighed ten (e) pounds. I was practicing my "one-crack" method, (f) that is, trying to split each piece with just one stroke, when I missed a piece and the maul smashed into my foot.

Father immediately took me to Charles Thompson, (g) Doctor of Medicine, but I had to wait until 1:10 (h) after noon before my foot could be examined. The doctor found no broken bones, and he prescribed pain medication to take (i) as needed. It was a (j) number of weeks before I could walk without limping.

(k) Postscript: My parents (l) and others have pointed out a valuable lesson that I can learn from this experience: Split wood in haste, and you can deplore the consequences (m) at pleasure.

A. 47 points
1. a. capitalization
   b. corporation
   c. cordial
   d. encourage
   e. manufacturer
   f. manager
   g. Incarnation
   h. carnality
2. corps, corpse
3. corporal, manual
4. corrupt
5. a. paternal
   b. maternal
   c. fraternal
   d. filial
6. patriarch
7. fraternity, patriots, affiliate
8. a. canine
   b. feline
   c. equine
9. canary
10. cows
11. swine
12. vaccine
13. a. juvenile, senile
    b. junior, senior
14. a. senator
    b. rejuvenate
15. a. A.D.
    b. viz.
    c. c.
    d. A.M.
    e. lb.
    f. i.e.
    g. M.D.
    h. P.M.
    i. p.r.n.
    j. no.
    k. P.S.
    l. et al.
    m. ad lib.

B. AFFIXING AFFIXES

Verb-forming Suffixes		Adjective-forming Suffixes	
-ate	do, make, become	*-ile, -ine*	of the quality or nature of
-fy, -ify	make		
-ize, -ise	make into *or* bring about		
Noun-forming Suffixes		**Diminutive Suffixes**	
-y, -ty, -ity	state of *or* condition of	*-ule, -let, -ette*	small

1. Use the correct suffixes to change these words into verbs.
   a. just [25] d. emphasis [26]
   b. vaccine e. dignity
   c. critic [25] f. humility
2. Use *-y, -ty,* or *-ity* to spell the noun forms of these words.
   a. carnal [25] c. difficulty [26]
   b. major [26] d. identify
3. The suffix *-y* may also mean "full of." Which word means "full of fire"? [26]
4. Form Lesson 27 words by attaching *-ile* or *-ine* to these Latin roots. Other letters may be needed between a root and a suffix.
   a. text (fabric) d. rep (crawl)
   b. fem (woman) e. can (dog)
   c. vacc (cow) f. vers (turn)
5. Write Lesson 28 words with these roots and diminutive suffixes.
   a. ring c. mol
   b. dine d. sched
6. a. Attach *-ette* to *farmer* and *usher.*
   b. In the words you wrote, *-ette* is a (masculine, feminine) suffix. [28]
7. Write the spelling words that have these prefixes or assimilated forms of them.
   a. ad- [25] d. re- [28]
   b. re- [26] e. de- [29]
   c. in- [27] f. ob- [29]
8. Which spelling words have these suffixes?
   a. -age [25] c. -ful [28]
   b. -less [27] d. -ous [29]

D. LANGUAGE LINEAGE

1. What characters were used in Old English writing that are not used today?
2. What is the source of endings such as *-ton* and *-ham* in many place names?
3. Why does Modern English have pairs of similar words such as *shirt—skirt*?
4. True or False: Danish invaders affected even the structure of the English language.
5. Write whether each underlined word is used with its *concrete* or *abstract* meaning.
   a. It takes backbone to stand for truth.
   b. This coin is a rarity that is seldom seen.

B. 34 points
1. a. justify
   b. vaccinate
   c. criticize
   d. emphasize
   e. dignify
   f. humiliate
2. a. carnality
   b. majority
   c. difficulty
   d. identity
3. fiery
4. a. textile
   b. feminine
   c. vaccine
   d. reptile
   e. canine
   f. versatile
5. a. ringlet
   b. dinette
   c. molecule
   d. schedule
6. a. farmerette, usherette
   b. feminine
7. a. associate
   b. remedy
   c. infantile
   d. rejuvenate
   e. descent
   f. occurrence
8. a. encourage
   b. doubtless
   c. joyful
   d. courteous

D. 10 points
1. the thorn (þ), the edh or eth (ð), the ash (æ)
2. These endings are Old English forms that have not changed since the early days of England.
3. In such pairs of words, one is a native English word and one is a Danish (Norse) word.
4. True
5. a. abstract
   b. concrete

LESSON 31

NEW WORDS

1. aquarium
2. aqueduct
3. export
4. import
5. importunity
6. navigator
7. occupation
8. opportunity
9. perceive
10. performance
11. permitted
12. persistent
13. persuade
14. pertaining
15. pierce
16. salary
17. transformed
18. translate
19. transparent
20. transportation

REVIEW WORDS

21. conscience
22. conscious
23. frequent
24. transferred
25. transgressions

A. UNEARTHING THE ROOTS

ROOT	MEANING	EXAMPLE
port	harbor, gate	port
aqua	water	aquarium
nav	ship	navigate

port

1. A wind blowing *toward port* (ob + port) was a favorable wind for sailors on an incoming ship. It gave them a good ____* to bring in the ship. (*Ob-* becomes *op-* by assimilation.)
2. A wind blowing *not toward port* (in + port) was unfavorable for an incoming ship; sailors had to use extra persistence to bring it in. Today, persistence in asking for something is ____*.
3. a. An ____* is an item going out of a port to another country.
   b. An ____* is an item coming into a port from another country.
4. As an English root, *port* has the idea of "carry." Carrying goods or people from one place to another is called ____*.
5. Choose from these words: *portable, portal, porter.*
   a. A gate may also be called a ____.
   b. A gatekeeper is a ____.
   c. Something ____ can easily be carried about.

aqua (ak′wə)

6. The huge [aqua]* contained many different kinds of (aerial, aquatic, praedial) creatures.
7. A large ____* brought water to the city.
8. From the name Aqua-Lung, you can tell that this device is made for breathing (in outer space, on high mountains, underwater).

nav

9. Magellan started on a trip around the world, but he was killed on the way. The voyage was completed by a man named Cano, who became the first ____* to sail around the earth.
10. Join the prefix *circum-* (around) with *navigate* to form a verb that expresses what Cano did in relation to the earth.
11. A military force that uses ships to do battle is (an army, a navy).
12. The *nav* root is sometimes spelled *nau*, as in *nausea, nautical,* and *nautilus*. Which word is associated with seasickness?

Lesson 31—55 points (A–C)

A. 16 points
1. opportunity
2. importunity
3. a. export
   b. import
4. transportation
5. a. portal
   b. porter
   c. portable
6. aquarium, aquatic
7. aqueduct
8. underwater
9. navigator
10. circumnavigate
11. a navy
12. nausea

Test Sentences

1. *perceive*	Did you *perceive* a change in the clouds?
2. *salary*	The businessman was paid a high *salary*.
3. *conscience*	If we continue in sin, our *conscience* is dulled.
4. *aquarium*	We bought goldfish for our *aquarium*.
5. *performance*	A road test measures a driver's *performance*.
6. *transformed*	Peter was *transformed* into a different man.
7. *aqueduct*	Romans invented the *aqueduct* for water.
8. *conscious*	Reflexes take no *conscious* thought.
9. *permitted*	Revenge was *permitted* in olden times.
10. *export*	Petroleum is Saudi Arabia's chief *export*.
11. *translate*	Can you *translate* German into English?
12. *persistent*	A judge helped the *persistent* widow.

B. AFFIXING AFFIXES

PREFIX	MEANING	EXAMPLE
trans-	across, over	transport
per-	through, thoroughly	persist

1. Write spelling words beginning with *trans-* and containing these roots.
   a. fer (carry)
   b. lat (bring)
   c. par (appear)
   d. form
   e. port (carry)
   f. gress (step)
2. Attach *trans-* to these words. Observe that each word you write has the idea of "across" or "over."
   a. plant
   b. oceanic
   c. action
   d. mission
3. Write New Words beginning with *per-* to match these definitions.
   a. Allowed to go through with (a request).
   b. Standing firm through difficulty or opposition.
4. Which New Word contains *per-* and a form of the root *ten* (hold)?
5. Since *per-* may mean "thoroughly," this prefix is a common intensifier. Write the spelling words with these meanings.
   a. Thoroughly urge (per + suad).
   b. Thoroughly form (per + form).
   c. Thoroughly grasp (per + ceiv).
6. In one New Word with *per-*, the prefix and root are blended into one syllable. Write this word; it is a synonym of *penetrate*.
7. Attach each suffix to the words after it.
   a. *-or*: navigate, dictate
   b. *-ation*: occupy, reform
   c. *-ent*: persist, consist

C. SOUND, STRUCTURE, AND MEANING

1. Write the spelling words in which you hear these sounds.
   a. /sw/ spelled *su*
   b. /p/ spelled *pp*
   c. /ē/ spelled *ei* after *c*
2. Write the two spelling words that are past forms in which the final consonant was doubled before adding *-ed*.
3. Answer with forms of *export* or *import*.
   a. Brazil raises coffee and ____ it to other countries.
   b. Because Paraguay has few factories, it ____ most of its machinery.
   c. Japan ____ much of its food because it has little farmland.
4. Write words to complete these analogies.
   a. bird : cage :: fish : ____*
   b. tractor : agriculture :: bus : ____*
   c. automobile : driver :: ship : ____*
   d. export : import :: rare : ____*
   e. knife : cut :: nail : ____*
   f. electricity : cable :: water : ____*
5. Which Review Words have the *sci* root?
6. Objects are distinctly visible through *transparent* glass. Objects are not distinctly visible through ____ glass. (See the Speller Dictionary.)
7. Roman soldiers received part of their pay in salt (Latin *sal*). Which New Word developed as a result of this practice?

97

B. 23 points
1. a. transferred
   b. translate
   c. transparent
   d. transformed
   e. transportation
   f. transgressions
2. a. transplant
   b. transoceanic
   c. transaction
   d. transmission
3. a. permitted
   b. persistent
4. pertaining
5. a. persuade
   b. performance
   c. perceive
6. pierce
7. a. navigator, dictator
   b. occupation, reformation
   c. persistent, consistent

C. 18 points
1. a. persuade
   b. opportunity
   c. perceive
2. permitted, transferred
3. a. exports
   b. imports
   c. imports
4. a. aquarium
   b. transportation
   c. navigator
   d. frequent
   e. pierce
   f. aqueduct
5. conscience, conscious
6. translucent
7. salary

13	*import*	Our country must *import* coffee from Brazil.
14.	*transparent*	We see through *transparent* glass.
15.	*frequent*	A desert has *frequent* sandstorms.
16.	*importunity*	Her *importunity* wearied the judge.
17.	*persuade*	I did *persuade* Titus to climb the tower.
18.	*transferred*	Amy *transferred* her seedlings.
19.	*navigator*	The *navigator* had worked ten years.
20.	*pertaining*	Nancy asked a question *pertaining* to grammar.
21.	*transportation*	Cars are *transportation*.
22.	*occupation*	Amos' *occupation* was herding sheep.
23	*pierce*	A balloon will burst if we *pierce* it.
24.	*transgressions*	God forgives *transgressions*.
25.	*opportunity*	Make friends at each *opportunity*.

D. LANGUAGE LINEAGE

THE NORMAN CONQUEST

An event occurred in the year 1066 that had a greater effect on English than did any other event in the history of the language. In that year William the Conqueror, duke of Normandy in France, defeated the king of England in the historic Battle of Hastings. Then William himself was crowned king of England.

King William placed Frenchmen in all the high government positions of England. He declared French to be the official language of the nation, and he required that French be used in all government and business transactions. Even church services and school sessions were to be conducted in French. The form of French that King William introduced was the Norman dialect of Old French.

But though the official language was French, the common people continued to speak English. Yet through their frequent dealings with the French, the English adopted hundreds of French words into their language. This strong French influence on English marked the end of the Old English period and the beginning of the Middle English period.

Many of the new words referred to the same things as native English words, but gradually they developed different shades of meaning. In general, the native English words are warm, simple, and forceful, whereas the French synonyms are cool, refined, and specific.

Native English	French	Native English	French
cow	beef	help	aid
calf	veal	might	power
swine	pork	wish	desire
sheep	mutton	shun	avoid
chicken	poultry	hate	detest

Of the one thousand English words most commonly used today, about three hundred are of French origin. Because the French language developed from Latin, it is easy to understand why there are so many words with Latin roots in the English language.

Exercises

1. Why did the Norman Conquest have a powerful effect on the English language?
2. On the table above, each pair of words on the left side is related in the same way. How is each pair related?
3. What is the general difference between native English words and their French synonyms?
4. How is it that *Latin* roots came into the English language through the *French* influence?

D. 8 points

1. William the Conqueror made French the official language of England. The common people continued to speak English, but they adopted hundreds of French words into their language.
2. In each pair, the first (English) word refers to an animal, and the second (French) word refers to the meat of that animal. (Note: The reason is that when the upper-class French referred to one of these animals, they were usually speaking about the meat of the animal.)
3. Native English words are warm, simple, and forceful whereas the French synonyms are cool, refined, and specific.
4. The French language developed from Latin.

LESSON 32

NEW WORDS

1. accidentally
2. awkward
3. dissect
4. fungicide
5. genuine
6. herbicide
7. incident
8. insecticide
9. occasion
10. oxygen
11. precisely
12. superficial
13. superlative
14. superscription
15. supersede
16. superstition
17. surrender
18. surrounded
19. ultimate
20. ultraviolet

REVIEW WORDS

21. advise
22. intercede
23. scissors
24. succeed
25. wrought

A. UNEARTHING THE ROOTS

ROOT	MEANING	EXAMPLE
cid	fall	accident
cid, cis	cut, kill	pesticide, scissors
sect	cut	section

cid (sid)

1. Write New Words with the *cid* root as described.
   a. A noun referring to any happening that falls on one.
   b. An adverb usually referring to something bad that falls on one.
2. When two things happen together in a remarkable way, possibly by God's providence, the event is (an accidence, a coincidence).
3. Another spelling of *cid* (fall) is *cas*. Write the New Word that contains this form; it is a synonym of *event*.

cid (sīd), cis (sīs)

4. The teacher used ____* to cut the paper ____* in half.
5. Write the New Words with these meanings.
   a. A substance that kills green plants.
   b. A substance that kills insects.
   c. A substance that kills fungi.
6. Choose from these words: *fratricide, infanticide, suicide.*
   a. Judas committed ____ after betraying Jesus.
   b. Both Pharaoh and Herod were guilty of ____.
   c. By killing his brother, Cain committed the crime of ____.
7. Choose from these words: *decision, excision, incision.*
   a. Cutting something out.
   b. Cutting into something.
   c. Cutting away all else and choosing one thing.

sect

8. To ____* something is to cut it apart.
9. Choose from these words: *bisect, insect, intersect, section.*
   a. A creature cut (segmented) into three distinct parts.
   b. To cut in two.
   c. To cut between; cross.
   d. The piece that lies between cuts.
10. In which New Word do you see both *sect* (cut) and *cid* (kill)?

99

Lesson 32—57 points (A–C)

A. 21 points
1. a. incident
   b. accidentally
2. a coincidence
3. occasion
4. scissors, precisely
5. a. herbicide
   b. insecticide
   c. fungicide
6. a. suicide
   b. infanticide
   c. fratricide
7. a. excision
   b. incision
   c. decision
8. dissect
9. a. insect
   b. bisect
   c. intersect
   d. section
10. insecticide

See page 108 for test sentences.

B. AFFIXING AFFIXES

PREFIX	MEANING	EXAMPLE
super-, sur-	over, above	supersede
ultra-	beyond	ultraviolet

1. Write the New Words beginning with *super-* that have these meanings.
   a. Something written above.
   b. To replace by being better.
   c. At or near the surface; not deep.
   d. Pertaining to the highest degree of comparison.
2. One New Word originally meant "act of standing over, as in fear or respect." Today the word means "a belief or practice based on ignorant fear." Write this word.
3. Attach *super-* to each word.
   a. vision c. sonic
   b. abound d. natural
4. The Latin prefix *super-* changed to *sur-* in the French language. Write the two New Words that have *sur-*.
5. Attach *sur-* to the following words.
   a. pass b. plus
   c. name d. charge
6. Write New Words beginning with *ultra-* or *ult-* to match these definitions.
   a. Last and greatest; beyond all others.
   b. Pertaining to light rays beyond the frequency of those for the color violet.
7. You would expect an ultramodern house to be (barely modern, especially modern).
8. A prefix with a meaning opposite that of *super-* and *ultra-* is *sub-*. Write the Review Word that has an assimilated form of *sub-*.
9. Which New Word has *ad-* (assimilated), *-al,* and *-ly*?

B. 20 points
1. a. superscription
   b. supersede
   c. superficial
   d. superlative
2. superstition
3. a. supervision
   b. superabound
   c. supersonic
   d. supernatural
4. surrender, surrounded
5. a. surpass
   b. surplus
   c. surname
   d. surcharge
6. a. ultimate
   b. ultraviolet
7. especially modern
8. succeed
9. accidentally

C. SOUND, STRUCTURE, AND MEANING

1. Write the spelling words in which you hear these sounds.
   a. /r/ spelled *rr* (2)
   b. /sīd/ spelled *cide* (3)
2. Write the spelling word in which /sēd/ is spelled *cede*. Remember that this is the most common spelling of /sēd/.
3. In which spelling word is /sēd/ spelled *ceed*? Remember that the only English words with /sēd/ spelled *ceed* are *exceed, proceed,* and this word.
4. Write the New Word in which /sēd/ is spelled *sede*. This is the only English word with /sēd/ spelled *sede*.
5. Write *advice* or *advise* for each sentence.
   a. Rehoboam rejected the old men's ____.
   b. I ____ you to be careful.
6. For each group of synonyms, write an antonym from the spelling list.
   a. artificial, synthetic, manmade
   b. purposely, intentionally, deliberately
   c. approximately, roughly, nearly
7. Write a spelling word for each description.
   a. Is an old past form of *work*.
   b. Has the suffix *-ward* and the original meaning "turned the wrong way."
   c. Comes from the Greek words *oxys* (acid) and *genēs* (born).

C. 16 points
1. a. surrender, surrounded
   b. fungicide, herbicide, insecticide
2. intercede
3. succeed
4. supersede
5. a. advice
   b. advise
6. a. genuine
   b. accidentally
   c. precisely
7. a. wrought
   b. awkward
   c. oxygen

Test Sentences

1. *accidentally*	He *accidentally* spilled milk.
2. *occasion*	On one *occasion*, Jesus healed ten lepers.
3. *surrender*	We must *surrender* to Christ as Lord.
4. *intercede*	Jonathan did *intercede* for David.
5. *oxygen*	A fire needs fuel and *oxygen* to burn.
6. *surrounded*	The village was *surrounded* by hills.
7. *awkward*	David did not wear Saul's *awkward* armor.
8. *precisely*	We arrived *precisely* at seven o'clock.
9. *scissors*	Doctors use *scissors* to snip stitches.
10. *dissect*	Students *dissect* animals to study them.
11. *superficial*	His accident wounds are only *superficial.*
12. *ultimate*	Serving Jesus brings the *ultimate* joy.

D. LANGUAGE LINEAGE

THE MIDDLE ENGLISH PERIOD

With England under the control of French-speaking rulers, Old English immediately lost its popularity. The West Saxon dialect was no longer the literary standard, and English became chiefly a spoken language used by the uneducated. The result was that the English language went through great changes in just a few centuries.

One important change was that the cumbersome inflections of Old English (Lesson 21) were greatly simplified. Some of this had already happened through the Danish influence, but now the inflections were lost even more rapidly.

Through this leveling of inflections, the order of words in sentences become more important. Word order has little significance in a highly inflected language because the ending of a word shows how the word functions in a sentence. In Old English, for example, the word for *hunter* has the forms *hunta* and *huntan* to show whether it is the subject or the object of a verb. But in Modern English, the position of *hunter* before or after the verb shows whether it is the subject or the object.

English was also affected during this period by traders from Germany, Holland, and Flanders. William the Conqueror encouraged the weavers from these countries to do business with England, and they came in large numbers. Among the words adopted from them are *deck, dock, freight,* and *guilder*.

During the 1100s, the English language slowly regained its popularity. A generation of people grew up who thought of themselves chiefly as Englishmen (even though many were of French descent), and French was used less and less. Then in 1204, the final tie between England and France was severed when England lost her control over Normandy. The decline of French continued through the 1300s; and finally in the 1400s, English was once again recognized as the official language of England. But by then the English language was vastly different from what it had been in 1066.

Exercises

1. After the Norman Conquest, why did the English language go through great changes in just a few centuries? Give two reasons.
2. In what way did Old English become considerably simpler? How did this simplifying process affect sentence structure?
3. What other outside influence (besides French) affected Middle English?
4. For what two reasons did use of the French language in England gradually decline during the 1200s and 1300s?

13. *fungicide* — A *fungicide* spray can stop plant rust.
14. *superlative* — Only God has *superlative* wisdom.
15. *succeed* — Who will *succeed* your schoolteacher then?
16. *genuine* — Carl's shoes are made of *genuine* leather.
17. *superscription* — Read the *superscription* on a dime.
18. *ultraviolet* — We cannot see *ultraviolet* rays.
19. *herbicide* — He sprinkled *herbicide* on the weeds.
20. *supersede* — Heaven will *supersede* all glory here.
21. *advise* — Doctors *advise* us to watch our salt intake.
22. *incident* — He told the *incident* of killing a bear.
23. *superstition* — We disbelieve all *superstition*.
24. *wrought* — God *wrought* miracles to free the Israelites.
25. *insecticide* — Will the *insecticide* also kill helpful insects?

D. 14 points

1. There were great changes because of the strong French influence, and because English was chiefly a spoken language used by the uneducated.
2. Many of the Old English inflections were lost. The order of words in sentences became more important.
3. the influence of traders and weavers from Germany, Holland, and Flanders
4. The people of England thought of themselves chiefly as Englishmen, even though many were of French descent. In 1204 the final tie between England and France was severed when England lost control over Normandy.

LESSON 33

NEW WORDS

1. betray
2. cafeteria
3. captivate
4. cashier
5. commander
6. delegate
7. discipline
8. exception
9. legislation
10. legitimate
11. mandate
12. mandatory
13. receipts
14. receiver
15. rectify
16. regiment
17. regulator
18. restrain
19. secede
20. selection

REVIEW WORDS

21. cassette
22. correction
23. extremely
24. gradually
25. pamphlet

A. UNEARTHING THE ROOTS

ROOT	MEANING	EXAMPLE
cap, cip, cept	seize, take	capture, accept
mand	order	command
reg, rect	rule, straighten	regulate, correct
leg, lect	choose, gather	select
leg	law	legal

cap, cip, cept

1. A visit to Washington, D.C., will ____* some tourists so much that they will return several more times.
2. Every citizen must pay taxes; even the president is no ____.*
3. Answer with New Words having the *ceiv* or *ceipt* spelling.
   a. The Internal Revenue Service is the ____* of federal taxes.
   b. These ____* are used to finance government operations.
4. Instruction and training are called ____*. (This word does not have the *cip* root even though it contains the letters *cip*.)

mand

5. a. The United States president is the supreme ____* of the United States military forces.
   b. An order from him may be called a presidential ____*.
6. It is ____* that Christians submit to the civil government.

reg, rect

7. Since the Pentagon is the [reg]* of the nation's military forces, it is responsible to [reg]* the activities of American soldiers.
8. Criminals are sent to prison as a means of [rect]*, but many of them still do not [rect]* their ways.

leg, lect

9. The Supreme Court reviews a ____* of cases decided by lower courts.
10. A large gathering of soldiers is a (legation, legion).

leg

11. Each member of Congress is a ____*, elected by his home state or district.
12. Congress proposes ____*, but it must be signed by the president before it becomes law.
13. The Federal Bureau of Investigation deals with persons whose activities are not ____*.

Lesson 33—64 points (A–C)

A. 17 points
1. captivate
2. exception
3. a. receiver
   b. receipts
4. discipline
5. a. commander
   b. mandate
6. mandatory
7. regulator, regiment
8. correction, rectify
9. selection
10. legion
11. delegate
12. legislation
13. legitimate

Test Sentences

1. *restrain*	Andrew tried to *restrain* the horses.
2. *discipline*	We need to *discipline* ourselves.
3. *betray*	A true friend will not *betray* our trust.
4. *receiver*	Listen to the voice in the telephone *receiver*.
5. *extremely*	It is *extremely* warm at the equator.
6. *secede*	Several states did *secede* from the Union.
7. *exception*	Is there any *exception* to the rule?
8. *cafeteria*	I ate lunch in the hospital *cafeteria*.
9. *gradually*	The air *gradually* fades into space.
10. *legislation*	The new *legislation* takes effect immediately.
11. *rectify*	Some problems are difficult to *rectify*.
12. *captivate*	The puppy seemed to *captivate* us.

B. AFFIXING AFFIXES

PREFIX	MEANING	EXAMPLE
re-	again, back	return
se-	apart	secede

1. Write New Words beginning with *re-* as described.
   a. Means "to draw or hold back."
   b. Is related to *receive.* (2)
2. The prefix *re-* may be used freely to add the idea of "again" to a verb. Attach *re-* to these words.
   a. occur d. deposit
   b. spread e. appear
   c. freeze f. sharpen
3. The initial letters *re* do not always form a prefix. Write three New Words in which initial *re* is not a prefix but is part of the *reg* or *rect* root.
4. Write spelling words beginning with *se-* and having these meanings.
   a. Choosing and setting apart (se + lect).
   b. To go apart; withdraw (se + cede).
5. Attach these suffixes to the words after them. One answer is not a spelling word.
   a. *-er* or *-or*: command, regulate
   b. *-ion*: except, correct
   c. *-ly*: gradual, extreme
   d. *-ary* or *-ory*: mandate, discipline
6. Write the Review Word that has the diminutive suffix *-ette*.
7. Which spelling words are related to these?
   a. cash c. disciple
   b. captive d. café

C. SOUND, STRUCTURE, AND MEANING

1. Write the spelling words in which you hear these sounds.
   a. /s/ spelled *sc*
   b. final /et/ spelled *ette*
   c. /ēt/ spelled *eipt*
   d. final /ā/ spelled *ay*
2. Write the word in which /sēd/ is spelled *cede*. Then write the one word from Lesson 32 that has /sēd/ spelled *sede*.
3. Write the spelling words that are synonyms for these.
   a. suppress d. controller
   b. booklet e. exceedingly
   c. choice f. compulsory
4. Write the two spelling words that are synonyms for *chastisement*.
5. A number of spelling words refer to persons who do certain things. Write the word that names
   a. a person who represents another.
   b. a person who directs soldiers.
   c. a person who receives cash payments.
6. Do not confuse *receipt* and *recipe*. Write the correct words.
   a. What is your ____ for success?
   b. Make sure this sales ____ is correct.
7. In the Speller Dictionary, what usage label is given to *captivated* as used in the following sentence?
   The spy was captivated and imprisoned.

103

B. 27 points
1. a. restrain
   b. receipts, receiver
2. a. reoccur
   b. respread
   c. refreeze
   d. redeposit
   e. reappear
   f. resharpen
3. rectify, regiment, regulator
4. a. selection
   b. secede
5. a. commander, regulator
   b. exception, correction
   c. gradually, extremely
   d. mandatory, disciplinary
6. cassette
7. a. cashier
   b. captivate
   c. discipline
   d. cafeteria

C. 20 points
1. a. discipline
   b. cassette
   c. receipts
   d. betray
2. secede; supersede
3. a. restrain
   b. pamphlet
   c. selection
   d. regulator
   e. extremely
   f. mandatory
4. discipline, correction
5. a. delegate
   b. commander
   c. cashier
6. a. recipe
   b. receipt
7. archaic

13. *selection* — They offer a good *selection* of shoes
14. *legitimate* — Do not overdo a *legitimate* activity.
15. *regiment* — Some governments *regiment* a citizen's life.
16. *cashier* — Mother paid the *cashier* for the groceries.
17. *mandate* — Did the king's *mandate* stop Daniel's prayers?
18. *cassette* — Norman recorded with a *cassette* player.
19. *commander* — The army's chief *commander* is the president.
20. *mandatory* — Elementary school is *mandatory*.
21. *regulator* — Is this a *regulator* for the furnace?
22. *delegate* — Good leaders *delegate* tasks to others.
23. *receipts* — Stores compute total *receipts* daily.
24. *correction* — We all need *correction* at times.
25. *pamphlet* — Read the *pamphlet* about highway safety.

D. LANGUAGE LINEAGE

MIDDLE ENGLISH LITERATURE

During the 1100s, little writing was done in English because the official language was French. When English was finally put in written form again, French scribes made several spelling changes. Both the thorn and the edh were replaced by *th* (*wiþ—with*, *deað—death*); *ū* was changed to *ou* (*clūd—cloud*); and *cw* was replaced by *qu* (*cwēn—queen*).

The Middle English period lasted from 1066 to about 1500. In this period, John Wycliffe and his assistants produced the first translation of the complete Bible in English. The Wycliffe version of the Lord's Prayer appears in Lesson 1.

Another noted writer of the Middle English period was Geoffrey Chaucer (1340?–1400). His best known work is *The Canterbury Tales,* a book containing poems about Catholics who went on pilgrimages to Canterbury (in southeastern England). A few lines from one poem appear below.

There were still numerous dialects in England, even to the point that Englishmen from different localities had difficulty conversing together. But gradually the English of London was accepted as the standard, and by about 1450 the majority of English literature was written in this dialect. London English was the earliest form of what we know today as standard English.

When that Aprille with his shoures sote
The droghte of Marche hath perced to the rote,
And bathed every veyne in swich licour,
Of which vertu engendred is the flour; . . .
Than longen folk to goon on pilgrimages
(And palmers for to seken straunge strondes)
To ferne halwes, couthe in sondry londes;
And specially, from every shires ende
Of Engelond, to Caunterbury they wende,
The holy blisful martir for to seke,
That hem hath holpen, whan that they were seke.

Exercises

1. Name three spelling changes that French scribes made when they wrote English.
2. What was the most important piece of literature produced in the Middle English period?
3. Give the modern spellings of the following words in the stanza from *The Canterbury Tales*. The numbers in parentheses show the lines in which the words appear.

Left column:	Right column:
(1) Aprille, shoures	(1) sondry, londes
(2) droghte, perced	(3) Engelond, wende
(5) longen, goon	(4) blisful, martir
(6) seken, straunge	(5) holpen, whan

4. The words *seek* and *sick* were apparently pronounced alike in Chaucer's day, because they are both spelled _____ in the last two lines above.
5. What was the earliest form of standard English as we know it today?

D. 22 points

Teacher: Canterbury was the ancient religious center of England. See below for a modern version of the excerpt.

1. The thorn and the edh were replaced by th, *ū* was changed to *ou*; and *cw* was changed to *qu*.
2. the Wycliffe translation of the complete Bible in English
3. Left column:
   (1) April, showers
   (2) drought, pierced
   (5) long, go
   (6) seek, strange
   Right column:
   (1) sundry, lands
   (3) England, wend
   (4) blissful, martyr
   (5) helped, when
4. seke
5. London English

Excerpt from *The Canterbury Tales* in Modern English

When April with his soothing showers
The drought of March has pierced to the root,
And bathed every vine in rich liquid,
Of which virtue the flower is engendered; . . .
Then folks long to go on pilgrimages
(And palmers [pilgrims bearing palm branches] to seek strange strands),
To faraway halves [parts], known in sundry lands,
And specially, from every shire's end
Of England, to Canterbury they wend,
The holy blissful martyr to seek,
That has helped them when they were sick.

Note: In the stanza above, seeking the "holy blissful martyr" apparently refers to the veneration of saints. Some poems in *The Canterbury Tales* have content that is even more objectionable.

Lesson 34—71 points (A–B)

LESSON 34

31	32	33
aquarium	accidentally	betray
aqueduct	awkward	cafeteria
export	dissect	captivate
import	fungicide	cashier
importunity	genuine	commander
navigator	herbicide	delegate
occupation	incident	discipline
opportunity	insecticide	exception
perceive	occasion	legislation
performance	oxygen	legitimate
permitted	precisely	mandate
persistent	superficial	mandatory
persuade	superlative	receipts
pertaining	superscription	receiver
pierce	supersede	rectify
salary	superstition	regiment
transformed	surrender	regulator
translate	surrounded	restrain
transparent	ultimate	secede
transportation	ultraviolet	selection

A. UNEARTHING THE ROOTS

port	harbor, gate	***cap, cip, cept***	seize, take
aqua	water	***mand***	order
nav	ship	***reg, rect***	rule, straighten
cid	fall	***leg, lect***	choose, gather
cid, cis	cut, kill	***leg***	law
sect	cut		

See page 121 for test sentences.

L31: port, aqua, nav

1. Write Lesson 31 words to match these meanings.
   a. An item going out of a port to another country.
   b. An item coming into a port from another country.

2. Which word referred originally to a wind
   a. blowing toward the port?
   b. not blowing toward the port?

3. Remember that *port* may have the idea of "carry." Which spelling word means "act of carrying from one place to another"?

4. Choose from these words: *deport, deportment, portable, report.*
   a. Something that can be carried easily is ____.
   b. To carry a person out of a country as a punishment is to ____ him.
   c. A story that is carried back from its source is a ____.
   d. A person's ____ is his conduct—how he carries himself.

5. A container that holds water and water creatures is an ____*.

6. A channel that brings water from a distance is an ____*.

7. One who directs a ship is a ____*.

8. A country with a large naval force would have many armed (cars, planes, ships).

L32: cid, cid–cis, sect

9. a. If something (usually unpleasant) "falls upon" someone, it happens [cid]*.
   b. Something more normal that "falls upon" a person is called an [cid]*.
   c. An [cas]* may be a normal or special happening.

10. Write three words from Lesson 32 in which final *cide* indicates "killing."

11. Match the following words with the phrases below: *fratricide, homicide, regicide, suicide.*
   a. King killing. c. Self killing.
   b. Brother killing. d. Man killing.

12. Write the spelling word with the *cis* root which means "exactly; accurately."

13. Write the spelling word with the *sect* root which means "cut apart."

L33: cap–cip–cept, mand, reg–rect

14. To ____* someone is to seize his attention.

15. An ____* is something taken or left out.

16. Write the two words in which the *cap* root is spelled *ceipt* or *ceiv.*

17. Write the spelling word that contains *cip* but not the *cip* root. It means "training."

18. It is [mand]* that soldiers obey every [mand]* of their [mand]*.

19. A colonel is the [reg]* of a [reg]* of soldiers.

20. To [rect]* a mistake is the same as to make a correction.

L33: leg–lect, leg

21. A ____* is something chosen from a number of other things.

22. A ____* activity is one that is acceptable according to the ____* of a country.

23. A ____* is someone who represents another person or group.

A. 40 points
1. a. export
   b. import
2. a. opportunity
   b. importunity
3. transportation
4. a. portable
   b. deport
   c. report
   d. deportment
5. aquarium
6. aqueduct
7. navigator
8. ships
9. a. accidentally
   b. incident
   c. occasion
10. fungicide, herbicide, insecticide
11. a. regicide
    b. fratricide
    c. suicide
    d. homicide
12. precisely
13. dissect
14. captivate
15. exception
16. receipts, receiver
17. discipline
18. mandatory, mandate, commander
19. regulator, regiment
20. rectify
21. selection
22. legitimate, legislation
23. delegate

B. AFFIXING AFFIXES

trans-	across, over
per-	through, thoroughly
super-, *sur-*	over, above
ultra-	beyond
re-	again, back
se-	apart

1. Write Lesson 31 words that contain these elements.
   a. trans + lat (bring)
   b. trans + form
   c. trans + port (carry)
   d. trans + par (appear)
2. Write Lesson 31 words beginning with *per-* that contain these elements.
   a. per + tain (hold)
   b. per + mit (send)
   c. per + sist (stand)
   d. per + ceiv (grasp)
   e. per + suad (urge)
3. Which meaning of *per-* makes this prefix especially suitable as an intensifier? [31]
4. Write Lesson 32 words with *super-* or *sur-* to replace the underlined words.
   a. This edition of the book is to <u>replace by being better</u> the previous edition.
   b. The huge army <u>encircled</u> the small city, and there was no choice but to <u>give up</u>.
   c. A <u>writing above</u> on Jesus' cross identified Him as the King of the Jews.
   d. It was a minor accident, and the damage was only <u>on the surface</u>.
5. Write the two words from Lesson 32 that have the element *ult* or *ultra*.
6. Write Lesson 33 words beginning with *re-* or *se-* to match these definitions.
   a. One who takes something.
   b. To draw or hold back; control.
   c. To go apart from others; withdraw.
   d. Things that are received.
   e. Act of picking out; choosing.
7. In which three spelling words does *ob-* have the assimilated form *oc-* or *op-*? [31, 32]
8. Form spelling words by attaching suffixes to these words.
   a. perform [31]
   b. navigate [31]
   c. accident [32]
   d. regulate [33]
   e. mandate [33]
   f. except [33]

D. LANGUAGE LINEAGE

1. After 1066, many ____ roots entered English through the ____ language.
2. Explain how the languages of Holland and Flanders came to affect Middle English.
3. What three spelling changes did French scribes make in English words?
4. Name two noted writers of the Middle English period.
5. What form of English developed into today's standard English?

B. 31 points
1. a. translate
   b. transformed
   c. transportation
   d. transparent
2. a. pertaining
   b. permitted
   c. persistent
   d. perceive
   e. persuade
3. thoroughly
4. a. supersede
   b. surrounded, surrender
   c. superscription
   d. superficial
5. ultimate, ultraviolet
6. a. receiver
   b. restrain
   c. secede
   d. receipts
   e. selection
7. occupation, opportunity, occasion
8. a. performance
   b. navigator
   c. accidentally
   d. regulator
   e. mandatory
   f. exception

D. 10 points
1. Latin, French
2. Traders and weavers from these countries did much business with England.
3. They replaced the edh and the thorn with *th*, they changed *ū* to *ou*, and they changed *cw* to *qu*.
4. John Wycliffe and Geoffrey Chaucer
5. the form used in London

Review Lesson 6—Test Sentences

1.	*hungrier*	What is *hungrier* than a bear?
2.	*graduating*	Keith is *graduating* his papers.
3.	*vacancies*	The sick pupils left four *vacancies*.
4.	*embargoes*	Some *embargoes* do more harm than good.
5.	*brethren*	Joseph was sold by his *brethren*.
6.	*pulleys*	Levers and *pulleys* are simple machines.
7.	*briefest*	My book review is the *briefest* of all.
8.	*quizzes*	Beth liked to work *quizzes* and puzzles.
9.	*canceled*	Linda *canceled* her dentist appointment.
10.	*tariff*	Colonists disliked British *tariff* policies.
11.	*amateur*	Albert was an *amateur* horseman.
12.	*mediator*	Our *mediator* is Jesus.
13.	*employer*	Glen's *employer* asked him to work late.
14.	*circular*	Our weekly *circular* came from the store.
15.	*finance*	The bank agreed to *finance* the purchase.
16.	*commence*	The song service will *commence* at seven.
17.	*medieval*	Many people were poor in *medieval* times.
18.	*initiative*	Take the *initiative* in forgiving.
19.	*definite*	Did they set a *definite* time for supper?
20.	*passenger*	Wanda was a *passenger* on a jet plane.
21.	*sanctuary*	A wildlife *sanctuary* protects animals.
22.	*worldliness*	Selfishness reveals *worldliness*.
23.	*Beatitudes*	Jesus spoke the *Beatitudes*.
24.	*separation*	Milk *separation* was done by hand.
25.	*Christendom*	*Christendom* is named after Christ.
26.	*discussion*	The *discussion* was on giving.
27.	*sacrifice*	They sold their land at a *sacrifice*.
28.	*confusion*	God brings order, not *confusion*.
29.	*suggestion*	Glenn offered a good *suggestion*.
30.	*possession*	Laban's *possession* was taken.
31.	*nuisance*	Ants are a *nuisance* at a picnic.
32.	*credence*	Paul gave no *credence* to wives' tales.
33.	*admonition*	His *admonition* grieved the man.
34.	*penitence*	With *penitence*, he confessed his sins.
35.	*fidelity*	A good speaker system has high *fidelity*.
36.	*summon*	Joe will *summon* me on time.
37.	*appearance*	His *appearance* was neat.
38.	*emergency*	Yield the telephone in an *emergency*.
39.	*conference*	A *conference* is recorded in Acts.
40.	*monitor*	I was *monitor* for the panel.
41.	*carriage*	Grandpa had a tall, erect *carriage*.
42.	*lunar*	Men visited the moon in a *lunar* module.
43.	*achievement*	Man's *achievement* will vanish.
44.	*diary*	Nathan kept a *diary* of his trip West.
45.	*anniversary*	I sent them an *anniversary* card.
46.	*solar*	Sunshine is the source of *solar* energy.
47.	*consideration*	Joseph showed *consideration*.
48.	*meridian*	The sun reaches its *meridian* at noon.

For numbers 49 and 50, write *only* the abbreviations.

49. *Thess.* *(Thessalonians)* Paul gives advice in *Thessalonians*.

50. *Isa.* *(Isaiah)* The prophet *Isaiah* foretold Christ's death.

Review Lesson 12—Test Sentences

1.	*clamor*	Jesus hated the *clamor* in God's house.
2.	*association*	We enjoy *association* with friends.
3.	*parallel*	The boards in our fence are *parallel*.
4.	*confession*	Achan's *confession* was forced.
5.	*aboard*	Everyone *aboard* the bus seemed excited.
6.	*proclaim*	He may *proclaim* it a disaster area.
7.	*accordingly*	We saw bears; *accordingly* we ran.
8.	*controlled*	Ann *controlled* her impulse to laugh.
9.	*professor*	Gamaliel was a Jewish law *professor*.
10.	*approximately*	I need *approximately* ten.
11.	*inquiries*	Jesus answered Nicodemus's *inquiries*.
12.	*benediction*	After the *benediction*, we parted.
13.	*proposed*	Three suggestions were *proposed*.
14.	*liquid*	The volcano spewed out fiery *liquid* rock.
15.	*controversy*	His miracles caused *controversy*.
16.	*indicate*	Chills and fever *indicate* an illness.
17.	*request*	Queen Esther's *request* was granted.
18.	*correspond*	Lives must *correspond* with words.
19.	*procession*	The animal *procession* entered
20.	*response*	A plant moves in *response* to light.
21.	*accomplish*	Did you *accomplish* much?
22.	*disappointment*	A *disappointment* hurts.
23.	*abnormal*	Albinos are *abnormal*.
24.	*interview*	William's job *interview* took an hour.
25.	*dismissal*	He got a *dismissal* for health reasons.
26.	*advise*	Did you *advise* him to go or stay?
27.	*apparent*	Rhoda's happiness was *apparent* to all.
28.	*spectator*	Saul was a *spectator* at the stoning.
29.	*expectation*	Planting brings an *expectation*.
30.	*visible*	The accident caused no *visible* injuries.
31.	*doctrine*	The Sadducees believed a false *doctrine*.
32.	*acknowledge*	We *acknowledge* the truth.
33.	*kindergarten*	Kevin is in *kindergarten*.
34.	*advantageous*	Math proved *advantageous*.
35.	*document*	A will is an important legal *document*.
36.	*antecedent*	Greece was *antecedent* to Rome.
37.	*prejudice*	Blind *prejudice* destroys friendships.
38.	*conscientious*	He was a *conscientious* bishop.
39.	*northwestern*	We took a *northwestern* route.
40.	*conscious*	They were *conscious* of God.
41.	*multiplicity*	God made a *multiplicity* of fish.
42.	*biscuit*	A cracker is a *biscuit* in Great Britain.
43.	*quartet*	Four people form a *quartet*.
44.	*century*	Not many people live a whole *century*.
45.	*quintuple*	If we *quintuple* two, we have ten.
46.	*duplicate*	Pam had a *duplicate* key.
47.	*septet*	A *septet* sang for Lois.
48.	*millipede*	The *millipede* scared her.
49.	*unique*	The rock was *unique*.
50.	*triune*	We worship a *triune* God.

Review Lesson 18—Test Sentences

1. *marvelous*	What a *marvelous* day!
2. *promotion*	Fred's *promotion* soon came.
3. *activity*	A hummingbird's *activity* is fascinating.
4. *thorough*	The diary was *thorough.*
5. *mischievous*	Monkeys are *mischievous* animals.
6. *agency*	We hear through the *agency* of sound waves.
7. *mobile*	An elaborate *mobile* hung from the ceiling.
8. *virtuous*	Hezekiah was a *virtuous* king.
9. *agitate*	Be careful not to *agitate* the bees.
10. *movement*	The sun's *movement* seems slow.
11. *changeable*	A chameleon has *changeable* color.
12. *affectionate*	She gave me an *affectionate* pat.
13. *effective*	Paul's ministry was *effective.*
14. *artificial*	The punch had *artificial* coloring.
15. *facility*	Elmer has great *facility* in woodcarving.
16. *believable*	A good story must seem *believable.*
17. *operation*	This machine's *operation* takes skill.
18. *sensible*	Be sure answers are *sensible.*
19. *beneficial*	Walking is a *beneficial* exercise.
20. *perfectly*	Is that sphere *perfectly* round?
21. *essential*	Food gives us *essential* vitamins.
22. *approval*	Father nodded in *approval* of our plan.
23. *subtrahend*	In 5 – 3 = 2, the *subtrahend* is 3.
24. *personal*	We should show a *personal* interest.
25. *attraction*	Explain its *attraction* to iron.
26. *spiritual*	Christians fight a *spiritual* battle.
27. *compel*	Jesus will not *compel* anyone to serve Him.
28. *impulsive*	You may regret an *impulsive* decision.
29. *repellent*	Philip dusted the cows with *repellent.*
30. *contracts*	Father signed two building *contracts.*
31. *maintenance*	A *maintenance* man fixed a window.
32. *absolutely*	God deals *absolutely* impartially.
33. *interrupt*	An alarm clock can *interrupt* dreams.
34. *resolve*	Ruth made an earnest *resolve* to do better.
35. *assistant*	The *assistant* pilot used the controls.
36. *liable*	The top-heavy wagon seemed *liable* to topple.
37. *obligation*	His *obligation* was to care for Mary.
38. *continuous*	The earth's rotation is *continuous.*
39. *obtained*	We *obtained* a wheelchair for Grandma.
40. *excellent*	Alligators are *excellent* swimmers.
41. *application*	Put an *application* of salve on it.
42. *curious*	On our walk, *curious* cows stared at us.
43. *pressure*	Mother uses a *pressure* cooker for meat.
44. *auxiliary*	They need an *auxiliary* heating system.
45. *extension*	We had a telephone *extension* upstairs.
46. *seize*	A drowning man will *seize* anything in sight.
47. *compressor*	The air *compressor* hose broke.
48. *flexible*	This job has *flexible* working hours.
49. *intention*	My *intention* was to write to you soon.
50. *reflected*	Vernon *reflected* over the past year.

Review Lesson 24—Test Sentences

1.	*exhibit*	Joseph did not *exhibit* a hateful attitude.
2.	*premium*	God places a *premium* on human life.
3.	*dependent*	We are *dependent* on God.
4.	*expenses*	Our living *expenses* increase every year.
5.	*eliminate*	Does this spray *eliminate* all weeds?
6.	*explanation*	What *explanation* was given?
7.	*estate*	Are we content with our *estate* in life?
8.	*extremely*	Our crops produced *extremely* well.
9.	*exemption*	Blindness receives tax *exemption.*
10.	*redemption*	Our *redemption* is by blood.
11.	*deferred*	Our meeting is *deferred* until next week.
12.	*collateral*	Property is *collateral* for loans.
13.	*sequence*	The *sequence* was difficult to follow.
14.	*substitute*	Grandmother uses a salt *substitute.*
15.	*difference*	Find a *difference* between the rocks.
16.	*submitted*	We *submitted* her best story.
17.	*covenant*	Israel made a *covenant* with God.
18.	*executive*	An *executive* decides company policies.
19.	*deduct*	A bank will *deduct* a monthly service charge.
20.	*persecution*	The early church had *persecution.*
21.	*compliance*	His *compliance* brought peace.
22.	*circuit*	The moon travels in a *circuit* each month.
23.	*diverse*	Insects are a most *diverse* group.
24.	*circumstances*	Her *circumstances* are poor.
25.	*conversation*	The *conversation* soon ended.
26.	*cooperation*	Firefighters need *cooperation.*
27.	*coarse*	We filled *coarse* burlap sacks with corn.
28.	*revolution*	Machines brought a new *revolution.*
29.	*communication*	Some *communication* is written.
30.	*converted*	Paul was *converted* near Damascus.
31.	*exceed*	Our income must *exceed* our spending.
32.	*remittance*	Send no cash *remittance* in the mail.
33.	*conceit*	Haman's *conceit* caused his own downfall.
34.	*precede*	Did Lincoln *precede* Johnson as president?
35.	*illustrate*	Artists *illustrate* many storybooks.
36.	*convenience*	Call at your *convenience.*
37.	*relieve*	Allen came to *relieve* the tired watchman.
38.	*intercede*	Lawyers *intercede* in behalf of others.
39.	*interior*	The earth's *interior* is very hot.
40.	*succession*	Four cars in *succession* turned left.
41.	*impossible*	The wreck was *impossible* to repair.
42.	*aggressive*	Bears are seldom *aggressive* to man.
43.	*opponent*	Goliath sneered at his young *opponent.*
44.	*constitution*	A *constitution* gives the goals.
45.	*negligent*	Eli was a *negligent* father to his sons.
46.	*disposition*	His kind *disposition* won friends.
47.	*statute*	Every *statute* was voted in by Congress.
48.	*gradually*	I *gradually* came to like my new home.
49.	*nonresistance*	Dirk showed *nonresistance.*
50.	*unnecessary*	Shouting was *unnecessary.*

Review Lesson 30—Test Sentences

1. *encourage*	Sugar will *encourage* ants.
2. *corporation*	Eight men formed a *corporation.*
3. *capitalization*	"I" receives *capitalization.*
4. *manual*	Shoveling is *manual* labor
5. *endeavor*	We want to help you in your *endeavor.*
6. *carnality*	Spirituality and *carnality* do not mix.
7. *corps*	A *corps* of rescue workers came to clean up.
8. *identify*	We can *identify* with Mary's joy.
9. *merchandise*	The *merchandise* sold well.
10. *Incarnation*	Jesus' *Incarnation* is a mystery.
11. *emphasize*	Underlining will *emphasize* the word.
12. *affiliate*	His store is an *affiliate* of a chain.
13. *patriarch*	An Indian chief was tribal *patriarch.*
14. *fiery*	Some *fiery* serpents bit the Israelites.
15. *difficulty*	A patient had *difficulty* breathing.
16. *patron*	Ken had long been a *patron* of that store.
17. *fraternity*	Many college boys join a *fraternity.*
18. *maternal*	She is our *maternal* grandmother.
19. *humility*	God values an attitude of calm *humility.*
20. *remedy*	Penicillin is a *remedy* for your sore throat.
21. *equine*	Mules and ponies are *equine* animals.
22. *canary*	Mother painted the kitchen a *canary* yellow.
23. *versatile*	A *versatile* man does many things well.
24. *cereal*	Farmers raise corn and other *cereal* grains.
25. *minor*	The old building contained some *minor* flaws.
26. *counsel*	Did you *counsel* with your parents?
27. *rite*	John first practiced the *rite* of Baptism.
28. *doubtless*	Do it, and you will *doubtless* succeed.
29. *feline*	Any *feline* animal eats meat.
30. *vaccine*	This *vaccine* will help resist the disease.
31. *senator*	A *senator* helps make laws.
32. *attached*	Baby Sue is *attached* to Mother.
33. *molecule*	The atoms joined to form a *molecule.*
34. *cassette*	Film for my camera comes in a *cassette.*
35. *schedule*	Did you *schedule* any time for reading?
36. *characters*	Two rough-looking *characters* came.
37. *senior*	My mother is thirty years my *senior.*
38. *dinette*	We ate lunch in a cozy *dinette.*
39. *rejuvenate*	Could you *rejuvenate* that old sofa?
40. *juvenile*	A *juvenile* may not sign the papers.
41. *occurrence*	Laws lessen the *occurrence* of fire.
42. *ancient*	The *ancient* Romans built sturdy roads.
43. *judgment*	God will bring *judgment* on all sin.
44. *argument*	Your *argument* is convincing.
45. *physician*	Ask a *physician* about an odd swelling.
46. *muscle*	The cardiac *muscle* never rests.
47. *courteous*	A *courteous* person wins many friends.
48. *temperature*	The *temperature* of water varies.
49. *mystery*	The fate of the Lost Colony is a *mystery.*
50. *descent*	Our neighbor is of Scottish *descent.*

Review Lesson 34—Test Sentences

1. *performance*	Rest aids *performance.*
2. *aquarium*	At the zoo *aquarium,* we fed a dolphin.
3. *permitted*	The weather *permitted* early plowing.
4. *aqueduct*	An *aqueduct* carries water.
5. *persistent*	Ray's *persistent* earache went away.
6. *export*	Does our country *export* wheat to Russia?
7. *pertaining*	Here are x-rays *pertaining* to teeth.
8. *importunity*	Her *importunity* brought justice.
9. *pierce*	Use this instrument to *pierce* the can.
10. *navigator*	The *navigator* sailed to Spain.
11. *salary*	Some workers are paid a fixed *salary.*
12. *occupation*	We enjoy the *occupation* of our home.
13. *translate*	Friends *translate* words into actions.
14. *opportunity*	Wait for an *opportunity* to speak.
15. *transparent*	Most glass is *transparent.*
16. *perceive*	Jesus could *perceive* hidden thoughts.
17. *transportation*	Air *transportation* ceased.
18. *oxygen*	The element *oxygen* is plentiful.
19. *accidentally*	Inventions do come *accidentally.*
20. *supersede*	New leaders *supersede* present ones.
21. *awkward*	Lucy felt *awkward* and shy.
22. *precisely*	You said *precisely* what I thought.
23. *dissect*	The scientist will *dissect* the odd plant.
24. *superstition*	Faith opposes all *superstition.*
25. *genuine*	John would baptize only *genuine* believers.
26. *herbicide*	Will this *herbicide* harm any wildlife?
27. *superficial*	He had only *superficial* friends.
28. *surrender*	A defeated army must then *surrender.*
29. *ultraviolet*	The *ultraviolet* rays cause a tan.
30. *insecticide*	An *insecticide* fights mosquitoes.
31. *surrounded*	An island is *surrounded* by water.
32. *occasion*	Pilate had no *occasion* to condemn Jesus.
33. *superscription*	I can read a *superscription.*
34. *ultimate*	Our God is the *ultimate* authority.
35. *discipline*	Learning to type takes *discipline.*
36. *betray*	Our face will often *betray* our thoughts.
37. *rectify*	Andy quickly tried to *rectify* his mistake.
38. *cafeteria*	The *cafeteria* offered Chinese food.
39. *exception*	They took *exception* to Christ's healings.
40. *captivate*	Bright colors *captivate* a small child.
41. *receipts*	Two sales *receipts* could not be found.
42. *restrain*	Eli did not *restrain* his wicked sons.
43. *cashier*	The *cashier* calculated the total bill.
44. *legitimate*	Eric's absence was *legitimate.*
45. *secede*	Poor health forced him to *secede* from them.
46. *commander*	Joab was David's *commander.*
47. *mandatory*	Is seat belt use *mandatory* here?
48. *regulator*	A faulty *regulator* makes a clock lose time.
49. *delegate*	Our state sent a *delegate* to a meeting.
50. *selection*	His *selection* of a drill took time.

Final Test

1.	*enrolled*	The hospital secretary *enrolled* my name.
2.	*brethren*	A group of *brethren* discussed the plan.
3.	*initial*	Your *initial* try may not succeed.
4.	*mediator*	A good *mediator* will be impartial.
5.	*sacrifice*	Some people *sacrifice* their health.
6.	*resurrection*	A *resurrection* of reading began.
7.	*credible*	Is your reason for tardiness *credible*?
8.	*admonition*	Isaac heeded the *admonition* given.
9.	*annually*	Robins generally fly south *annually*.
10.	*commitment*	His *commitment* to quality is kept.
11.	*proclaim*	The Jews would often *proclaim* a fast.
12.	*attitude*	Glen knelt in an *attitude* of prayer.
13.	*indicate*	Budding trees *indicate* springtime.
14.	*requirements*	What *requirements* are needed?
15.	*interview*	Newsmen often *interview* the president.
16.	*apparent*	Was this *apparent* burglary reported?
17.	*conscience*	To sin willfully dulls a *conscience*.
18.	*advantageous*	It was *advantageous* to farmers.
19.	*century*	Life in our *century* keeps changing.
20.	*mobile*	Our lower jaw is *mobile*; it is not fixed.
21.	*agitate*	Do not *agitate* this muddy water.
22.	*beneficial*	Most snakes are *beneficial* to man.
23.	*feasible*	Joshua gave a *feasible* plan of action.
24.	*impelling*	A wind is *impelling* our boat to shore.
25.	*attraction*	Samson's *attraction* to her hurt him.
26.	*solution*	Judas found no *solution* to his problems.
27.	*interrupt*	Did I *interrupt* your conversation?
28.	*extension*	Please plug in the *extension* cord.
29.	*complicated*	An infection *complicated* matters.
30.	*dependent*	Its pressure is *dependent* on depth.
31.	*redemption*	The *redemption* price is very costly.
32.	*difference*	Does it make any *difference* to you?
33.	*consequently*	I was ill; *consequently* I slept.
34.	*involved*	The long trip *involved* much planning.
35.	*circumstances*	None chose his *circumstances*.
36.	*convenience*	Leon found the ramp a *convenience*.
37.	*admission*	Judas's *admission* did not save him.
38.	*gradually*	His bricklaying *gradually* improved.
39.	*negotiations*	Legal *negotiations* take months.
40.	*endeavor*	She will *endeavor* to do right.
41.	*Incarnation*	The *Incarnation* was miraculous.
42.	*patriarch*	Abraham was a respected *patriarch*.
43.	*affiliate*	He was a business *affiliate* of Lewis.
44.	*feminine*	Karen has a fragile *feminine* appearance.
45.	*junior*	Mr. Smith needed a *junior* business partner.
46.	*cassette*	Dan put a *cassette* into the tape player.
47.	*mosquitoes*	Only female *mosquitoes* will bite.
48.	*opportunity*	Study nature at each *opportunity*.
49.	*superstition*	Is her fear from a *superstition*?
50.	*discipline*	They have good *discipline* in school.

The Speller Dictionary

Full Pronunciation Key

Each entry word in the Speller Dictionary is followed by a phonetic spelling that shows its pronunciation. This pronunciation key lists all the symbols used in the phonetic spellings, and it shows how they should be pronounced.

A heavy accent mark is placed after the syllable that receives the primary accent. A light accent mark follows a syllable with a secondary accent. Observe the primary and secondary accents in the word *pronunciation*: (prə nun′sē ā′shən).

a	man, had
ā	ate, made
ä	ah, father
är	park, star
âr	care, fair
b	boy, tab
ch	choose, such
d	deer, lid
e	red, then
ē	me, east
f	for, if
g	girl, peg
h	have, his
i	it, dim
ī	hide, wire
îr	dear, deer
j	jar, rejoice
k	kin, week
l	lot, deal
m	my, some
n	need, win
ng	sing, rang
o	not, fox
ō	home, so
ô	fall, paw
ôr	cord, or
oi	oil, point
o͝o	pull, took
o͞o	blue, pool
ou	loud, round
p	pay, dip
r	rod, near
s	saw, gas
sh	she, dish
t	top, wet
th	thank, with
t͟h	the, weather
u	bud, sun
ûr	turn, herd
v	very, over
w	we, away
y	you, canyon
z	zone, daze
zh	treasure, vision
ə	represents *a* in ago, *e* in open, *i* in pencil, *o* in wagon, *u* in cactus

Abbreviations

adj.	adjective
adv.	adverb
conj.	conjunction
interj.	interjection
n.	noun
prep.	preposition
pron.	pronoun
v.	verb
abbr.	abbreviation
cap.	capitalized
def.	definition
pl.	plural
sing.	singular
<	from
E	English
F	French
G	German
Gk.	Greek
Ital.	Italian
L	Latin
M	Middle
O	Old
Scand.	Scandinavian
Sp.	Spanish

A

ab nor mal (ab nôr′məl), *adj.* Not normal; not average; unusual; irregular. [< L *ab-* from + *norma* rule] **—ab nor′mal ly,** *adv.*

a board (ə bôrd′), *adv., prep.* On board; in, into, or on a train, bus, ship, plane, etc. [< OE *a-* on + board]

a broad (ə brôd′), *adv.* 1. Outside one's home or country. 2. In circulation; heard or told by many people: *A strange story was abroad.* [< OE *a-* at + *brād* broad]

ab scess (ab′ses′), *n.* An infected area where pus has collected. [< L *abscedere* < *ab-* away + *cedere* to go; in reference to body fluids that flow to the area]

ab so lute (ab′sə lo͞ot′), *adj.* 1. Unrestricted; not limited by any outside influence: *absolute authority.* 2. Complete; perfect: *absolute holiness.* —*n.* Something that is absolute. [< L *absolutus* < *ab-* from + *solvere* to loosen]

ab so lute ly (ab′sə lo͞ot′lē, ab′sə lo͞ot′lē), *adv.* Completely; perfectly.

ac ci den tal ly (ak′si den′tə lē), *adv.* By accident; not purposely. [< L *accidens* chance < *ad-* upon + *cadere* to fall]

ac com plish (ə kom′plish), *v.* To perform; carry out; get done. [< L *accomplere* < *ad-* to + *complere* to fill up, complete] **—ac com′plish er,** *n.*

ac cord ing ly (ə kôr′ding lē), *adv.* 1. In accord; in agreement. 2. Thus; consequently; so. [< L *accordare* agree < *ad-* to + *cor* heart]

ac cu mu late (ə kyo͞om′yə lāt′), *v.,* **-lat ed, -lat ing.** To pile up; collect. [< L *accumulatus* heaped < *ad-* to + *cumulare* to heap]

a chieve ment (ə chēv′mənt), *n.* Something accomplished, especially by unusual strength, skill, or bravery. [< OF *a chief (venir)* (to come) to a head, finish < L *ad caput (venire)*]

ac knowl edge (ak nol′ij), *v.,* **-edged, -edg ing.** 1. To admit as being true; confess. 2. To recognize as being valid: *acknowledge the king's authority.* 3. To report the receipt of: *acknowledge a letter.* [< ME *aknow* to admit] **—ac knowl′edg ment,** *n.*

had, māde, stär, câre, red, mē, dim, hīde, not, hōme, ôr, oil, to͝ok, po͞ol, loud, sun, tûrn; ch, such; ng, sing; sh, she; th, with; th, the; zh, vision

ə represents *a* in ago, *e* in open, *i* in pencil, *o* in wagon, *u* in cactus

ac quaint (ə kwānt′), *v.* To cause (someone) to know personally; make (a person) familiar. [< OF *acointer* < L *adcognitare* to make known to < *ad-* to + *cognoscere* to know < *com-* together + *gnoscere* to come to know]

ac tiv i ty (ak tiv′i tē), *n., pl.* **-ties.** 1. The state of being active. 2. A set of actions carried out at a given time or place: *the activity of the evening.* [< L *actus* a doing, *actum* a thing done]

ac tor (ak′tər), *n.* A person who acts, especially one who acts in a play. [< L *actus*]

ac tu al ly (ak′cho͞o əl ē), *adv.* In fact; in reality; really. [< L *actualis* < *actus*]

ad (ad), *n.* An advertisement.

ad journ ment (ə jûrn′mənt), *n.* 1. The act of adjourning; discontinuation of proceedings for a time. 2. A period during which proceedings are discontinued. [< L *adjurnare* to set a day < *ad-* to + *diurnus* daily < *dies* day]

ad min is tra tion (ad min′i strā′shən), *n.* 1. The act of administering. 2. A body of persons who manage a government, business, etc. [< L *ad-* to + *ministrare* to serve]

ad mi ra tion (ad′mə rā′shən), *n.* 1. The act of admiring. 2. A feeling of wonder and delight because of high esteem for a person or thing. 3. Something that is admired. [< L *ad-* at + *mirari* to wonder < *mirus* strange, wonderful]

ad mis sion (ad mish′ən), *n.* 1. The act of admitting or the condition of being admitted; access;

adj.	adjective	*pl.*	plural
adv.	adverb	*prep.*	preposition
conj.	conjunction	*pron.*	pronoun
interj.	interjection	*sing.*	singular
n.	noun	*v.*	verb

entrance. 2. An acknowledgment that a statement is true; a confession. [< L *ad-* to + *mittere* to send, let go]

ad mo ni tion (ad′mə nish′ən), *n.* Counsel, warning, or reproof in regard to an error, an oversight, etc. [< L *ad-* to, toward + *monere* to warn]

ad van ta geous (ad′van tā′jəs), *adj.* Providing an advantage; favorable; profitable. [< OF *avant* before < L *ab ante* from before] **—ad′van ta′geous ly,** *adv.*

ad ven ture (ad ven′chər), *n.* 1. An undertaking that involves danger. 2. An experience that is notable for its excitement and danger. *—v.,* **-tured, -tur ing.** To dare to undertake; take the chance of; venture. [< L *adventura* about to happen < *ad-* to + *venire* to come]

ad ver tise ment (ad′vər tīz′mənt, ad vûr′tis mənt), *n.* A public notice of an offer to buy or sell. [< L *ad-* to + *vertere* to turn]

ad vise (ad vīz′), *v.,* **-vised, -vis ing.** To give counsel to; caution or recommend. [< L *ad-* to + *visum* seen < *videre* to see] **—ad vis′er,** *n.*

af fect ed (ə fek′tid), *v.* Past form of *affect. —adj.* Pretended; feigned: *affected friendliness.* [< L *affectus* influenced < *ad-* to + *facere* to do] **—af fect′ed ly,** *adv.* **—af fect′ed ness,** *n.*

af fec tion ate (ə fek′shə nit), *adj.* Expressing affection; loving; fond. [< L *affectus*] **—af fec′tion ate ly,** *adv.*

af fil i ate (ə fil′ē āt′), *v.,* **-at ed, -at ing.** 1. To associate or unite with: *Do not affiliate with evildoers.* 2. To receive as a child; adopt. *—n.* (ə fil′ē it, ə fil′ē āt′). A person or group that is united with another; an associate. [< L *affiliare* to adopt < *ad-* to + *filius* son]

a gen cy (ā′jən sē), *n., pl.* **-cies.** 1. The ability to act or the state of acting; an operation; activity. 2. A person or thing through which something is done; means; instrumentality. 3. A company that does business for others. [< L *agentia* < *agere* to do]

a gen da (ə jen′də), *n., pl. of* agendum *but considered singular.* A list or plan of things to be done, especially at a meeting; program. [< L *agere* to do]

ag gres sive (ə gres′iv), *adj.* 1. Able and willing to attack; militant. 2. Inclined to put forth vigorous effort; enterprising. [< L *aggressus* attack < *ad-* to + *gradi* to step, go] **—ag gres′sive ly,** *adv.* **—ag gres′sive ness,** *n.*

ag i tate (aj′i tāt′), *v.,* **-tat ed, -tat ing.** 1. To stir up; set in irregular motion. 2. To disturb the emotions of; excite. [< L *agitare* to set in motion < *agere* to drive, move]

ag ri cul ture (ag′ri kul′chər), *n.* The science or business of raising crops and livestock; farming. [< L *ager* field + *cultura* cultivation] **—ag′ri cul′tur al,** *adj.*

al ley (al′ē), *n., pl.* **-leys.** A narrow street, usually providing access to the rear of buildings. [< OF *aler* to go < L *ambulare* to walk]

am a teur (am′ə tûr′, am′ə cho͝or, am′ə chər), *n.* A person who engages in an activity as a pastime rather than a profession. *—adj.* Having to do with an amateur; characteristic of an amateur: *an amateur photographer.* [< F < L *amator* lover]

an a lyze (an′ə līz′), *v.,* **-lyzed, -lyz ing.** 1. To separate (something) into its parts or elements, especially to determine its make-up. 2. To examine closely; investigate in detail. [< Gk. *analyein* to dissolve < *ana* completely + *lyein* to loosen] Also *British* **analyse.**

an cient (ān′shənt), *adj.* 1. Of times very long

ago. 2. Very old; existing from times long past: *an ancient custom.* —*n.* A person who lived in ancient times. [< OF *ancien* < *ante* before] **—an′cient ly,** *adv.*

an ni ver sa ry (an′ə vûr′sə rē), *n., pl.* **-ries.** A date that marks a notable event which happened on the same day in a previous year. [< L *annus* year + *versus* turned]

an nounce ment (ə nouns′mənt), *n.* 1. The act of announcing. 2. Something that is announced; a declaration; public notification. [< OF *anoncier* < L *annuntiare* < *ad-* to + *nuntiare* to report]

an nu al ly (an′yo͞o əl ē), *adv.* Every year. [< L *annualis* yearly < *annus* year]

an te ce dent (an′ti sēd′ənt), *adj.* Going or being before; preceding. —*n.* The noun to which a pronoun refers. [< L *ante-* before + *cedere* to go]

an te room (an′tē ro͞om′), *n.* A room placed before another room, often serving as an entranceway and used as a waiting room. [< L *ante-* before + room]

ap par ent (ə pâr′ənt, ə par′ənt), *adj.* 1. Easily seen or understood. 2. Seeming, but not necessarily true: *an apparent injustice.* [< L *apparere* < *ad-* to + *parere* to come forth, show itself]

ap pear ance (ə pîr′əns), *n.* 1. The act of coming into view. 2. The act of coming before a public audience. 3. The external aspect of something; how something looks. [< L *apparere*]

ap pe tite (ap′i tīt′), *n.* A desire for food; also, any physical desire. [< L *appetitus* < *appetere* to strive for < *ad-* to + *petere* to seek]

ap pli ca tion (ap′li kā′shən), *n.* 1. The act of applying. 2. That which is applied. 3. A use of a rule in a practical way. [< L *applicare* to join to < *ad-* to + *plicare* to fold]

ap ply (ə plī′), *v.,* **-plied, -ply ing.** 1. To bring into contact with. 2. To put to practical use. 3. To devote in a diligent manner: *apply oneself to a lesson.* 4. To make a formal request: *apply for a job.* [< L *applicare*]

ap pre ci ate (ə prē′shē āt′), *v.,* **-at ed, -at ing.** 1. To be grateful for. 2. To have a proper esteem for; value rightly. 3. To increase in value. [< L *appretiare* to appraise < *ad-* to + *pretium* price]

ap prov al (ə pro͞o′vəl), *n.* 1. Consent; permission. 2. A favorable opinion; commendation. [< OF *aprover* < L *approbare* < *ad-* to + *probare* to prove, approve < *probus* good]

ap prox i mate ly (ə prok′sə mit lē), *adv.* About; not exactly, but nearly. [< L *approximare* to come near < *ad-* to + *proximus* nearest < *prope* near]

a quar i um (ə kwâr′ē əm), *n., pl.* **a quar i ums** or **a quar i a.** A tank or pool in which fish or other water animals are kept. [< L *aquarius* < *aqua* water]

aq ue duct (ak′wi dukt′), *n.* A water channel, usually for bringing water from a distance. [< L *aqua* water + *ductus* < *ducere* to lead]

ar gu ment (är′gyə mənt), *n.* 1. A discussion by persons who disagree; a debate or dispute. 2. A reason offered as proof of something. 3. A discourse or an essay that urges the audience to accept a viewpoint or do a certain thing. [< L *arguere* to clarify, prove]

a rise (ə rīz′), *v.,* **a rose, a ris en, a ris ing.** 1. To get up or go up. 2. To come into being, as a river; originate. [< OE *ā-* up + *rīsan* to rise]

ar ti fi cial (är′tə fish′əl), *adj.* 1. Manmade rather

had, māde, stär, câre, red, mē, dim, hīde, not, hōme, ôr, oil, to͝ok, po͞ol, loud, sun, tûrn; ch, such; ng, sing; sh, she; th, with; th, the; zh, vision

ə represents *a* in ago, *e* in open, *i* in pencil, *o* in wagon, *u* in cactus

adj.	adjective	*pl.*	plural
adv.	adverb	*prep.*	preposition
conj.	conjunction	*pron.*	pronoun
interj.	interjection	*sing.*	singular
n.	noun	*v.*	verb

than natural: *artificial flowers.* 2. Pretended; not sincere: *artificial friendliness.* [< L *artificialis* < *artis* art + *facere* to make] **—ar′ti fi′cial ly,** *adv.*

as sign ment (ə sīn′mənt), *n.* 1. The act of assigning; an appointment. 2. Something that is assigned, as a lesson or task. [< L *assignare* < *ad-* to + *signare* make a sign < *signum* sign]

as sist ance (ə sis′təns), *n.* Help; aid; support. [< L *assistere* < *ad-* to + *sistere* to cause to stand]

as sist ant (ə sis′tənt), *n.* A helper; an aide. *—adj.* Working as a helper: *an assistant teacher.*

as so ci ate (ə sō′shē āt′, ə sō′sē āt′), *v.,* **-at ed, -at ing.** 1. To unite as a league; work together; ally. 2. To keep company (with someone). 3. To connect (ideas) in the mind. *—n.* (n. *and* adj. *also* ə sō′shē it, ə sō′sē āt′). One who is associated with; a partner or friend. *—adj.* Joined in a common interest or pursuit: *an associate doctor.* [< L *associatus* < *ad-* to + *sociare* to join < *socius* ally]

as so ci a tion (ə sō′sē ā′shən, ə sō′shē ā′shən), *n.* 1. The act of associating or the state of being associated. 2. A union of two or more persons, businesses, etc. for a common cause; league; alliance. 3. A mental connection between ideas, feelings, etc.

as sort ment (ə sôrt′mənt), *n.* A collection of varied items. [< OF *assorter* < L *ad-* to + *sorte* < *sors* lot]

as sume (ə so͞om′), *v.,* **-sumed, -sum ing.** 1. To take and use as one's own; adopt. 2. To take up and fulfill: *assume a responsibility.* 3. To consider as being true; take for granted; suppose. [< L *assumere* to take up, adopt < *ad-* to + *sumere* to take]

as sure (ə sho͝or′), *v.,* **-sured, -sur ing.** 1. To make sure; establish. 2. To cause to be confident; reassure; convince; encourage. [< OF *aseurer* < L *assecurare* < *ad-* to + *securus* safe] **—as sur′ance,** *n.*

at mos phere (at′mə sfîr′), *n.* 1. The envelope of gases that surrounds the earth or some other body in space. 2. The general feeling of a place or a group of people; mood: *an atmosphere of contentment.* [< Gk. *atmos* vapor + L *sphaera* sphere] **—at′mos pher′ic,** *adj.*

at tach (ə tach′), *v.* 1. To fasten; affix. 2. To feel close (to) because of personal affection: *be attached to one's family.* [< OF *atachier* < L *ad-* to + *tache* nail]

at tack (ə tak′), *v.* 1. To set upon violently; begin battle; assail. 2. To begin working on with determination: *attack a problem. —n.* 1. An act of attacking; an assault. 2. A sudden onset, as of a disease. [< F *attaquer* < L *ad-* to + *tache* nail] **—at tack′er,** *n.*

at ten dance (ə ten′dəns), *n.* 1. The act of attending. 2. The number of persons attending (a meeting). [< L *attendere* to give heed to < *ad-* toward + *tendere* to stretch]

at ten dant (ə ten′dənt), *n.* A person who attends, especially as a helper or servant. *—adj.* Accompanying; following, as a consequence. [< L *attendere*]

at ti tude (at′i to͞od′, at′i tyo͞od′), *n.* A feeling or state of mind with regard to some matter. [< Ital. *attitudine* < L *aptitudo* fitness < *aptus* fitted, suited]

at trac tion (ə trak′shən), *n.* 1. The act or power of attracting. 2. A person or thing that attracts. [< L *attractus* < *attrahere* to draw toward < *ad-* toward + *trahere* to draw, drag]

au thor i ty (ə thôr′i tē), *n., pl.* **-ties.** 1. The right to require and enforce obedience. 2. *pl.* Those who have this right, especially policemen and others who enforce law. 3. A person with superior knowledge about a subject; expert. [< OF *autoritē* < L *auctoritas* power, authority < *augere* to increase]

aux il ia ry (ôg zil′yə rē, ôg zil′ə rē), *adj.* 1. Giving help; assisting. 2. Additional; reserve: *auxiliary equipment.* —*n., pl.* **-ries.** 1. A person who helps; assistant. 2. A verb that helps to express certain shades of meaning; helping verb. [< L *auxilium* help < *augere* to increase]

a vail a ble (ə vā′lə bəl), *adj.* Capable of being obtained and used. [< L *ad-* to + *valoir* < *valere* to be strong] **—a vail′a bil′i ty,** *n.*

a vi a tor (ā′vē ā′tər), *n.* A person who flies airplanes; pilot. [< F < L *avis* bird]

awk ward (ôk′wərd), *adj.* 1. Not skillful; clumsy. 2. Perplexing or embarrassing: *an awkward moment.* [< Scand. *öfugr* turned the wrong way + *-ward* (toward)] **—awk′ward ly,** *adv.* **—awk′ward ness,** *n.*

B

bank rupt cy (bangk′rəpt sē, bangk′rəp sē), *n., pl.* **-cies.** The condition of being bankrupt; the state of having more debts than assets. [< Ital. *banca* bench + L *ruptus* broken < *rumpere* to break, burst]

bap tize (bap tīz′, bap′tīz′), *v.,* **-tized, -tiz ing.** To apply water to (a person) as a sign of his commitment to Christ and his acceptance into a Christian church. [< Gk. *baptizein* to wash] Also *British* **baptise.** **—bap tiz′er,** *n.*

bar gain (bär′gin), *n.*1. An agreement to buy or sell. 2. Something offered or sold at a low price. —*v.* To discuss in order to reach an agreement; negotiate. [< OF *bargaine*]

bass[1] (bas), *n., pl.* **bass** or **basses.** A food fish with spiny fins. [< OE *baers,* related to OE *byrst* bristle]

bass[2] (bās), *n.* The lowest singing part for men and boys. —*adj.* Having a deep, low pitch: *a bass voice.* [< OF *bas* low, related to Ital. *basso*]

Be at i tudes (bē at′i to͞odz′, bē at′i tyo͞odz′), *n., pl.* The nine statements of blessing that Jesus pronounced at the beginning of the Sermon on the Mount (Matthew 5:3–12). [< L *beatitudo* blessedness < *beatus* blessed, happy]

be liev a ble (bi lē′və bəl), *adj.* Capable of being believed; credible. [< ME *beleven* < *be-* completely + *lēfan* to allow, believe] **—be liev′a bly,** *adv.*

ben e dic tion (ben′i dik′shən), *n.* The pronouncing of a blessing, especially at the end of a worship service. [< L *bene* well + *dictum* spoken < *dicere* to speak]

ben e fi cial (ben′ə fish′əl), *adj.* Providing a benefit; advantageous. [< L *beneficium* favor < *bene* well + *facere* to make, do]

be tray (bi trā′), *v.* 1. To help an enemy of; be treacherous to. 2. To reveal unintentionally: *words that betray anger.* [< ME *be-* over, to + *trayen* to deliver < L *tradere* to hand over] **—be tray′al,** *n.* **—be tray′er,** *n.*

bi an nu al (bī an′yo͞o əl), *adj.* Coming or happening twice a year; semiannual. [< bi- (twice) + annual < L *annualis* yearly < *annus* year] **—bi an′nu al ly,** *adv.*

bi en ni al (bī en′ē əl), *adj.* 1. Coming or happening every two years. 2. Of plants, living two years. —*n.* A plant with a life cycle of two years. [< L *biennis* < *bi* two + *annus* year] **—bi en′ni al ly,** *adv.*

had, māde, stär, câre, red, mē, dim, hīde, not, hōme, ôr, oil, to͝ok, po͞ol, loud, sun, tûrn; ch, such; ng, sing; sh, she; th, with; th, the; zh, vision

ə represents *a* in ago, *e* in open, *i* in pencil, *o* in wagon, *u* in cactus

adj.	adjective	*pl.*	plural
adv.	adverb	*prep.*	preposition
conj.	conjunction	*pron.*	pronoun
interj.	interjection	*sing.*	singular
n.	noun	*v.*	verb

bis cuit (bis′kit), *n.* 1. In America, a kind of bread baked in small cakes. 2. In England, a thin, crisp wafer; cracker or cookie. [< OF *bescuit* < L *bis* twice + *coctus* < *coquere* to cook]

book let (bo͝ok′lit), *n.* A little book; pamphlet. [< book + -let (small)]

bound a ry (boun′də rē, bound′drē), *n., pl.* **-ries.** Anything that marks the limit or extent of something, as a dividing line. [< OF *bodne* < L *bodina* limit]

breth ren (breth′rən), *n., pl.* 1. *Archaic.* Brothers. 2. Men who are fellow members of a church; spiritual brothers. [< ME *pl.* of brother]

brief (brēf), *adj.* Short; ending quickly. —*n.* A short document, usually about a legal matter or a news item.—*v.* To give precise instructions in advance: *brief an interviewer.* [< OF *bref* < L *brevis* short] **—brief′ly,** *adv.*

broad cast (brôd′kast′), *v.,* **-cast** or **-cast ed, -cast ing.** 1. To scatter abroad, as seed. 2. To transmit over a wide area by radio or television. —*n.* Something that is broadcast; a radio or television program.

busi ness (biz′nis), *n.* 1. That in which a person is engaged; an activity. 2. An occupation or profession; a vocation. 3. Affair(s); matter(s): *other people's business.* [< OE *bisignis* activity < *bisig* active, busy]

C

caf e te ri a (kaf′i tîr′ē ə), *n.* A restaurant or lunchroom in which the diners serve themselves. [< American Sp. *cafetería* coffee store < *Sp. café* coffee]

cal en dar (kal′ən dər), *n.* A table showing the months, weeks, and days of the year. [< L *calendarium* account book < *calendae* the first days of months (when bills were due)]

Cal va ry (kal′və rē), *n.* The hill outside Jerusalem where Jesus was crucified. [< L *calvaria* skull]

ca nar y (kə nâr′ē), *n., pl.* **-ies.** 1. A small finch with yellow or greenish yellow feathers, native in the Canary Islands and popular as a cage bird because of its song. 2. A bright yellow color. [< Sp. *Islas Canarias* Canary Islands < L *Canaria Insula* Dog Island < *canis* dog]

can cel (kan′səl), *v.* 1. To call off, as an appointment; annul. 2. To divide the numerator and the denominator of (two fractions) by the same number to simplify computation. [< L *cancelli* small lattices (from the appearance of lines used to mark out something) < *cancer* lattice, related to *carcer* prison]

ca nine (kā′nīn), *adj.* Of or like a dog. —*n.* 1. A member of the dog family, which includes the wolf and the fox. 2. One of the pointed teeth next to the incisors; cuspid. [< L *caninus* < *canis* dog]

cap i tal i za tion (kap′i təl i zā′shən), *n.* The act or practice of beginning a word with a capital letter. [< L *capitalis* < *caput* head]

cap ti vate (kap′tə vāt′), *v.,* **-vat ed, -vat ing.** 1. To attract and hold the attention of; charm; fascinate. 2. *Archaic.* To capture; take captive. [< L *captivatus* captured < *capere* to take, seize]

car nal i ty (kär nal′i tē), *n.* The fact or condition of being controlled by fleshly desires; sensuality. [< L *carnalis* fleshly < *carnis* flesh]

car riage (kar′ij), *n.* 1. A vehicle (usually horse-drawn) in which people ride. 2. A manner of carrying oneself; bearing. [< ME *cariage* < L *carricare* to transport in a vehicle < *carrus* cart]

cash ier[1] (ka shîr′), *n.* A person employed to receive and keep record of payments. [< F *cassier* < *casse* money box < L *capsa* box]

cash ier[2] (ka shîr′), *v.* 1. To dismiss (a military officer, etc.) from service for a dishonorable act; discharge in disgrace. 2. To discard; scrap: *cashier the whole project.* [< F *casser* < L *cassare* to annul and *quassare* to destroy]

cas sette (kə set′), *n.* A cartridge containing film for use in a camera, or magnetic tape for use in a tape recorder. [< F *cassette* little box < *casse* box, case]

cat e go ry (kat′i gôr′ē), *n., pl.* **-ries.** One of the divisions in a system of classification; class; group. [< L *categoria* < Gk. *katēgoria* < *katēgoreein* to allege, declare < *kata-* against + *agora* public assembly]

cau tion (kô′shən), *n.* Carefulness so as to avoid injury or accident; wariness. —*v.* To advise to use caution; warn. [< L *cautio* precaution < *cavere* to be on guard, take heed]

ce dar (sē′dər), *n.* An evergreen tree in the pine family, having durable, fragrant wood; also, wood from this tree. —*adj.* Made of cedar: *a cedar chest.* [< L *cedrus* < Gk. *kedros*]

cei ling (sē′ling), *n.* 1. The overhead inside lining of a room. 2. An upper limit, as on a price; maximum. 3. The distance from the ground to the base of the lowest layer of clouds. [< F *ciel* roof < L *caelum* sky]

cen sus (sen′səs), *n.* An official count of the population in a city, nation, etc. [< L *censere* to assess, because taxes in the Roman Empire were assessed on the number of people and the value of the property they owned]

cen ti pede (sen′tə pēd′), *n.* A wormlike arthropod having one pair of legs for each segment of its body. [< L *centipeda* < *centum* hundred + *pedis* foot]

cen tu ry (sen′chə rē), *n., pl.* **-ries.** A period of one hundred years. [< L *centuria* < *centum* hundred]

had, māde, stär, câre, red, mē, dim, hīde, not, hōme, ôr, oil, to͝ok, po͞ol, loud, sun, tûrn; ch, such; ng, sing; sh, she; th, with; th̲, the; zh, vision

ə represents *a* in ago, *e* in open, *i* in pencil, *o* in wagon, *u* in cactus

ce re al (sîr′ē əl), *n.* 1. A grain that is used as food, such as wheat, rice, corn, etc. 2. A breakfast food made of grain. —*adj.* Relating to grain. [< L *cerealis* of grain < *Ceres* the goddess of grain]

cer tif i cate (sər tif′i kit), *n.* An official document that states a fact, as the date of one's birth. —*v.* (sər tif′i kāt′), **-cat ed, -cat ing.** To prove by using a certificate. [< L *certificatus* certified < *certus* certain + *facere* to make]

change a ble (chān′jə bəl), *adj.* Changing frequently; variable. [< OF *changer* < L *cambiare* to exchange] **—change′a bly,** *adv.* **—change′a bil′i ty, change′a ble ness,** *n.*

char ac ter (kar′ək tər), *n.* 1. A person in a story. 2. The basic moral quality of a person; also, good moral quality: *a man of character.* 3. A letter, numeral, or other symbol used in printing or writing. [< L < Gk. *charaktēr* stamp, mark < *charassein* to carve, engrave]

cheer ful (chîr′fəl), *adj.* Full of cheer; showing or contributing to a pleasant mood: *a cheerful worker, a cheerful color.* [< OF *chere* face < L *cara*] **—cheer′ful ly,** *adv.* **—cheer′ful ness,** *n.*

chem is try (kem′is trē), *n., pl.* **-tries.** 1. The science dealing with the composition, structure, and properties of substances and with their reactions to one another. 2. Make-up; composition: *the chemistry of water.* [< L *alchimia* alchemy < Arabic *al-kīmīa* the alchemy < Gk. *chēmia* transmutation of metals]

chil dren (chil′drən), *n.* Plural of *child.* [< ME]

adj.	adjective	*pl.*	plural
adv.	adverb	*prep.*	preposition
conj.	conjunction	*pron.*	pronoun
interj.	interjection	*sing.*	singular
n.	noun	*v.*	verb

cho rus (kôr′əs), *n.* 1. An organized group of singers; choir. 2. The part of a song repeated after each stanza; refrain. 3. An instance of several people speaking at once. —*v.* To say in unison. [< L < Gk. *choros* dance]

Chris ten dom (kris′ən dəm), *n.* All professing Christians collectively. [< OE *cristen* Christian]

cir cuit (sûr′kit), *n.* 1. A circular route. 2. The path of electricity from its source, through an electrical device, and back to the source. [< L *circuitus* < *circumire* to go around < *circum-* around + *ire* to go]

cir cu lar (sûr′kyə lər), *adj.* In the shape of a circle; round. —*n.* An advertisement or a notice printed for circulation among many people. [< L *circulus* small ring < *circus* ring]

cir cum fer ence (sər kum′fər əns), *n.* The distance around a circle; periphery. [< L *circumferentia* < *circum-* around + *ferre* to carry; translation of Gk. *periphereia* < *peri-* around + *pherein* to carry]

cir cum stance (sûr′kəm stans′), *n.* 1. A fact or happening, usually incidental, that is connected with a more important occurrence. 2. **circumstances.** All the conditions in which a person finds himself: *unusual circumstances.* [< L *circumstare* to stand around < *circum-* around + *stare* to stand]

clam or (klam′ər), *n.* 1. A loud outcry; noisy shouting. 2. Any loud, continuous noise. —*v.* To make loud, insistent demands; make a public outcry. [< L *clamere* to cry out] Also *British* **clamour.**

coarse (kôrs), *adj.* 1. Having large particles; not fine. 2. Not delicate or refined; vulgar; crude. [< *course* with the meaning "common; customary"; thus, "usual; ordinary"]

col lat er al (kə lat′ər əl), *adj.* 1. Running alongside, in a literal or figurative sense; parallel. 2. Guaranteed by a security: *a collateral loan.* —*n.* Property used as security for a loan. [< L *collateralis* < *com-* together + *later* side]

Co los si ans (kə losh′ənz), *n.* The New Testament book consisting of Paul's epistle to the Christians at Colossae. *Abbr.* **Col.**

com fort a ble (kum′fər tə bəl), *adj.* 1. Providing physical comfort: *a comfortable chair.* 2. Free from physical or mental stress, discomfort, etc.; at ease: *comfortable in her presence.* [< L *com-* with + *fortis* strong]

com mand er (kə man′dər), *n.* One who commands, especially as an officer in an army. [< L *com-* thoroughly + *mandare* to order]

com mem o rate (kə mem′ə rāt′), *v.,* **-rat ed, -rat ing.** To keep (something) in remembrance by taking part in a ceremony; observe; celebrate. [< L *com-* together + *memorare* to remember]

com mence (kə mens′), *v.,* **-menced, -menc ing.** 1. To begin; start, as an undertaking. [< OF *comencer* < L *com-* thoroughly + *initiare* to begin] **—com mence′ment,** *n.*

com mit ment (kə mit′mənt), *n.* 1. The act of committing (a person or thing) into the charge of someone. 2. A promise to do something, along with the obligation that results; pledge. [< L *com-* together + *mittere* to send]

com mit tee (kə mit′ē), *n.* A group of people appointed to investigate a matter, to direct an undertaking, etc. [< F *commettre* entrusted < L *committere*]

com mu ni ca tion (kə myōō′ni kā′shən), *n.* 1. The transmission of ideas, as by speech or writing. 2. The ideas transmitted; message. [< L *communicatus* shared < *communis* common]

com mun ion (kə myōōn′yən), *n.* 1. An intimate

sharing of thoughts and feelings; close fellowship. 2. **Communion.** The Christian ordinance in which the bread and the cup are shared together in memory of Christ's suffering and death; the Lord's Supper. [< L *communis* common]

com pel (kəm pel′), *v.,* **-pelled, -pel ling.** 1. To urge (a person) so strongly that he yields; constrain. 2. To force (a person) to do something; drive. [< L *com-* together + *pellere* to drive]

com pen sa tion (kom′pən sā′shən), *n.* 1. Suitable payment for (damage, etc.); amends; reimbursement. 2. Wages; salary. 3. Something that makes up for (a lack); that which offsets. [< L *compensare* < *com-* together + *pensare* < *pendere* to weigh]

com plex ion (kəm plek′shən), *n.* The general appearance of the skin, especially of the face. [< L *complexionis* the constitution of the body < *com- together* + plectere *to twist, braid*]

com pli ance (kəm plī′əns), *n.* A yielding to the request or demand of another; obedience. [< Ital. *complire* < Sp. *cumplir* to complete (an act of courtesy) < *com-* thoroughly + *plere* to fill]

com pli cat ed (kom′pli kā′tid), *adj.* Consisting of so many interrelated parts that understanding is difficult; complex; involved. [< L *complicare* < *com-* together + *plicare* to fold]

com pres sor (kəm pres′ər), *n.* Something that compresses, especially a machine that compresses gases. [< L *compressus* < *comprimere* to press hard < *com-* together + *premere* to press]

con ceit (kən sēt′), *n.* 1. An exalted opinion of oneself; excessive self-esteem. 2. *Archaic.* A thought; idea: *wise in one's own conceit.* [< conceive < L *concipere* < *com-* thoroughly + *capere* to grasp, take]

con dem na tion (kon′dem nā′shən), *n.* 1. An act of condemning; a finding (of someone) to be guilty. 2. The state or feeling of being found guilty. [< L *condemnare* < *com-* thoroughly + *damnare* to condemn]

had, māde, stär, câre, red, mē, dim, hīde, not, hōme, ôr, oil, to͝ok, po͞ol, loud, sun, tûrn; ch, such; ng, sing; sh, she; th, with; t͟h, the; zh, vision

ə represents *a* in ago, *e* in open, *i* in pencil, *o* in wagon, *u* in cactus

con fer ence (kon′fər əns), *n.* 1. An instance of conferring; a meeting of persons to discuss an important matter. 2. An association of church districts working together under one group of church leaders. [< L *conferre* < *com-* together + *ferre* to bring]

con fes sion (kən fesh′ən), *n.* 1. An act of confessing (a sin, etc.); admission; acknowledgment. 2. A formal statement of the beliefs held by a person or church: *confession of faith* [< L *confessus* confessed < *com-* thoroughly + *fateri* to declare]

con fi dence (kon′fi dəns), *n.* Trust; assurance. [< L *confidere com-* thoroughly + *fidere* to trust]

con firm (kən fûrm′), *v.* 1. To make firm; strengthen; establish. 2. To assure of the validity of (information, an appointment, etc.). [< L *confirmare* < *com-* thoroughly + *firmare* to make firm, strong < *firmus* firm]

con fu sion (kən fyo͞o′zhən), *n.* The state of being confused; perplexity; bewilderment. [< L *confusus* < *com-* together + *fundere* to pour]

con grat u late (kən grach′ə lāt′, kən graj′ə lāt′), *v.,* **-lat ed, -lat ing.** To express pleasure at the happiness, good fortune, etc., of another. [< L *congratulari* < *com-* together + *gratulari* to rejoice]

con gress (kong′gris), *n.* 1. An assembly held to discuss a matter. 2. **Congress.** The legislative body of the United States, consisting of the Senate and the House of Representives. [< L *congressus* a coming together < *com-* together + *gradi* to walk]

adj.	adjective	*pl.*	plural
adv.	adverb	*prep.*	preposition
conj.	conjunction	*pron.*	pronoun
interj.	interjection	*sing.*	singular
n.	noun	*v.*	verb

con quer (kong′kər), *v.* To overcome; defeat; be victorious over. [< L *conquirere* < *com-* thoroughly + *quaerere* to ask, search]

con science (kon′shəns), *n.* Moral sense; ability to discern between right and wrong. [< L *conscire* to be conscious < *com-* together + *scire* to know]

con sci en tious (kon′shē en′shəs), *adj.* Sensitive to the directives of the conscience; scrupulous; honest. [< L *conscire*] **—con′sci en′tious ly,** *adv.* **—con′sci en′tious ness,** *n.*

con scious (kon′shəs), *adj.* 1. Aware of one's surroundings and of one's own existence; mentally awake. 2. Aware of a particular object or fact: *conscious of a need.* 3. Intentional; deliberate: *conscious disobedience.* [< L *conscius* knowing inwardly < *com-* together + *scire* to know] **—con′scious ly,** *adv.* **—con′scious ness,** *n.*

con se quent ly (kon′si kwent′lē), *adv.* As a result (of a previous act, condition, etc.); therefore. [< L *consequentis* < *com-* together + *sequi* to follow]

con sid er a tion (kən sid′ə rā′shən), *n.* 1. The act or process of considering; careful thought; deliberation. 2. A factor to be considered in forming an opinion; relevant fact. 3. Kindness and courtesy; thoughtfulness. [< L *considerare* to observe the stars (with reference to astrology) < *com-* thoroughly + *sideris* star]

con sti tu tion (kon′sti to͞o′shən), *n.* 1. The makeup of something; composition. 2. The principles by which a nation, state, school, or other institution is governed; also, a document that states these principles. 3. **Constitution.** The set of principles by which the United States is governed. [< L *constituere* to set up < *com-* together + *statuere* to station] **—con′sti tu′tion al,** *adj.*

con tin u ous (kən tin′yo͞o əs), *adj.* 1. Continuing; going on or keeping on without interruption; constant. [< L *continere* to hold together < *com-* together + *tenere* to hold] **—con tin′u ous ly,** *adv.*

con tract (kən trakt′), *v.* 1. To make or become smaller or shorter; draw together. 2. (*also* kon′trakt). To enter into a formal agreement. 3. To shorten (words) by leaving out some letters and replacing them with an apostrophe. *—n.* (kon′trakt′). A formal agreement, usually signed by all who enter into it; also, a document that states the terms of an agreement. [< L *contractus* < *contrahere* < *com-* together + *trahere* to draw]

con trac tor (kon′trak′tər), *n.* 1. (*also* kən trak′tər). One who contracts to work for others, especially to erect buildings. 2. Something that contracts, as a muscle. [< L *contractus*]

con tra dic tion (kon′trə dik′shən), *n.* 1. A statement that opposes another statement. 2. Any inconsistency or disagreement between two things: *contradiction between words and actions.* [< L *contradictus* < *contradicere* < *contra-* against + *dicere* to speak]

con trar y (kon′trer′ē), *adj.* 1. Opposite; opposed; adverse. 2. (*also* kən trâr′ē). Inclined to oppose and contradict. *—n., pl.* **-ies.** That which is contrary; the opposite. [< L *contrarius* < *contra* against] **—con′trar′i ness,** *n.*

con tri tion (kən trish′ən), *n.* Humble awareness of wrongdoing and sincere sorrow for it; penitence. [< L *contritus* < *conterere* < *com-* thoroughly + *terere* to rub, grind]

con trol (kən trōl′), *v.,* **-trolled, -trol ling.** 1. To direct; regulate; govern. 2. To restrain, as an emotion: *control one's anger.* *—n.* 1. The power to keep (a person or thing) under one's command. 2. That which controls, as a device on a machine. 3. A standard used to check the results of a scientific experiment. [< ME *controllen* < OF *contreroller* to keep a copy of an account (as a check list) < L *contrarotulus* check list < *contra-* against + *rotulus* list] **—con trol′ler,** *n.*

con tro ver sy (kon′trə vûr′sē), *n., pl.* **-sies.** 1. A difference of opinion on a matter; strong disagreement; also, the matter on which opinions differ. 2. A discussion marked by disagreement; debate; dispute. [< L *controversus* turned against, disputed < *contra* against + *versus* < *vertere* to turn] **—con′tro ver′si al** (kon′trə vûr′shəl, kon′trə vûr′sē əl), *adj.*

con ven ience (kən vēn′yəns), *n.* 1. The quality of being well fitted to one's needs or desires; suitability. 2. Personal ease or comfort: *for your convenience.* 3. Something that saves work or affords comfort, as an electrical device. [< L *convenire* to come together, be proper < *com-* together + *venire* to come]

con ven tion (kən ven′shən), *n.* 1. A meeting for a specific purpose, as to discuss a matter; congress. 2. An accepted rule or practice; custom. [< L *convenire* to come together < *com-* together + *venire* to come] **—con ven′tion al,** *adj.*

con ver sa tion (kon′vər sā′shən), *n.* 1. An oral exchange of ideas; informal, unplanned discussion. 2. *Archaic.* Behavior; conduct; manner of life. [< L *conversari* to live with, keep company with < *com-* together + *vertere* to turn]

con ver sion (kən vûr′zhən), *n.* 1. The act of changing or the state of being changed. 2. The spiritual change through which a person turns from a life of sin to a life of righteousness; the new birth. [< L *convertere* < *com-* thoroughly + *vertere* to turn]

con vert (kən vûrt′), *v.* 1. To change to another state, form, etc; transform. 2. To turn from a life of sin to a life of righteousness through the new birth. *—n.* (kon′vərt′). A person who has

had, māde, stär, câre, red, mē, dim, hīde, not, hōme, ôr, oil, to͝ok, po͞ol, loud, sun, tûrn; ch, such; ng, sing; sh, she; th, with; t͟h, the; zh, vision

ə represents *a* in ago, *e* in open, *i* in pencil, *o* in wagon, *u* in cactus

experienced conversion, or who has changed from one set of religious beliefs to another. [< L *convertere*]

con vic tion (kən vik′shən), *n.* 1. The act of convicting or the state of being convicted; convincing or being convinced. 2. In court, the finding of accused person to be guilty. 3. A firm belief: *a religious conviction.* [< L *convictus* < *convincere* to refute, overcome < *com-* thoroughly + *vincere* to conquer]

co op er ate (kō op′ə rāt′), *v.,* **-at ed, -at ing.** To work together for a common purpose. [< L *cooperari* < *co-* together + *operari* to work < *opus* work, labor]

co op er a tion (kō op′ə rā′shən), *n.* A working together for a common purpose; joint action. [< L *cooperari*]

co or di nate (kō ôr′dən āt′), *v.,* **-nat ed -nat ing.** 1. To place in the same order or rank. 2. To act or cause to act harmoniously; synchronize. *—adj.* (*adj.* and *n.; also* kō ôr′də nit). Equal in rank or importance. *—n.* 1. A person or thing that is equal. 2. One of two or more lines, numbers, etc., used in specifying the location of something. [< L *coordinare* to arrange < *co-* together + *ordinare* to set in order < *ordinis* rank] **—co or′di na′tion,** *n.*

cor dial (kôr′jəl, kôr′dyəl), *adj.* 1. Warm and sincere; hearty. 2. *Archaic.* Having to do with the heart. [< L *cordialis* < *cor* heart] **—cor′dial ly,** *adv.*

cor po ral (kôr′pər əl, kôr′prəl), *adj.* Of or to the body; physical. [< L *corpus* body]

cor po ra tion (kôr′pə rā′shən), *n.* A body of persons recognized by law as a unit and having

adj.	adjective	*pl.*	plural
adv.	adverb	*prep.*	preposition
conj.	conjunction	*pron.*	pronoun
interj.	interjection	*sing.*	singular
n.	noun	*v.*	verb

privileges and responsibilities distinct from those of the persons as individuals. [< L *corporatus* formed into a body < *corpus* body]

corps (kôr), *n., pl.* **corps** (kôrz). A group of trained persons acting together. [< OF *cors* < L *corpus* body]

corpse (kôrps), *n.* A dead body. [< L *corpus* body]

cor rec tion (kə rek′shən), *n.* 1. The act of correcting; also, that which is used as an improvement. 2. Punishment; chastisement. [< L *correctus* straightened < *corrigere* < *com-* together + *regere* to make straight] **—cor rec′ tion al,** *adj.*

cor re spond (kôr i spond′), *v.* 1. To be consistent; agree; match. 2. To communicate by writing letters. [< L *correspondere* < *com-* together + *respondere* to answer < *re-* back + *spondere* to promise]

cor re spon dent (kôr′i spon′dənt), *n.* One who or that which corresponds, especially a person who writes letters regularly to another person. *—adj.* In accord; corresponding; agreeing. [< L *correspondere*]

cor rupt (kə rupt′), *v.* To make or become unclean, evil, rotten, etc.; pervert; debase. *—adj.* 1. Immoral; depraved; wicked. 2. Guilty of or open to bribery, as a government official. [< L *corruptus* < *corrumpere* < *com-* thoroughly + *rumpere* to break]

coun cil (koun′səl), *n.* 1. A group of persons who come together to discuss a matter. 2. A group appointed to perform certain government responsibilities. [< ME *counceil* < OF *concile* < L *concilium* < *com-* together + *calare* to call]

coun sel (koun′səl), *v.* 1. To give advice to. 2. To seek advice from; consult: *counsel with one's parents.* *—n.* 1. Advice; guidance. 2. One or more lawyers engaged to give advice in a civil or criminal case. 3. *Archaic.* Purpose; intention. [< ME *conseil* < L *consilium* < *consulere* to deliberate, consult] **—coun sel or,** *n.*

cour te ous (kûr′tē əs), *adj.* Polite; respectful; considerate. [< OF *corteis* befitting a court < *cort* court] **—cour′te ous ly,** *adv.*

cov e nant (kuv′ə nənt), *n.* A solemn agreement between two persons, especially one that involves a religious matter. *—v.* To make a covenant. [< OF *covenir* < L *covenire* to meet together, agree < *com-* together + *venire* to come]

cre dence (krēd′əns), *n.* Credit; belief. [< L *credentia* < *credere* to believe]

cre den tial (kri den′shəl), *n.* Something (as a document) used to prove one's ability, trustworthiness, etc. [< L *credentia*]

cred i ble (kred′ə bəl), *adj.* Capable or worthy of being believed; probably true or reliable. [< L *credibilis* < *credere* to believe]

creed (krēd), *n.* 1. A brief formula that states religious belief or doctrine; confession of faith. 2. Any principle or set of principles by which a person lives. [< L *credo* I believe < *credere* to believe]

crim i nal (krim′ə nəl), *adj.* Involving or guilty of crime. *—n.* A person who has commited a crime; malefactor. [< L *criminalis* < *crimen* charge, crime] **—crim′i nal ly,** *adv.*

crit i cize (krit′ə sīz′), *v.,* **-cized, -ciz ing.** 1. To point out the positive and negative qualities of; evaluate. 2. To find fault with; judge severely. [< L *criticus* < Gk. *kritikos* able to judge < *krinein* to judge] **—crit′i ciz er,** *n.*

crys tal (kris′təl), *n.* 1. A kind of transparent quartz. 2. A mass having a regular shape that

had, māde, stär, câre, red, mē, dim, hīde, not, hōme, ôr, oil, to͝ok, po͞ol, loud, sun, tûrn; ch, such; ng, sing; sh, she; th, with; t͟h, the; zh, vision

ə represents *a* in ago, *e* in open, *i* in pencil, *o* in wagon, *u* in cactus

forms when a liquid becomes solid: *salt crystals.* 3. Sparkling, perfectly clear glass; also, dishes made of such glass. 4. The glass or plastic cover over the face of a watch. *—adj.* Clear and sparkling like crystal: *a crystal stream.* [< L *crystallus* < Gk. *krystallos* ice < *kryos* frost]

cu ri ous (kyo͝or′ē əs), *adj.* 1. Eager to know; inquisitive. 2. Attracting attention because of being unusual; strange. 3. *Archaic.* Skillfully made. [< L *curiosus* careful, inquisitive < *cura* care] **—cu′ri ous ly,** *adv.*

cur rent (kûr′ənt), *n.* A flow or stream, as of electricity, air, or water. *—adj.* 1. Belonging to the present time; now in progress or practice. 2. Generally accepted or done at a given time: *a current belief in the 1200s.* [< L *currere* to run] **—cur′rent ly,** *adv.*

D

de cent (dē′sənt), *adj.* 1. Proper; fit; suitable. 2. Morally proper; free from immorality, immodesty, etc. [< L *decens* < *decere* to be fitting, proper] **—de′cent ly,** *adv.*

dec i mal (des′ə məl), *adj.* Pertaining to or based upon ten: *a decimal system of measures. —n.* A fraction or mixed number written in decimal form, as 0.25 or 8.76. [< L *decimus* tenth < *decem* ten]

dec la ra tion (dek′lə rā′shən), *n.* 1. The act of declaring; also, that which is declared; proclamation. 2. A naming of goods that are subject to customs or other taxation. [< L *de-* completely + *clarare* to make clear < *clarus* clear]

de duct (di dukt′), *v.* To take away (one amount from another); subtract. [< L *deductus* < *deducere* < *de-* down + *ducere* to lead] **—de duct′i ble,** *adj.* **—de duc′tion,** *n.*

de fense (di fens′), *n.* 1. The act of defending; also, something used to defend. 2. A person called to answer a charge in court, along with his legal counsel. [< L *defensus* < *defendere* < *de-* down, away + *fendere* to strike] **—de fen′sive,** *adj.*

de fer[1] (di fûr′), *v.,* **-ferred, -fer ring.** To delay; put off; postpone. [< L *differre* < *dis-* apart + *ferre* to carry]

de fer[2] (di fûr′), *v.,* **-ferred, -fer ring.** To yield to the wishes of another person. [< L *deferre* < *de-* down + *ferre* to carry]

def er ence (def′ər əns), *n.* Courteous regard for or yielding to the wishes of another person. [< L *deferre*]

def i nite (def′ə nit), *adj.* 1. Clear and exact. 2. Referring to a particular item or number: *definite adjectives.* [< L *definere* < *de-* down + *finere* to limit, end < *finis* boundary, end]

del e gate (del′i gāt′), *v.,* **-gat ed, -gat ing.** 1. To send (a person) as a representative. 2. To commit to another person: *to delegate authority. —n.* (*also* del′i git). A person sent to act for another; representative. [< L *delegare* < *de-* down + *legare* to send as a deputy < *leg-, lex* law] **—del′e ga′tion,** *n.*

de nom i na tion (di nom′ə nā′shən), *n.* 1. The act of naming; calling by name. 2. The name of a thing or of the class to which it belongs; category. 3. A large religious group. [< L *denominare* < *de-* down + *nominare* to name < *nomen* name] **—de nom′i na′tion al,** *adj.*

de pend ent (di pen′dənt), *adj.* 1. Depending on or conditioned by something else. 2. Depending on another for material support. *—n.* A person who depends on another for support. [< L *dependere* < *de-* down + *pendere* to hang]

de pos it (di poz′it), *v.* 1. To set down; place;

adj.	adjective	*pl.*	plural
adv.	adverb	*prep.*	preposition
conj.	conjunction	*pron.*	pronoun
interj.	interjection	*sing.*	singular
n.	noun	*v.*	verb

lay. 2. To entrust to (a person or business) for safekeeping: *deposit money in a bank.* —*n.* Something that is deposited. [< L *depositus* < *deponere* < *de-* down + *ponere* to put, place] **—de pos′i tor,** *n.*

de scent (di sent′), *n.* 1. The act of descending; movement from a higher to a lower level. 2. A downward inclination; slope. 3. Family line; ancestry: *of royal descent.* [< L *descendere* < *de-* down + *scandere* to climb]

de sire (di zīr′), *v.,* **-sired, -sir ing.** 1. To want; wish for. 2. To make a request for; ask for. —*n.* 1. An act of wanting; wish. 2. Something that is wanted. [< OF *desirer* < L *desiderare* < *de-* from + *sideris* star (with reference to astrology)]

des per ate (des′pər it), *adj.* 1. Ready to do anything (to relieve a severe difficulty); reckless because of despair. 2. Very severe; extreme; dire: *in desperate need.* [< L *desperare* < *de-* down, away + *sperare* to hope < *spes* hope] **—des′per ate ly,** *adv.*

de spise (di spīz′), *v.,* **-spised, -spis ing.** To look down upon as being inferior, worthless, or contemptible; disdain; scorn. [< OF *despis-* < L *despicere* < *de-* down + *specere* to look at] **—de spis′er,** *n.*

des sert (di zûrt′), *n.* Fruit, cake, pie, etc., served as the last course of a meal. [< F *desservir* to clear a table < *des-* away + *servir* to serve < L *servire*]

de tract (di trakt′), *v.* To draw away or take away: *detract attention.* [< L *detractus* < *detrahere* < *de-* away + *trahere* to draw, drag] **—de trac′tor,** *n.*

de vel op ment (di vel′əp mənt), *n.* 1. The act or process of developing; also, the stage resulting from a developing. 2. A happening; occurrence: *the latest development at school.* [< F *développer* < *dé-* away + OF *volupere* to fold, wrap up] **—de vel′op er,** *n.*

de vise (di vīz′), *v.,* **-vised, -vis ing.** To form in the mind; invent; contrive. [< L *devisus* < *dividere* to separate, divide < *dis-* apart + *videre* to see] **—de vis′er,** *n.*

di a ry (dī′ə rē), *n., pl.* **-ries.** A book in which to record daily events; journal. [< L *diarium* < *dies* day]

dif fer ence (dif′ər əns), *n.* 1. The quality of being different; variation. 2. A disagreement of opinions. 3. The amount by which one number differs from another, determined by subtraction. [< L *differre* < *dis-* apart + *ferre* to carry]

dif fi cul ty (dif′i kul′tē), *n., pl.* **-ties.** The fact or quality of being difficult; also, something that is difficult; problem. [< L *difficultas* < *difficilis* < *dis-* not + *facilis* easy < *facere* to make, do]

dig ni ty (dig′ni tē), *n., pl.* **-ties.** 1. Formal reserve in speech and action; stateliness. 2. Something worthy of honor and esteem: *the dignity of hard work.* [< L *dignitas* < *dignus* worthy]

di nette (dī net′), *n.* A small dining room or eating area, usually attached to a larger room; also, furniture for such a place. [< dine + -ette (small)]

di rec tor (di rek′tər, dī rek′tər), *n.* A person who directs an organization such as a business or school. [< L *directus* < *diregere* to arrange, direct < *dis-* apart + *regere* to guide]

dis a gree a ble (dis′ə grē′ə bəl), *adj.* 1. Unpleasant; repulsive; offensive. 2. Peevish; bad-tempered; quarrelsome. [< L *dis-* not + agree < OF *agreer* < *a gre* to one's liking] **—dis′a gree′a bly,** *adv.*

had, māde, stär, câre, red, mē, dim, hīde, not, hōme, ôr, oil, to͝ok, po͞ol, loud, sun, tûrn; ch, such; ng, sing; sh, she; th, with; t͟h, the; zh, vision

ə represents *a* in ago, *e* in open, *i* in pencil, *o* in wagon, *u* in cactus

dis ap point ment (dis′ə point′mənt), *n.* 1. The act of disappointing; frustration of hopes. 2. The feeling of being disappointed; frustration because of unfulfilled hopes. 3. Something that disappoints. [< L *dis-* not + appoint < MF *apointier* to arrange < L *ad-* to + *punctum* point]

dis ap prove (dis′ə pro͞ov′), *v.,* **-proved, -prov ing.** To consider with disfavor; condemn or reject. [< L *dis-* not + approve < L *approbare* < *ad-* to + *probare* to prove, approve < *probus* good]

dis ci pline (dis′ə plin), *n.* 1. Training that includes instruction, control, and practice. 2. Correction; chastisement. 3. The condition that results from subjection to authority; order and control. —*v.,* **-plined, -plin ing.** 1. To train by instruction, control, and practice. 2. To give correction to; chasten. [< L *disciplina* instruction < *discipulus* pupil < *discere* to learn]

dis count (dis′kount′), *n.* A deduction from the regular price, as for cash payment. —*v.* (*also* dis kount′). 1. To deduct a certain amount from the regular price of (merchandise). 2. To disregard in full or in part; hesitate to believe (someone's words). [< OF *descompter* < L *discomputare* < *dis-* away + *computare* to count < *com-* together + *putare* to reckon]

dis cus sion (di skush′ən), *n.* An oral or written treatment of a topic, often by an oral exchange between two persons. [< L *discussionis* < *discutere* to discuss < *dis-* apart + *quatere* to shake]

dis miss al (dis mis′əl), *n.* The act of dismissing or the state of being dismissed; also, a written notice of being dismissed. [< L *dimittere* to send away < *dis-* away + *mittere* to send]

dis patch (di spach′), *v.* 1. To send to a particular destination, as a letter or a messenger. 2. To take care of (a matter) quickly and efficiently. —*n.* 1. Speed and efficiency in taking care of a matter. 2. (*also* dis′pach′). An important message or news item sent speedily to its destination. [< Sp. *despacher* or Ital. *dispacciare* < MF *despeechier* to set free < *des-* not + *peechier* to hinder] **—dis patch′er,** *n.*

dis po si tion (dis′pə zish′ən), *n.* 1. One's prevailing mood or tendency: *a cheerful disposition.* 2. The act or manner of disposing (of a matter). [< L *dis-* away + *ponere* to place]

dis sect (di sekt′, dī sekt′, dī′sekt′), *v.* 1. To cut apart (a plant or an animal) so as to examine its structure. 2. To examine in detail; analyze. [< L *dissecare* < *dis-* apart + *secare* to cut]

dis solve (di zolv′), *v.,* **-solved, -solv ing.** 1. To cause (a solid) to go into solution: *dissolve sugar in water.* 2. To bring to an end; terminate: *dissolve an alliance.* [< L *dis-* apart + *solvere* to loosen]

di verse (di vûrs′, dī vûrs′), *adj.* Different from each other; unlike; varied. [< L *diversus* different < *divertere* < *dis-* apart + *vertere* to turn]

doc ile (dos′əl; *British* dō′sīl), *adj.* Easily taught and managed; gentle and obedient. [< L *docilis* teachable < *docere* to teach] **—doc′ile ly,** *adv.*

doc trine (dok′trin), *n.* 1. Something taught, especially an established teaching of a religious group. 2. An official statement of a government's position on a matter: *the Monroe Doctrine.* [< L *doctrina* < *docere* to teach] **—doc′tri nal,** *adj.* **—doc′tri nal ly,** *adv.*

doc u ment (dok′yə mənt), *n.* A written or printed record that furnishes proof of something. —*v.* (dok′yə ment′). To prove by referring to a document. [< L *documentum* lesson < *docere* to teach]

adj.	adjective	*pl.*	plural
adv.	adverb	*prep.*	preposition
conj.	conjunction	*pron.*	pronoun
interj.	interjection	*sing.*	singular
n.	noun	*v.*	verb

do mes tic (də mes′tik), *adj.* 1. Not wild; tame. 2. Having to do with the home or family: *domestic interests.* —*n.* A household servant. [< L *domesticus* < *domus* house] **—do mes′ti cal ly,** *adv.*

doubt less (dout′lis), *adj.* Free from doubt; sure. —*adv.* Most likely; surely: *Doubtless you are tired.* [< doubt < L *dubium* + -less (without)]

du al (do͞o′əl, dyo͞o′əl), *adj.* Having two parts; double. [< L *dualis* < *duo* two] **—du′al ly,** *adv.* **—du al′i ty,** *n.*

du pli cate (do͞o′plə kāt′, dyo͞o′plə kāt′), *v.,* **-cat ed, -cat ing.** To make an exact copy of; reproduce. —*n.* (*n.* and *adj.* do͞o′plə kit, dyo͞o′plə kit). Something that is an exact copy; reproduction. —*adj.* 1. Made exactly like the original: *a duplicate photograph.* 2. Having two corresponding parts; twofold; double: *The kidneys are duplicate.* [< L *duplicare* to double < *duo* two + *plicare* to fold] **—du′pli cate ly,** *adv.*

E

ear nest[1] (ûr′nist), *adj.* 1. Determined and purposeful; zealous. 2. Sincere and heartfelt: *an earnest plea.* [< OE *eornoste*] **—ear′nest ly,** *adv.*

ear nest[2] (ûr′nist), *n.* Something given as a token of what is to come. [< OF *erres* < L *arra, arrhabo* < Gk. *arrhabōn* < Hebrew ‘*ērābôn*]

e di tion (i dish′ən), *n.* 1. All the books, magazines, etc., produced in one printing from one set of plates. 2. One of the several forms in which a publication is produced: *a revised edition.* [< L *editionis* < *edere* < *e-* out + *dare* to give]

ed u ca tion al (ej′ə kā′shə nəl), *adj.* 1. Having to do with education. 2. Providing education: *an educational experience.* [< L *educare* to bring up < *educere* < *e-* out + *ducere* to lead] **—ed′u ca′tion al ly,** *adv.*

ef fec tive (i fek′tiv), *adj.* Producing the desired result. [< L *effectus* < *efficere* to bring about < *ex-* out + *facere* to do, make] **—ef fec′tive ly,** *adv.* **—ef fec′tive ness,** *n.*

ef fort (ef′ərt), *n.* The use of energy to accomplish something. [< OF *esfort* < *esforcier* to force < L *ex-* out + *forcier* to force]

e lim i nate (i lim′ə nāt′), *v.,* **-nat ed, -nat ing.** To get rid of; stamp out or expel. [< L *eliminare* to expel < *e-* out + *limen* threshold] **—e lim′i nat′or,** *n.* **—e lim′i na′tion,** *n.*

em bar go (em bär′gō), *n., pl.* **-goes.** A government order forbidding certain trade with certain nations. —*v.* To establish an embargo. [< L *in-* in + *barricare* to barricade]

e mer gen cy (i mûr′jən sē), *n., pl.* **-cies.** A sudden, unexpected happening that requires immediate action. [< L *emergere* < *e-* out + *mergere* to plunge]

em pha size (em′fə sīz′), *v.,* **-sized, -siz ing.** To give emphasis to; stress. [< Gk. *emphainein* to indicate < *en-* in + *phainein* to show]

em ploy ee (em ploi′ē), *n.* A person employed to work for another on a regular basis. [< F *employer* to employ < L *in-* in + *plicare* to fold, involve]

em ploy er (em ploi′ər), *n.* A person or business that employs people to work on a regular basis. [< F *employer*]

en cour age (en kûr′ij), *v.,* **-aged, -ag ing.** 1. To inspire with courage, cheer, etc.; hearten. 2. To be favorable to; promote: *encourage rapid growth.* [< OF *encoragier* < *en-* in + *corage* courage < L *cor* heart] **—en cour′age ment,** *n.*

had, māde, stär, câre, red, mē, dim, hīde, not, hōme, ôr, oil, to͝ok, po͞ol, loud, sun, tûrn; ch, such; ng, sing; sh, she; th, with; th, the; zh, vision

ə represents *a* in ago, *e* in open, *i* in pencil, *o* in wagon, *u* in cactus

en deav or (en dev′ər), *v.* To make an effort to do something; try. *—n.* An earnest effort; a determined attempt. [< ME *en-* in + *dever* duty < L *debere* to owe] Also *British* **endeavour.**

en gi neer ing (en′jə nîr′ing), *n.* The application of scientific knowledge to the design and construction of roads, bridges, dams, etc. [< OF *engin* < L *ingenium* natural ability < *in-* in + *gignere* to beget]

e nor mous (i nôr′məs), *adj.* 1. Very great in size or number; immense. 2. *Archaic.* Very wicked; shocking; abominable. [< L *e-* out + *norma* rule] **—e nor′mous ly,** *adv.*

en roll (en rōl′), *v.* 1. To place (or have placed) one's name on a list, as in joining a group; register. 2. To roll or wrap up. [< OF *en-* in + *rolle* roll] Also **enrol.**

en ter prise (en′tər prīz′), *n.* 1. A task that requires extraordinary determination, effort, etc.; a major undertaking. 2. Readiness to engage in bold, energetic action; fearless initiative. [< OF *entreprise* < *entre-* (L *inter-*) between + *prendre* (L *prehendere*) to take]

e quine (ē′kwīn′), *adj.* Of or like a horse. *—n.* A member of the horse family, which includes the donkey and the zebra. [< L *equinus* < *equus* horse]

e rupt (i rupt′), *v.* 1. To throw out lava, steam, etc., as a volcano. 2. To become suddenly active or violent: *Fighting erupted.* 3. To break out on the skin, as a rash. [< L *eruptus* < *erumpere* < *e-* out + *rumpere* to burst, break] **—e rup′tion,** *n.*

es sen tial (i sen′shəl), *adj.* 1. Having to do with the essence of something; fundamental; basic. 2. Of utmost importance; absolutely necessary. *—n.* Something that is of utmost importance; an absolute necessity. [< L *essentia* < *esse* to be] **—es sen′tial ly,** *adv.*

es tate (i stāt′), *n.* 1. Condition; standing. 2. An extensive tract of land, usually with a large house on it. 3. All of one's possessions; especially, the possessions left by a deceased person. [< OF *estat* < L *status* condition, state < *stare* to stand]

ev er last ing (ev′ər las′ting), *adj.* Lasting forever; eternal. *—n.* **Everlasting.** God. **—ev′er last′ing ly,** *adv.*

ev i dence (ev′i dəns), *n.* That which supports or contradicts something; proof or disproof. *—v.,* **-denced, -denc ing.** To support or prove by the use of evidence. [< L *evidere* < *ex-* out + *videre* to see]

ex ag ger ate (ig zaj′ə rāt′), *v.,* **-at ed, -at ing.** To represent as being greater, worse, etc., than what is actually true; misrepresent the truth by overstating it. [< L *exaggerare* < *ex-* out + *agger* a heap < *ad-* to *gerere* to carry] **—ex ag′ger a′tor,** *n.* **—ex ag′ger a′tion,** *n.*

ex am (ig zam′), *n.* An examination.

ex am i na tion (ig zam′ə nā′shən), *n.* The act of examining; inspection. 2. A test of one's knowledge and skills. [< L *examinare* < *examen* tongue of a balance < *ex-* out + *agere* to move, drive]

ex ceed (ik sēd′), *v.* 1. To be more than; surpass. 2. To go beyond (a limit, restriction, etc.): *exceed the speed limit.* [< L *ex-* out, beyond + *cedere* to go]

ex cel lent (ek′sə lənt), *adj.* Of the best quality; superior. [< L *excellere* < *ex-* out, beyond + *cellere* to rise] **—ex′cel lent ly,** *adv.*

ex cep tion (ik sep′shən), *n.* 1. The act of leaving (something) out; also, that which is left out. 2. Something that does not conform: *an exception to the rule.* [< L *excipere* < *ex-* out

adj.	adjective	*pl.*	plural
adv.	adverb	*prep.*	preposition
conj.	conjunction	*pron.*	pronoun
interj.	interjection	*sing.*	singular
n.	noun	*v.*	verb

+ *capere* to take] **—ex cep′tion al,** *adj.* **—ex cep′tion al ly,** *adv.*

ex com mu ni cate (eks′kə myōō′nə kāt′), *v.,* **-cat ed, -cat ing.** To expel from a church; deprive of church membership. [< L *excommunicare* < *ex-* out + *communicare* to share < *communis* common] **—ex′com mu′ni ca′tion,** *n.*

ex ec u tive (ig zek′yə tiv), *adj.* Having to do with the executing of laws, policies, etc.; pertaining to the putting into effect of what is proposed. *—n.* 1. A person who causes laws, policies, etc., to go into effect, as a president or governor. 2. A person holding an administrative position in a business or other institution; a director or manager. [< L *executus* < *exsecutus* < *exsequi* to follow through < *ex-* throughout + *sequi* to follow]

ex emp tion (ig zemp′shən), *n.* 1. The act of freeing, or state of being freed, from something that is required of others. 2. In computing income taxes, an amount allowed as a deduction from one's taxable income for the support of oneself or his dependents. [< L *exemptus* < *eximere* < *ex-* out + *emere* to take, buy]

ex hib it (ig zib′it), *v.* To put on display; show. *—n.* A display; public presentation. [< L *exhibere* < *ex-* out + *habere* to have, hold]

ex ist (ig zist′), *v.* To be or be real. 2. To continue to be or to live: *No animal can exist without water.* [< L *existere* < *ex-* out + *sistere* to stand]

ex or bi tant (ig zôr′bi tənt), *adj.* Much too high, as a price: *an exorbitant fee.* [< L *exorbitare* to go astray < *ex-* out + *orbita* track]

ex pec ta tion (ek′spek tā′shən), *n.* 1. The act or state of expecting; anticipation. 2. That which is expected. [< L *ex-* out + *spectare* to look at < *spectus* < *specere* to look]

ex pen di ture (ik spen′də chər), *n.* 1. The act of spending; outlay. 2. That which is spent; expense. [< L *expendere* < *ex-* out + *pendere* to weigh]

ex pense (ik spens′), *n.* 1. Something on which money is spent. 2. The amount of money needed to pay for something; cost. [< L *expensa* < *expendere* < *ex-* out + *pendere* to weigh]

ex pe ri ence (ik spîr′ē əns), *n.* 1. Actual contact with something; real practice. 2. An occurrence; something that happens to a person. *—v.,* **-enced, -enc ing.** To have happen to one; enjoy or endure. [< L *experientia* < *ex-* out + *periri* to try]

ex per i ment (ik sper′ə mənt), *n.* A trial or test to discover something, especially of a scientific nature. *—v.* To make a test or trial. [< L *experimentum* < *experiri* to try out < *ex-* out + *periri* to try] **—ex per′i ment′ er,** *n.*

ex pla na tion (ek′splə nā′shən), *n.* 1. The act of explaining; also, that which explains. 2. A discussion that clears up a misunderstanding. [< L *explanare* < *ex-* out + *planare* to level < *planus* level, flat]

ex port (ik spôrt′, ek′spôrt), *v.* To take or send (goods) out of a country for sale in other countries. *—n.* (ek′spôrt). Something that is exported. [< L *exportare* < *ex-* out + *portare* to carry; related to *portus* harbor, *porta* gate] **—ex port′er,** *n.*

ex pose (ik spōz′), *v.,* **-posed, -pos ing.** 1. To remove cover or shelter from. 2. To present to view by uncovering; reveal. 3. To make known, as something secret, dishonest, etc. 4. To admit light to (photographic film). [< MF *exposer* < L *exponere* < *ex-* out + *ponere* to put, place] **—ex pos′er,** *n.*

ex pres sion (ik spresh′ən), *n.* 1. The act of

putting thoughts into words; also, a word or phrase having a special meaning. 2. Effort put forth to express the meaning, feeling, etc., of what is uttered. 3. The look on one's face. [< L *expressionis* < *exprimere* < *ex-* out + *premere* to press]

ex ten sion (ik sten′shən), *n.* 1. The act of extending or the state of being extended. 2. A lengthening of an alloted time. 3. An additional outlet, as for a telephone. [< L *extendere* < *ex-* out + *tendere* to stretch]

ex treme ly (ik strēm′lē), *adv.* To an extreme degree; exceedingly. [< L *extremus* farthest outside < *exterus* outside]

F

fa cil i ty (fə sil′i tē), *n., pl.* **-ties.** 1. Ease of performance; freedom from difficulty or hindrance: *to work with facility.* 2. A building or room with equipment to be used for a certain purpose. [< F *facilité* < L *facilitas* < *facilis* easy to do < *facere* to do]

fac to ry (fak′tə rē), *n., pl.* **-ries.** An establishment where goods are manufactured or assembled. [< L *factoria* < *factor* maker < *facere* to make, do]

faint (fānt), *v.* 1. To lose consciousness through a lack of blood supply to the brain; swoon. 2. *Archaic.* To become weary and discouraged. —*adj.* 1. Very light or dim; hard to see. 2. Ready to faint; weak and dizzy. [< OF *faindre* to be lazy, shirk < L *fingere* to shape] **—faint′ly,** *adv.* **—faint′ness,** *n.*

faith ful ly (fāth′fəl ē), *adv.* In a faithful manner; conscientiously and loyally. [< ME *faith* < OF *feid* < L *fides* < *fidere* to trust]

fa mil iar (fə mil′yər), *adj.* 1. Very well known: *familiar territory.* 2. Well acquainted: *familiar friends.* [< L *familiaris* of the family < *familia* family] **—fa mil′iar ly,** *adv.* **—fa mil′iar′i ty,** *n.*

had, māde, stär, câre, red, mē, dim, hīde, not, hōme, ôr, oil, to͝ok, po͞ol, loud, sun, tûrn; ch, such; ng, sing; sh, she; th, with; t͟h, the; zh, vision

ə represents *a* in ago, *e* in open, *i* in pencil, *o* in wagon, *u* in cactus

fare well (fâr wel′), *interj.* May you fare well; good-bye. —*n.* A parting salutation; bidding of farewell; also, a service held in connection with a person's departure. —*adj.* Having to do with a departure; parting: *a farewell hymn.* [< fare + well]

fash ion a ble (fash′ə nə bəl), *adj.* Conforming to the prevailing fashion; stylish. [< ME *fasoun* shape, manner < L *factionis* < *factus* < *facere* to make, do] **—fash′ion a bly,** *adv.*

fa vor a bly (fā′vər ə blē), *adv.* In a favorable manner; agreeably; approvingly. [< OF *favor* friendly regard < L *favere* to favor] Also *British* **favourably.**

fea si ble (fē′zə bəl), *adj.* 1. Capable of being carried out; practical. 2. Reasonable; likely to be true: *a feasible explanation.* [< OF *faisable* < *faire* to do < L *facere* to do, make] **—fea′si bly,** *adv.* **—fea′si bil′i ty, fea′si ble ness,** *n.*

fe line (fē′līn′), *adj.* Of or like a cat. —*n.* A member of the cat family, which includes lions, cougars, and leopards. [< L *felinus* < *felis* cat]

fem i nine (fem′ə nin), *adj.* 1. Of or like females. 2. Characteristic of or suitable for women and girls; womanly. 3. In grammar, pertaining to the gender that applies to females: *a feminine suffix.* [< L *femina* woman]

fi del i ty (fī del′i tē, fi del′i tē), *n., pl.* **-ties.** 1. Faithfulness; loyalty. 2. Exactness; adherence to the truth. [< F *fidéleté* < L *fidelitas* < *fideles* faith < *fidere* to trust]

fier y (fīr′ē, fī′ə rē), *adj.,* **-i er, -i est.** 1. Full of fire; burning; blazing. 2. Full of strong feeling; passionate. [< ME *fier* fire] **—fier′i ness,** *n.*

fil i al (fil′ē əl), *adj.* Of, by, or from a son or

adj.	adjective	*pl.*	plural
adv.	adverb	*prep.*	preposition
conj.	conjunction	*pron.*	pronoun
interj.	interjection	*sing.*	singular
n.	noun	*v.*	verb

daughter; also, befitting a son or daughter: *filial honor.* [< L *filialis* < *filius* son] **—fil′i al ly,** *adv.*

fi nance (fī nans′, fī′nans, fī′nans′), *n.* 1. The science of money matters. 2. **finances.** Money available for immediate use; funds. *—v.* To supply money for. [< OF *finer* to settle, pay < *fin* settlement < L *finis* end]

flex i ble (flek′sə bəl), *adj.* 1. Easily bent or twisted without breaking; pliant. 2. Readily adjustable for different needs or purposes: *a flexible schedule.* [< L *flexus* < *flectere* to bend] **—flex′i bly,** *adv.* **—flex′i bil′i ty, flex′i ble ness,** *n.*

fra ter nal (frə tûr′nəl), *adj.* Of or like a brother; brotherly. [< L *fraternus* < *frater* brother] **—fra ter′nal ly,** *adv.*

fra ter ni ty (frə tûr′ni tē), *n., pl.* **-ties.** 1. The quality or state of being brothers; brotherhood; also, a brotherly spirit. 2. An organization of male students usually having a name composed of Greek letters and engaging in secret rites at their meetings. [< L *fraternitas* brotherhood < *frater* brother]

free dom (frē′dəm), *n.* The quality or state of being free; liberty; independence. [< OE *freodom* < *freo* free]

fre quent (frē′kwənt), *adj.* Happening or coming often. *—v.* (*also* frē kwənt′).To visit often; be present (at a place) regularly. [< L *frequentis* crowded] **—fre′quent ly,** *adv.*

fun gi cide (fun′ji sīd′, fung′gi sīd′), *n.* A substance used to destroy fungi. [< fungi + cide < L *-cida* killer < *caedere* to kill]

G

gen u ine (jen′yo͞o in), *adj.* Actually having the quality, origin, character, etc., that is claimed; authentic; real. [< L *genuinus* native, innate] **—gen′u ine ly,** *adv.* **—gen′u ine ness,** *n.*

Geth sem a ne (geth sem′ə nē), *n.* The garden at the foot of the Mount of Olives, where Jesus prayed just before His arrest and crucifixion. [< Aramaic *gath shemānīm* oil press]

gra cious (grā′shəs), *adj.* Full of kindness, compassion, courtesy, and generosity; loving and considerate. [< MF *gracieus* < L *gratiosus* favored, agreeable < *gratia* favor] **—gra′cious ly,** *adv.* **—gra′cious ness,** *n.*

grad u al ly (graj′o͞o ə lē), *adv.* Slowly and by degrees; little by little. [< L *gradualis* < *gradus* a step]

grad u ate (graj′o͞o āt′), *v.,* **-at ed, -at ing.** 1. To receive a diploma (from a school) for completing a course of study. 2. To give a diploma (to a student) for completing a course of study. 3. To mark (a scale) with units of measurement; calibrate. *—n.* (graj′o͞o it). A student who has graduated from an institution of learning. [< L *graduare* < *gradus* a step]

grease (grēs), *n.* A thick, oily substance, especially a thick lubricant. *—v.* (*also* grēz), **greased, greas ing.** To smear or lubricate with grease. [< OF *graisse* < L *crassus* fat]

guard i an (gär′dē ən), *n.* Someone who guards or cares for a person or thing, especially a person legally appointed to care for a child until he is of age. *—adj.* Protecting: *a guardian angel.* [< OF *guarden* < *guarder* to guard, defend] **—guard′i an ship,** *n.*

H

heart y (här′tē), *adj.,* **-i er, -i est.** 1. From the heart; warm and sincere. 2. Abundant and nourishing: *a hearty meal.* [< OE *heorte* heart] **—heart′i ly,** *adv.* **—heart′i ness,** *n.*

had, māde, stär, câre, red, mē, dim, hīde, not, hōme, ôr, oil, to͝ok, po͞ol, loud, sun, tûrn; ch, such; ng, sing; sh, she; th, with; th, the; zh, vision

ə represents *a* in ago, *e* in open, *i* in pencil, *o* in wagon, *u* in cactus

her bi cide (hûr′bi sīd′, ûr′bi sīd), *n.* A substance used to kill weeds. [< herb < L *herba* grass + -cide < L *-cida* killer < *caedere* to kill]

here to fore (hîr′tə fôr′), *adv.* Until now; previously.

high school, *n.* A school for students who have completed elementary school, consisting of grades 9 or 10 to 12.

his tor i cal (hi stôr′i kəl), *adj.* Pertaining to or belonging to history. [< L *historia* < Gk. *histōr* knowing] **—his tor′i cal ly,** *adv.*

hoarse (hôrs), *adj.* 1. Deep and harsh in sound; grating. 2. Having a husky voice, as from a cold. [< ME *hors* < OE *has, hars* hoarse] **—hoarse′ly,** *adv.* **—hoarse′ness,** *n.*

hon est ly (on′ist lē), *adv.* In an honest manner; fairly; justly. [< L *honestus* honorable < *honos* honor]

hu mil i ty (hyo͞o mil′i tē), *n.* The quality or state of being humble; modest view of one's own importance and accomplishments. [< L *humilitas* lowness < *humilis* low < *humus* ground]

hun gry (hung′grē), *adj.,* **-gri er, -gri est.** 1. Desiring or needing food. 2. Indicating a desire for food: *a hungry look.* 3. Earnestly desiring; eager (for): *hungry for affection.* [< OE *hungrig* < *hungor* hunger] **—hun′gri ly,** *adv.*

hy giene (hī′jēn), *n.* Practices that contribute to good health, especially those involving cleanliness. [< F *hygiĕne* < Gk. *hygieinos* healthful < *hygiēs* healthy] **—hy gi en′ic,** *adj.*

I

i den ti fy (ī den′tə fī′), *v.,* **-fied, -fy ing.** 1. To recognize or prove to be a particular person or thing. 2. To consider oneself as sharing the circumstances or feelings of another person; put oneself in another's situation. 3. To consider the same; equate: *identify wealth with happiness.* [< L *identificare* < *identicus* < *idem* the same] **—i den′ti fi′er,** *n.*

ig no rance (ig′nər əns), *n.* The fact or state of being ignorant; lack of knowledge, information, or awareness. [< L *ignorare* to have no knowledge of < *in-* not + *gnoscere* to know]

il lus trate (il′ə strāt′), *v.,* **-trat ed, -trat ing.** 1. To use pictures or examples to clarify what is expressed in words. 2. To provide (a book, magazine, etc.) with pictures. [< L *illustrare* to light up < *in-* thoroughly + *lustrare* to light, make bright]

im mi grant (im′i grənt), *n.* A person who comes into a foreign country to live. [< L *immigrare* < *in-* in + *migrare* to migrate]

im pa tient (im pā′shənt), *adj.* Not patient; not willing to endure trouble or delay. [< L *in-* not + *patiens* < *pati* to suffer] **—im pa′tient ly,** *adv.*

im pel (im pel′), *v.,* **-pelled, -pel ling.** 1. To cause (a person) to act by strong urging. 2. To drive (something) forward; propel. [< L *impellere* < *in-* on + *pellere* to drive] **—im pel′ler,** *n.*

im port (im pôrt′, im′pôrt′), *v.* To take or bring (goods) into a country to be sold. *—n.* (im′pôrt′). 1. Something that is imported. 2. Meaning; significance: *the import of the message.* 3. Major consequence: *the import of Adam's sin.* [< L *importare* < *in-* in + *portare* to carry; related to *portus* harbor, *porta* gate] **—im port′er,** *n.*

im por tu ni ty (im′pôr to͞o′ni tē, im′pôr tyo͞o′ni tē), *n., pl.* **-ties.** Persistence in asking for something; also a request that is repeated frequently.

adj.	adjective	*pl.*	plural
adv.	adverb	*prep.*	preposition
conj.	conjunction	*pron.*	pronoun
interj.	interjection	*sing.*	singular
n.	noun	*v.*	verb

[< L *importunus* (a wind) not blowing toward port, and thus unfavorable < *in-* not + *portus* harbor]

im pos si ble (im pos′ə bəl), *adj.* 1. Not possible; not capable of occuring or existing. 2. So difficult that there appears to be no solution; hopeless: *an impossible problem.* [< L *impossibilis* < *in-* not + *possibilis* possible] **—im pos′si bly,** *adv.* **—im pos′si bil′i ty, im pos′si ble ness** *n.*

im pul sive (im pul′siv), *adj.* Motivated by impulse; not premeditated: *an impulsive answer.* [< L *impulsivus* < *impellere* < *in-* on + *pellere* to drive] **—im pul′sive ly,** *adv.*

In car na tion (in′kär nā′shən), *n.* The union of Jesus' divine nature with a (sinless) human nature in a human body. [< L *incarnare* to embody in flesh < *in-* in + *carnis* flesh]

in ci dent (in′si dənt), *n.* A happening; event; occurrence. *—adj.* Normally happening in connection with something; to be expected; *a risk incident to surgery.* [< L *incidure* to fall upon < *in-* on + *cadere* to fall] **—in′ci den′tal,** *adj.* **—in′ci den′tal ly,** *adv.*

in debt ed ness (in det′id nis), *n.* 1. The state of being indebted; liability. 2. The amount owed; total of one's debts. [< ME *indetted* < OF *endette* < *en-* in + *dette* debt < L *debitum*]

in de pend ence (in′di pen′dəns), *n.* Freedom from the control, support, and help of another. [< in- (not) + dependence < L *dependere* < *de-* down + *pendere* to hang]

in di cate (in′di kāt′), *v.,* **-cat ed, -cat ing.** 1. To point out or point to: *indicate which person.* 2. To be a sign of; suggest strongly: *Smoke indicates fire.* 3. To show; make known: *A barometer indicates air pressure.* [< L *in-* in + *dicare* to point out, proclaim]

in dict (in dīt′), *v.* 1. To make an official charge against a person: said of a grand jury. 2. To charge with an offense; accuse. [< L *indictare* to accuse < *in-* in + *dictare* to declare < *dicere* to say, speak] **—in dict′er, in dict′or,** *n.*

in fan tile (in′fən tīl′, in′fən til), *adj.* 1. Having to do with infants or infancy. 2. Like an infant; babyish or childish. [< L *infantilis* < *infans* not speaking < *in-* not + *fans* < *fari* to speak]

in fi nite (in′fə nit), *adj.* Not finite; not limited in extent, duration, power, etc.; boundless; endless. *—n.* **the Infinite.** God. [< L *infinitus* < *in-* not + *finis* limit, bound]

in flec tion (in flek′shən), *n.* 1. A change in the pitch or loudness of the voice. 2. In grammar, a change in the form of a word to show tense, number, case, etc. [< L *in-* in + *flectere* to bend] Also *British* **inflexion.**

in iq ui ty (i nik′wi tē), *n., pl.* **-ties.** A sin; evil deed. [< L *iniquitas* < *iniquus* unequal, unjust < *in-* not + *aequus* equal, just]

in i tial (i nish′əl), *adj.* Of or at the beginning; first. *—n.* The first letter of one's first or last name. [< L *initialis* < *initium* beginning < *inire* to enter upon < *in-* in + *ire* to go] **—in i′tial ly,** *adv.*

in i tia tive (i nish′ə tiv), *n.* 1. Inclination and ability to start something; enterprise. 2. An active part in leading out: *to take the initiative.* [< L *initium*]

in quiry (in kwī′rē, in′kwə rē), *n., pl.* **-quir ies.** 1. An act of inquiring; asking; also, an extensive search for information. 2. A question. [< L *inquirere* < *in-* into + *quaerere* to ask, seek] Also **enquiry.**

in sec ti cide (in sek′ti sīd), *n.* A substance used to kill insects. [< insect < L *(animal) insectum* divided animal < *in-* into + *secare* to cut, divide + -cide < L *cida* killer < *caedere* to kill]

in spect (in spekt′), *v.,* To look at carefully; examine closely. [< L *inspectus* < *inspicere* to look into < *in-* into + *specere* to look]

in spire (in spīr′), *v.,* **-spired, -spir ing.** 1. To breathe in; inhale. 2. To stir up or motivate by a thought or feeling. [< L *in-* into + *spirare* to breathe] **—in spir′er,** *n.*

in sti tute (in′sti to͞ot′, in′sti tyo͞ot′), *v.,* **-tut ed, -tut ing.** To establish; start, as an operation or a practice. *—n.* An organization estabished for a particular purpose, as for education or research; also, the building or buildings used by such an organization. [< L *instituere* to establish < *in-* in, on + *statuere* to set up < *status* position]

in tel li gent (in tel′ə jənt), *adj.* 1. Having or displaying a perceptive mind; quick to learn. 2. Showing understanding; discerning: *an intelligent answer.* [< L *intelligere* to perceive < *inter-* between + *legere* to choose] **—in tel′li gent ly,** *adv.*

in ten tion (in ten′shən), *n.* An intended action, purpose, or goal. [< L *intendere* to stretch toward < *in-* at + *tendere* to stretch] **—in ten′tion al,** *adj.* **—in ten′tion al ly,** *adv.*

in ter cede (in′tər sēd′), *v.,* **-ced ed, -ced ing.** To go between (two parties) in an effort to establish an agreement between them; mediate. [< L *inter-* between + *cedere* to go] **—in′ter ced′er,** *n.*

in ter fere (in′tər fîr′), *v.,* **-fered, -fer ing.** 1. To get in the way; be a hindrance. 2. To get involved in (a person's affairs) without a valid reason; meddle. 3. In sports, to obstruct an opposing player in violation of the rules. [< L *inter-* between + *ferire* to strike] **—in′ter fer′er,** *n.*

in te ri or (in tîr′ē ər), *adj.* Pertaining to the inside; inner; internal. *—n.* The internal part; the inside. [< L *inter* within, between]

had, māde, stär, câre, red, mē, dim, hīde, not, hōme, ôr, oil, to͝ok, po͞ol, loud, sun, tûrn; ch, such; ng, sing; sh, she; th, with; t͟h, the; zh, vision

ə represents *a* in ago, *e* in open, *i* in pencil, *o* in wagon, *u* in cactus

in ter nal (in tûr′nəl), *adj.* Pertaining to the inside; inner; interior. [< L *internus* within] **—in ter′nal ly,** *adv.*

in ter rupt (in′tə rupt′), *v.* 1. To break in on (work, a conversation, etc.); intrude. 2. To break the uniformity or continuity of: *interrupt a row of circles with a square.* [< L *interruptus* < *interrumpere* < *inter-* between + *rumpere* to break, burst] **—in′ter rupt′er,** *n.* **—in′ter rup′tive,** *adj.*

in ter view (in′tər vyo͞o′), *n.* A meeting in which (usually) two persons talk something over, especially when one seeks information from the other. *—v.* To have an interview; meet and talk with (a person). [< MF e*ntrevue* < L *inter-* between, within + *videre* to see] **—in′ter view′er,** *n.*

in va lid[1] (in′və lid), *n.* A person who is weak and sickly because of an injury or a long illness. *—adj.* Weak and sickly; infirm. [< L *in-* not + *validus* strong < *valere* to be strong]

in val id[2] (in val′id), *adj.* Not valid; without force or effect; void: *an invalid signature.* [< L *invalidus*] **—in val′id ly,** *adv.*

in ves ti gate (in ves′ti gāt′), *v.,* **-gat ed, -gat ing.** To search or inquire into; examine thoroughly. [< L *investigare* < *in-* in + *vestigare* to track, trace < *vestigium* a track]

in volve (in volv′), *v.,* **-volved, -volv ing.** 1. To have or cause to have part in; take in or bring in; include. 2. To hold one's attention; occupy; absorb: *be deeply involved in solving a problem.* [< L *involvere* to roll up, enfold < *in-* in + *volvere* to roll] **—in volve′ment,** *n.*

adj.	adjective	*pl.*	plural
adv.	adverb	*prep.*	preposition
conj.	conjunction	*pron.*	pronoun
interj.	interjection	*sing.*	singular
n.	noun	*v.*	verb

in volved (in volvd′), *adj.* Complex; complicated: *a long, involved explanation.* [< L *involvere* to roll up, enfold < *in-* in + *volvere* to roll]

I sa iah (ī zā′ə, ī zī′ə), *n.* 1. An Israelite prophet of the eighth century B.C. 2. The Old Testament book written by Isaiah. *Abbr.* **Isa.** [< Hebrew *yesha'yāhu* Salvation of God]

J

Jer e mi ah (jer′ə mī′ə), *n.* 1. An Israelite prophet of the seventh century B.C. 2. The Old Testament book written by Jeremiah. *Abbr.* **Jer.** [< Hebrew *yirmĕyāhu* God loosens]

jour ney (jûr′nē), *n., pl.* **-neys.** 1. An instance of traveling; trip. 2. The distance traveled: *a day's journey.* —*v.,* **-neyed, -ney ing.** To go on a trip; travel. [< OF *journee* a day's travel < L *diurnus* daily < *dies* day]

joy ful (joi′fəl), *adj.* Full of joy; happy; glad. [< OF *joie* < L *gaudium* < *gaudere* to rejoice] **—joy′ful ly,** *adv.* **—joy′ful ness,** *n.*

judg ment (juj′mənt), *n.* 1. An act of judging; also, an opinion or a decision reached by judging. 2. Ability to judge well; discernment: *poor judgment.* 3. **Judgment.** Judgment Day, when God will judge the world. [< OF *juge* < L *judicus* < *jus* law + dicere *to speak*]

jun ior (jo͞on′yər), *adj.* Younger in age or lower in rank, as opposed to *senior.* —*n.* A younger person: *his junior by ten years. Abbr.* **jr.; Jr.** (after a name). [< L *junior* younger < *juvenis* young]

jus ti fy (jus′tə fī′), *v.,* **-fied, -fy ing.** 1. To consider or declare just; clear (a person) of guilt. 2. To show (something questionable) to be proper or right; defend. 3. To adjust lines of type with spaces so that the lines are of equal length. [< L *justus* just + *facere* to make]

ju ve nile (jo͞o′və nīl′, jo͞o′və nəl), *adj.* 1. Young; youthful; also, childish; immature. 2. Of or for young people: *juvenile interests.* —*n.* A young person, especially one who is not of legal age; minor. [< L *juvenis* young]

K

kin der gar ten (kin′dər gär′tən), *n.* A school or class for children four to six years old. [< G *kinder* children + *garten* garden]

kitch en ette (kich′ən et′), *n.* A small, compactly arranged kitchen. [< kitchen < OE *cycene* < L *coquina* < *coquere* to cook + -ette (small)]

knight (nīt), *n.* 1. In medieval times, a soldier who helped protect the castle and the surrounding territory of his lord. 2. In England, a man who has been raised to a status of nobility for an outstanding service or accomplishment. 3. In chess, a piece shaped like a horse's head and moving in an L-shaped pattern. —*v.* To make (a person) a knight. [< OE *cniht* boy, military attendant]

knowl edge (nol′ij), *n.* 1. The act or state of knowing. 2. That which is known; information. [< ME *knowlegen* to admit, recognize < OE *cnāwan* to know]

L

lat i tude (lat′i to͞od′, lat′i tyo͞od′), *n.* 1. Distance north or south of the equator, measured in degrees and marked off by parallels. 2. A region of a certain latitude. 3. Freedom from narrow restrictions; liberty to think, speak, and act in a given way. [< L *latitudo* < *latus* wide]

league[1] (lēg), *n.* A union of persons, nations, etc. that have agreed to help each other. —*v.,* **leagued, leagu ing.** To form a league. [< MF *ligue* < L *ligare* to bind]

league[2] (lēg), *n.* An old unit of measurement equal to three or four miles. [< OF *legue* < L *leuga* < Celtic]

leg is la tion (lej′i slā′shən), *n.* The process of making laws; also, the laws made. [< L *legis* < *lex* law + *lationis* a bringing, proposing < *latus* < *ferre* to bring]

le git i mate (lə jit′ə mit), *adj.* 1. Permitted by law; legal. 2. Acceptable; reasonable: *a legitimate reason for being late.* —*v.* (lə jit′ə māt′), **-mat ed, -mat ing.** To declare or establish as being legal. [< L *legis* law] **—le git′i mate ly,** *adv.*

li a ble (lī′ə bəl), *adj.* 1. Responsible, as for damage; obliged to pay. 2. Likely (to happen): *That child is liable to get hurt.* [< OF *lier* < L *ligare* to bind]

li brar i an (lī brâr′ē ən), *n.* A person working or trained to work in a library. [< L *librarium* book case < *liber* book]

li cense (lī′səns), *n.* 1. Legal permission to do something; authorization. 2. A document that shows such permission: *a driver's license.* 3. Unrestricted liberty, especially when it is abused; lack of restraint. —*v.,* **-censed, -cens ing.** To give permission to; authorize. [< L *licere* to be allowed] Also *British* **licence.**

lig a ment (lig′ə mənt), *n.* A band of strong tissue that holds a joint together or holds an organ in place. [< L *ligamentum* band < *ligare* to bind]

liq uid (lik′wid), *n.* A substance that flows and that can be poured, as water. —*adj.* 1. In the form of a liquid: *liquid fertilizer.* 2. Readily convertible into cash: *liquid assets.* 3. Clear and flowing, as sounds: *the songbird's liquid melody.* [< L *liquidus* < *liquere* to be fluid]

lis ten (lis′ən), *v.* 1. To try to hear. 2. To give heed; pay attention: *Listen to your parents' advice.* [< OE *hlysnan,* related to *hlyst* hearing] **—lis′ten er,** *n.*

had, māde, stär, câre, red, mē, dim, hīde, not, hōme, ôr, oil, to͝ok, po͞ol, loud, sun, tûrn; ch, such; ng, sing; sh, she; th, with; <u>th</u>, the; zh, vision

ə represents *a* in ago, *e* in open, *i* in pencil, *o* in wagon, *u* in cactus

live ly (līv′lē), *adj.,* **-li er, -li est.** 1. Active and energetic: *lively children.* 2. *Archaic.* Living; alive. —*adv.* In a lively manner; briskly. [< OE *līfelīce* < *līf* life] **—live′li ness,** *n.*

lo cal i ty (lō kal′i tē), *n., pl.* **-ties.** A specific place; area; neighborhood. [< F *localité* < L *localitas* < *locus* place]

lu nar (lo͞o′nər), *adj.* Of, from, or to the moon. [< L *lunaris* < *luna* moon]

M

ma chin er y (mə shē′nə rē), *n., pl.* **-ies.** A group of machines or machine parts. [< L *machina* < Gk. *mēchanē* device]

main te nance (mān′tə nəns), *n.* 1. A maintaining or being maintained; upkeep. 2. Means of living; support; livelihood. [< OF *maintenir* < L *manu tenere* to hold in one's hand < *manus* hand + *tenere* to hold]

ma jor i ty (mə jôr′ə tē), *n., pl.* **-ties.** 1. A portion greater than one-half; the greater part. 2. In voting, the number by which the elected candidate's votes exceed the total number of votes cast for all other candidates. [< MF *majorité* < L *majoritas* < *major* greater < *magnus* great]

man age ment (man′ij mənt), *n.* 1. A managing or being managed. 2. A group of persons who manage a business; administration. [< Ital. *maneggiare* to train (horses) < L *manus* hand]

man ag er (man′ij ər), *n.* A person who manages (a business, institution, etc.); director. [< Ital. *maneggiare*]

man date (man′dāt′), *n.* A command given by

adj.	adjective	*pl.*	plural
adv.	adverb	*prep.*	preposition
conj.	conjunction	*pron.*	pronoun
interj.	interjection	*sing.*	singular
n.	noun	*v.*	verb

someone in authority; an order. [< L *mandare* to order < *manus* hand + *dare* to give]

man da to ry (man′də tôr′ē), *adj.* Required by (or as if by) a mandate; compulsory. [< L *mandare*]

man u al (man′yo͞o əl), *adj.* Pertaining to the hands: *manual labor.* —*n.* A book of instructions or a small reference book; handbook. [< L *manualis* < *manus* hand] **—man′u al ly,** *adv.*

man u fac tur er (man′yə fak′chər ər), *n.* A person or an establishment that manufactures; a factory or factory owner. [< L *manus* hand + *factura* a making < *facere* to make, do]

mar vel ous (mar′vəl əs), *adj.* Arousing wonder and admiration; wonderful; amazing. [< OF *marveille* < L *mirabilis* wonderful < *mirari* to wonder < *mirus* strange, wonderful] **—mar′vel ous ly,** *adv.*

mas cu line (mas′kyə lin), *adj.* 1. Of or like males. 2. Characteristic of or suitable for men and boys; manly. 3. In grammar, pertaining to the gender that applies to males: *a masculine noun.* [< L *masculus* male]

ma ter nal (mə tûr′nəl), *adj.* 1. Of or like a mother; motherly. 2. Related through one's mother: *a maternal uncle.* [< L *maternus* < *mater* mother] **—ma ter′nal ly,** *adv.*

mat ri mo ny (mat′rə mō′nē), *n., pl.* **-nies.** 1. The state of being married; marriage. 2. A ceremony in which a man and woman are married; wedding. [< L *matrimonium* < *mater* mother]

me di a tor (mē′dē ā′tər), *n.* A person who mediates; intercessor. [< L *mediatus* < *mediare* to stand between, mediate < *medius* middle]

me di e val (mē′dē ē′vəl), *adj.* Belonging to or like the Middle Ages (the period from the fall of Rome in 476 to about 1450 or 1500). [< L *medius* middle + *aevum* age] Also **mediaeval.**

me di um (mē′dē əm), *adj.* Of a middle quality, position, degree, etc.; not extreme. —*n., pl.* **-di ums** or **-di a.** 1. A middle condition. 2. That through which something is done; agency. [< L *medius* middle]

mer chan dise (mûr′chən dīz′, mûr′chən dīs′), *n.* Goods that are bought and sold for profit; wares. —*v.,* **-dised, -dis ing.** To buy and sell (goods) for profit; trade. [< OF *marchant* merchant < L *mercari* to traffic, buy < *mercis* wares] Also **merchandize. —mer′chan dis′er,** *n.*

me rid i an (mə rid′ē ən), *n.* 1. In geography, a line that compasses the globe and passes through both the North Pole and the South Pole, used to mark off degrees of longitude. 2. The highest point in the duration of something; peak; zenith: *the meridian of Solomon's reign.* —*adj.* 1. Pertaining to a meridian. 2. Pertaining to midday: *the meridian sun.* [< L *meridies* noon, south < *medidies* < *medius* middle + *dies* day]

mil li pede (mil′ə pēd′), *n.* A wormlike arthropod having two pairs of legs for almost every segment of its body. [< L *millepeda* < *mille* thousand + *pedis* foot] Also **millepede.**

mi nor (mī′nər), *adj.* Of a lesser degree, importance, etc., as opposed to *major.* —*n.* A person who is not of legal age; juvenile. [< L *minor* smaller, lesser]

mir a cle (mir′ə kəl), *n.* A happening that is impossible according to natural laws, usually associated with the power of God. [< L *miraculum* < *mirari* to wonder < *mirus* wonderful]

mis chie vous (mis′chə vəs), *adj.* Having to do with mischief; troublesome, annoying, or teasing. [< OF *meschevous* < *meschever* to come to grief < *mes-* (mis-) wrong + *chever* to come to an end < *chief* end, head < L *caput* head] **—mis′chie vous ly,** *adv.*

mis er a ble (miz′ər ə bəl), *adj.* Very unhappy or uncomfortable; wretched. [< L *miserabilis* pitiable < *miserari* to pity < *miser* wretched] **—mis′er a bly,** *adv.*

mis er y (miz′ə rē), *n., pl.* **-ies.** 1. A feeling or state of extreme unhappiness or discomfort; wretchedness. 2. Something that causes misery. [< L *miser* wretched]

mis sion ar y (mish′ə ner′ē), *n., pl.* **-ies.** A person who helps to spread the Gospel. *—adj.* Of or about missionaries: *missionary life.* [< L *missionis* < *mittere* to send]

mo bile (mō′bəl, mō′bēl′), *adj.* 1. Moving or changing readily. 2. Easily movable; designed to be moved from place to place: *a mobile home.* *—n.* (mō′bēl′). A decoration consisting of rods or wires suspended on strings and moved by air currents. [< L *mobilis* movable < *movere* to move]

mol e cule (mol′i kyo͞ol′), *n.* The smallest particle into which a susbstance can be divided without losing its physical and chemical properties. [< L *molecula* little mass < *moles* mass]

mon i tor (mon′i tər), *n.* 1. A person who gives advice or caution. 2. A student appointed to help maintain order, keep records, etc. *—v.* To watch (something) in order to control or regulate it. [< L *monitus* < *monere* to warn, remind]

mon u ment (mon′yə mənt), *n.* An object (such as a pillar) set up to keep alive the memory of some person or event; memorial. [< L *monumentum* < *monere* to remind, warn]

mor al (môr′əl), *adj.* 1. Having to do with principles of right and wrong: *a moral issue.* 2. Upright; true to principles of right and wrong: *a moral person.* *—n.* 1. **morals.** Principles of behavior: *sound morals.* 2. The lesson

had, māde, stär, câre, red, mē, dim, hīde, not, hōme, ôr, oil, to͝ok, po͞ol, loud, sun, tûrn; ch, such; ng, sing; sh, she; th, with; t͟h, the; zh, vision

ə represents *a* in ago, *e* in open, *i* in pencil, *o* in wagon, *u* in cactus

that a story teaches. [< L *moralis* < *mores* manners, morals] **—mor′al ly,** *adv.*

mos qui to (mə skē′tō), *n., pl.* **-toes** or **-tos.** A small insect, the female of which pierces the skin of man and animals and draws blood. [< Sp. *mosquito* small fly < *mosca* < L *musca* fly]

mo ti vate (mō′tə vāt′), *v.,* **-vat ed, -vat ing.** To provide with a motive; induce to think, speak, or act in a certain way. [< L *motivus* < *movere* to move]

move ment (mo͞ov′mənt), *n.* 1. The act or process of moving. 2. The plans and actions of people who work together over a period of time to achieve a goal: *the pacifist movement.* 3. The mechanism of a clock or similar device; works. [< OF *movoir* < L *movere* to move]

mul ti plic i ty (mul′tə plis′i tē), *n., pl.* **-ties.** The condition of being multiple and diverse; the fact of being many and varied. [< L *multiplicare* to multiply < *multus* many + *plicare* to fold]

mus cle (mus′əl), *n.* A body tissue that moves a part of the body by contracting. [< L *musculus* little mouse < *mus* mouse (from the appearance of some muscles)]

mys te ri ous (mi stîr′ē əs), *adj.* Hard to understand; strange and puzzling. [< L *mysterium* Gk. *mystērion* < *mystos* keeping silence < *myein* to close (the lips or eyes)] **—mys te′ri ous ly,** *adv.*

mys ter y (mis′tə rē), *n., pl.* **-ies.** Something difficult or impossible to understand; a secret. [< L *mysterium*]

adj.	adjective	*pl.*	plural
adv.	adverb	*prep.*	preposition
conj.	conjunction	*pron.*	pronoun
interj.	interjection	*sing.*	singular
n.	noun	*v.*	verb

N

nav i ga tor (nav′i gā′tər), *n.* 1. One who navigates the seas; a sailor. 2. One who steers a ship or an aircraft; a helmsman or pilot. [< L *navigare* < *navis* boat + *agere* to drive, direct]

neg li gent (neg′li jənt), *adj.* Showing neglect; careless or inattentive. [< L *negligere* to disregard < *nec-* not + *legere* to pick up] **—neg′li gent ly,** *adv.*

ne go ti a tion (ni gō′shē ā′shən), *n.* 1. The act or process of negotiating. 2. A conference held to discuss terms of an agreement. [< L *negotiari* to do business < *negotium* business < *nec-* not + *otium* ease, leisure]

non re sis tance (non′ri zis′təns), *n.* The doctrine or policy of refusing to retaliate for wrong, but returning good instead. [< non- (not) + resistance < L *resistere* to withstand < *re-* back + *sistere* to cause to stand]

north west ern (nôrth′west′ərn), *adj.* Of, from, or toward the direction midway between north and west.

nui sance (no͞o′səns, nyo͞o′səns), *n.* A person or thing that is bothersome or troublesome; annoyance. [< OF *nuisir* to harm < L *nocere*]

O

o be di ence (ō bē′dē əns), *n.* An act of obeying or a condition of being obedient; submission; compliance. [< L *obedire* < *ob-* toward + *audire* to hear, listen]

ob li ga tion (ob′li gā′shən), *n.* Something that one is required to do, especially because of a promise; duty; responsibility. [< L *obligare* < *ob-* toward + *ligare* to bind]

ob ser va tion (ob′zər vā′shən), *n.* 1. An act of observing or an item that is observed. 2. A brief comment; remark. [< L *observare* to watch < *ob-* over + *servare* to watch]

ob tain (əb tān′, ob tān′), *v.* To get; come to have; gain. [< L *ob-* to + *tenere* to hold]

oc ca sion (ə kā′zhən), *n.* 1. A particular event, usually one that is special. 2. A cause; reason: *no occasion to worry.* —*v.* To be the reason for; bring about: *an accident occasioned by carelessness.* [< L *occidere* to fall toward < *ob-* toward + *cadere* to fall]

oc cu pa tion (ok′yə pā′shən), *n.* 1. One's regular business or vocation; job. 2. An occupying by force, as the holding of land by invading soldiers. [< L *occupare* to seize < *ob-* against + *capere* to take]

oc cur rence (ə kûr′əns), *n.* Something that occurs; happening; event. [< L *occurrere* < *ob-* toward + *currere* to run]

oc tave (ok′tiv, ok′tāv), *n.* 1. In music, the distance from low *do* to high *do* or between any two tones separated by an interval of that size. 2. Any group of eight things. [< L *octavus* eighth < *octo* eight]

op er a tion (op′ə rā′shən), *n.* 1. The act or process of operating. 2. In mathematics, the changing of a value by computation, as by adding, subtracting, etc. 3. A surgical procedure done by a doctor; surgery. [< L *operari* to work < *opus* work]

o pin ion (ə pin′yən), *n.* A personal judgment or conclusion about a matter; what one thinks about something. [< L *opinari* to think]

op po nent (ə pō′nənt), *n.* A person on the opposite side in a game, a battle, etc. —*adj.* Opposing or opposite; contrary. [< L *opponere* to set against < *ob-* against + *ponere* to place]

op por tu ni ty (op′ər to͞o′ni tē, op′ər tyo͞o′ni tē), *n., pl.* **-ties.** A favorable time; convenient occasion or circumstance. [< L *opportunus* (a wind) blowing toward port, and thus favorable < *ob-* toward + *portus* harbor]

op pose (ə pōz′), *v.,* **-posed, -pos ing.** To be against; resist. [< L *opponere* < *ob-* against + *ponere* to place]

or di nance (ôr′dən əns), *n.* A rule or law established by someone in authority, especially an observance ordained by God. [< L *ordinare* to set in order < *ordo* order, arrangement]

or di nar y (ôr′dən er′ē), *adj.* Common; everyday; usual. *—n., pl.* **-ies.** Something that is common or usual. [< L *ordinarius* < *ordo* order, arrangement] **—or′di nar′i ly,** *adv.*

o ver look (ō′vər lo͝ok′), *v.* 1. To fail to notice; miss. 2. To disregard; ignore. 3. To provide an elevated view of. *—n.* (ō′vər lo͝ok′). An elevated place, as on a mountain, that affords a view of the scene below.

ox y gen (ok′si jən), *n.* A gas that forms 21 percent of the atmosphere and that is necessary for the existence of life. [< Gk. *oxys* sharp, acid + *-genēs* born, produced (because it was once considered essential to all acids)]

P

pam phlet (pam′flit), *n.* A booklet with paper covers; brochure. [< OF *pamphilet* < *Pamphilus,* title of a popular poem published in this form in the 1100s]

par a graph (pâr′ə graf′), *n.* In a composition, a division that covers a unit of thought and that usually begins with an indented first line. *—v.* To divide (a composition) into paragraphs. [< Gk. *paragraphos* a short line in a text marking a break in the sense < *para* beside + *graphein* to write]

par al lel (pâr′ə lel′), *adj.* 1. Of lines and planes, the same distance apart at all points. 2. Similar in many ways; corresponding. *—n.* Something that is parallel; an illustration, as a parable, that improves one's understanding of a new idea by showing its similarity to something familiar. *—v.* 1. To be or cause to be parallel. 2. To show how one thing is similar to another; show correspondence. [< Gk. *para allēlos* beside one another]

had, māde, stär, câre, red, mē, dim, hīde, not, hōme, ôr, oil, to͝ok, po͞ol, loud, sun, tûrn; ch, such; ng, sing; sh, she; th, with; th, the; zh, vision

ə represents *a* in ago, *e* in open, *i* in pencil, *o* in wagon, *u* in cactus

par tic u lar (pər tik′yə lər), *adj.* 1. Considered by itself; single. 2. Wanting all the details to one's liking; choosy. *—n.* A detail; item; point. [< L *particula* small part < *partis* part]

par tic u lar ly (pər tik′yə lər lē), *adv.* 1. In particular; in detail; distinctly: *an item particularly mentioned.* 2. Unusually; especially: *particularly interesting.* [< L *particula*]

pas sen ger (pas′ən jər), *n.* One who rides in a vehicle that he is not driving. [< OF *passagier* < *passer* to pass < L *passus* a step; related to *pace*]

pa ter nal (pə tûr′nəl), *adj.* 1. Of or like a father; fatherly. 2. Related through one's father: *one's paternal grandmother.* [< L *paternus* < *pater* father] **—pa ter′nal ly,** *adv.*

pa tri arch (pā′trē ärk′), *n.* 1. A father of the human race; one of the men from Adam to Noah. 2. A father and ruler of a great tribe or race, especially Abraham, Isaac, and Jacob, the ancestors of the Hebrew race. [< Gk. *patriarchēs* < *patria* family, tribe + *archein* to rule; related to L *pater* father]

pa tri ot (pā′trē ət, pā′trē ot′), *n.* A person who loves his country and actively defends and supports it. [< L *patriota* fellow countryman < Gk. *patrios* < *patris* fatherland; related to L *pater* father]

pa tron (pā′trən), *n.* 1. Someone who fosters,

adj.	adjective	*pl.*	plural
adv.	adverb	*prep.*	preposition
conj.	conjunction	*pron.*	pronoun
interj.	interjection	*sing.*	singular
n.	noun	*v.*	verb

protects, or otherwise supports a person or a cause; benefactor. 2. A person who does regular business with a company; a regular customer. [< L *patronus* protector < *pater* father]

pen i tence (pen'i təns), *n.* Sincere regret and sorrow for wrongdoing; contrition. [< L *paenitere* to repent]

per ceive (pər sēv'), *v.*, **-ceived, -ceiv ing.** 1. To become aware of through the physical senses. 2. To take in mentally; understand, apprehend. [< OF *perceivre* < L *percipere* < *per-* thoroughly + *capere* to take, grasp]

per en ni al (pə ren'ē əl), *adj.* 1. Lasting though the whole year or for a long time. 2. Of plants living more than two years. —*n.* A plant that lives more than two years. [< L *perennis* < *per-* through + *annus* year] **—per en'ni al ly,** *adv.*

per fect ly (pûr'fikt lē), *adv.* 1. In a perfect manner; without any error, defect, etc.; flawlessly. 2. Completely; fully: *perfectly satisfied.* [< L *perfectus* completed < *perficere* < *per-* thoroughly + *facere* to do, make]

per form ance (pər fôr'məns), *n.* 1. An act of performing; doing. 2. A manner of performing; how one does. 3. A show, as in a circus. [< OF *parfournir* < *par-* thoroughly + *fournir* to accomplish; related to L *performare* < *per-* thoroughly + *formare* to form]

per mit (pər mit'), *v.*, **-mit ted, -mit ting.** To let (someone) do something; allow. —*n.* (pûr'mit, pər mit'). A document showing that a person has permission to do something: *a building permit.* [< L *per-* through + *mittere* to send, let go]

per se cu tion (pûr'si kyōō'shən), *n.* The act of persecuting or the state of being persecuted; oppression, usually because of religious beliefs. [< L *persecutus* < *persequi* to pursue < *per-* through + *sequi* to follow]

per sist ent (pər sis'tənt), *adj.* 1. Pressing on, especially in the face of trouble or opposition; persevering. 2. Not going away; continuing: *a persistent cough.* [< L *persistere* < *per-* through + *sistere* to stand firm] **—per sist'ent ly,** *adv.*

per son al (pûr'sə nəl), *adj.* 1. Of or pertaining to one person; individual; private. 2. Done in person: *a personal visit.* 3. In grammar, referring to person: *personal pronouns.* [< L *persona* actor, person] **—per'son al ly,** *adv.*

per suade (pər swād'), *v.*, **-suad ed, -suad ing.** To cause (a person) to do or believe something by urging, reasoning, etc.; convince. [< L *per-* thoroughly + *suadere* to urge, advise] **—per suad'er,** *n.*

per tain (pər tān'), *v.* To have to do with; be associated with or belong to. [< L *pertinere* to extend < *per-* through + *tenere* to hold]

phrase (frāz), *n.* A group of words, especially one that functions as a unit: *a verb phrase.* —*v.*, **phrased, phras ing.** To put into words; express: *phrase the explanation carefully.* [< Gk. *phrasis* speech < *phrazein* to point out, express]

phys i cal (fiz'i kəl), *adj.* 1. Of the body, as opposed to *mental* or *spiritual: a physical illness.* 2. Of natural matter and the laws that govern it; material. [< L *physica* < Gk. *physis* nature < *phyein* to produce] **—phys'i cal ly,** *adv.*

phy si cian (fi zish'ən), *n.* A doctor. [< L *physica*]

pierce (pirs), *v.*, **pierced, pierc ing.** 1. To make a hole with something sharp; puncture. 2. To go through as if by stabbing: *A shriek pierced the air.* 3. To affect sharply (with a feeling): *pierced with sorrow.* [< OF *percier* < L *pertundere* to perforate < *per-* through + *tundere* to beat] **—pierc'er,** *n.* **—pierc'ing ly,** *adv.*

pil grim age (pil′grə mij), *n.* The journey of a pilgrim. [< OF *pelrimage* < *pelerin* pilgrim < L *peregrinus* foreigner < *per-* through + *ager* land]

poi son ous (poi′zə nəs), *adj.* 1. Containing poison; harmful or deadly to plants, animals, or people. 2. Dangerous; destructive: *poisonous teachings.* [< L *potionis* potion, poisonous drink < *potare* to drink] **—poi′son ous ly,** *adv.*

pos ses sion (pə zesh′ən), *n.* 1. The state of possessing; ownership. 2. Something possessed; property. [< L *possidere* < *potis* in power or ability + *sedere* to sit]

pos si bil i ty (pos′ə bil′i tē), *n., pl.* **-ties.** The fact of being possible; also, something that is possible. [< L *possibilis* < *posse* to be able]

prai rie (prâr′ē), *n.* A vast, level grassland, especially in central North America. [< F < L *pratum* meadow]

pre cede (pri sēd′), *v.,* **-ced ed, -ced ing.** To be or go before. [< L *praecedere* < *prae-* before + *cedere* to go]

pre cise ly (pri sīs′lē), *adv.* Very accurately; exactly. [< L *praecidere* to cut off < *prae-* before + *cidere* to cut]

prej u dice (prej′ə dis), *n.* 1. An idea or attitude, usually unfair, adopted before a person knows all the facts. 2. Dislike for all persons of a particular race, nationality, etc. *—v.,* **-diced, -dic ing.** To cause a prejudice in (a person). [< L *praejudicium* prior judgment < *prae-* before + *judicium* judgment]

pre mi um (prē′mē əm), *n.* 1. Something extra given as a reward for good work or as an inducement to buy; a bonus. 2. High regard; special value: *to put a premium on strict honesty.* 3. A specified amount that must be paid for insurance. [< L *praemium* reward < *prae-* before + *emere* to take, buy]

had, māde, stär, câre, red, mē, dim, hīde, not, hōme, ôr, oil, to͝ok, po͞ol, loud, sun, tûrn; ch, such; ng, sing; sh, she; th, with; th, the; zh, vision

ə represents *a* in ago, *e* in open, *i* in pencil, *o* in wagon, *u* in cactus

pres sure (presh′ər), *n.* 1. A steady pressing, as by the weight of something. 2. Any steady compulsion; compelling force: *the pressure of many responsibilities.* *—v.,* **-sured, -sur ing.** To use pressure to persuade someone; urge strongly. [< L *pressura* < *premere* to press]

pre vail (pri vāl′), *v.* 1. To be victorious; win; triumph. 2. To be found or practiced in many places; abound. 3. To pressure (someone) to do something; urge strongly: *The angels prevailed upon Lot to leave Sodom.* [< L *praevalere* < *prae-* before + *valere* to be strong, have power]

prin ci pal (prin′sə pəl), *adj.* Most important; main; chief. *—n.* One who is the head of an institution, especially a school. 2. An amount of money that is borrowed, upon which interest is paid. [< L *princeps* first, chief < *primus* first + *capere* to take] **—prin′ci pal ly,** *adv.*

pro ces sion (prə sesh′ən), *n.* 1. An instance of proceeding; a going foward. 2. A line of persons or vehicles going somewhere together: *a funeral procession.* [< L *procedere* < *pro-* forward + *cedere* to go]

pro claim (prō klām′), *v.* To announce publicly; declare openly. [< OF *proclamer, proclaimer* < L *pro-* forth + *clamare* to call, shout] **—pro claim′er,** *n.*

pro duc tion (prə duk′shən, prō duk′shən), *n.* 1. The act or process of producing; also, that which is produced. 2. An amount produced: *increasing production.* [< L *producere* < *pro-* forward + *ducere* to lead]

pro fes sion al (prə fesh′ə nəl), *adj.* 1. Having to do with a profession: *a doctor's professional*

adj.	adjective	*pl.*	plural
adv.	adverb	*prep.*	preposition
conj.	conjunction	*pron.*	pronoun
interj.	interjection	*sing.*	singular
n.	noun	*v.*	verb

duties. 2. Doing for an occupation what most people do for pleasure: *a professional singer.* —*n.* A person engaged in a profession. [< L *professus* < *profiteri* to profess, confess < *pro-* forth + *fateri* to acknowledge] **—pro fes′sion al ly,** *adv.*

pro fes sor (prə fes′ər), *n.* 1. One who professes: *a professor of Christianity.* 2. One who teaches in a college or university. [< L *professus*]

pro mo tion (prə mō′shən), *n.* An act of promoting; advancing or being advanced. [< L *promotus* < *promovere* < *pro-* forward + *movere* to move]

pro nun ci a tion (prə nun′sē ā′shən), *n.* The act or manner of pronouncing; utterance. [< L *pronuntiatus* < *pronuntiare* to pronounce < *pro-* forth + *nuntiare* to announce]

proph e sy (prof′i sī′), *v.,* **-sied, -sy ing.** To speak under divine inspiration, especially in foretelling the future. [< Gk. *prophētia* < *pro-* before + *phanai* to speak] **—proph′e si′er,** *n.*

pro por tion (prə pôr′shən), *n.* 1. The relationship between two sizes, amounts, etc. 2. A proper relationship between parts: *in good proportion.* —*v.* To cause to be in correct proportion. [< L *pro-* for + *portionis* share, portion]

pro pose (prə prōz′), *v.,* **-posed, -pos ing.** To set forth for consideration; suggest. [< L *proponere* < *pro-* forth + *ponere* to put, place]

pul ley (pŏŏl′ē), *n., pl.* **-leys.** 1. A wheel with a rim that is grooved to receive a rope, used to lift heavy objects. 2. A wheel on which a belt turns. [< OF *poulie* < L *poleia* < Gk. *polos* pivot, axis]

Q

quar tet (kwôr tet′), *n.* A group of four items or persons, especially singers. [< F *quartette* < L *quartus* fourth < *quattuor* four] Also **quartette.**

ques tion naire (kwes′chə nâr′), *n.* A written form containing a list of questions, used to obtain opinions or information from a number of people. [< F < L *quaerere* to ask]

quin tu ple (kwin tōō′pəl, kwin tyōō′pəl, kwin tup′əl, kwin′tə pəl), *v.,* **-pled, -pling.** To multiply by five; make five times as great. —*n.* A number or quantity that is five times as great. —*adj.* 1. Five times as great. 2. Consisting of five things or five parts. [< L *quintuplex* < *quintus* fifth < *quinque* five + *plicare* to fold] **—quin tup′ly,** *adv.*

quiz (kwiz), *n., pl.* **quiz zes.** A short test, usually given orally. —*v.,* **quizzed, quiz zing.** To question; ask. [Origin unknown]

R

re ceipt (ri sēt′), *n.* 1. A receiving or being received. 2. A written statement showing that something (usually money) has been received. [< ME *receit* < L *recipere* to receive < *re-* back + *capere* to take]

re ceiv er (ri sē′vər), *n.* 1. A person or thing that receives. 2. A device that converts electrical impulses into sound or a visible display, as the part of a telephone held in the hand or the screen of a radar system. [< L *recipere*]

rec ti fy (rek′tə fī′), *v.,* **-fied, -fy ing.** 1. To make (a wrong) right; correct; remedy. 2. To change (an alternating electric current) into a direct current. [< L *rectificare* < *rectus* right, straight + *facere* to make] **—rec′ti fi ca′tion,** *n.*

re demp tion (ri demp′shən), *n.* 1. A redeeming or being redeemed; ransom; recovery. 2. Deliverance, especially from sin; salvation. [< L *redimere* to redeem < *re-* back + *emere* to buy]

re duc tion (ri duk′shən), *n.* A reducing or being reduced; decrease. 2. The amount by which something is reduced. [< L *reducere* < *re-* back + *ducere* to lead]

re flect (ri flekt′), *v.* 1. To send back, as sound, light, or heat. 2. To send back an image; mirror. 3. To consider seriously; think carefully; ponder. [< L *re-* back + *flectere* to bend]

re flex (rē′fleks′), *n.* An involuntary action, as sneezing or blinking. —*adj.* 1. Of or pertaining to an involuntary action. 2. Of angles, measuring between 180 and 360 degrees. [< L *reflexus* < *re-* back + *flectere* to bend]

reg i ment (*n.* rej′ə mənt; *v.* rej′ə ment), *n.* 1. A military unit of intermediate size, usually commanded by a colonel. 2. A large group of people. —*v.* 1. To form into an orderly group; organize. 2. To rule (people) in a strict and systematic way, usually at the expense of their freedom. [< L *regere* to rule]

reg u la tor (reg′yə lā′tər), *n.* A person or a mechanical device that regulates; controller. [< L *regula* straight rod < *regere* to rule, direct, straighten]

rein deer (rān′dîr′), *n., pl.* **-deer.** A large deer of the North, sometimes kept as a domestic animal. [< Scand. *hreindyri* < *hreinn* reindeer + *dyr* deer, animal]

re ju ve nate (ri jo͞o′və nāt′), *v.* **-nat ed, -nat ing.** To make young again; restore youth or youthful qualities to. [< re- (again) + L *juvenis* young] **—re ju′ve na′tor,** (ri jo͞o′və nā′tər), *n.* **—re ju′ve na′tion,** *n.*

re la tion (ri lā′shən), *n.* 1. The fact of being related; association; connection. 2. A person who is related; kinsman; relative. 3. Reference; regard: *in relation to this matter.* [< L *relatus* < *re-* back + *latus* < *ferre* to carry]

re lieve (ri lēv′), *v.,* **-lieved, -liev ing.** 1. To reduce or remove (pain, anxiety, etc.); alleviate. 2. To release (a person) from a duty by taking his place. [< L *relevare* to lift, lighten < *re-* again + *levare* to lift < *levis* light] **—re liev′er,** *n.*

had, māde, stär, câre, red, mē, dim, hīde, not, hōme, ôr, oil, to͝ok, po͞ol, loud, sun, tûrn; ch, such; ng, sing; sh, she; th, with; th, the; zh, vision

ə represents *a* in ago, *e* in open, *i* in pencil, *o* in wagon, *u* in cactus

re lig ious (ri lij′əs), *adj.* 1. Pertaining to or devoted to religion. 2. Very careful; conscientious. [< L *religio* reverence, respect < *religare* < *re-* back + *ligare* to bind] **—re lig′ious ly,** *adv.*

rem e dy (rem′i dē), *n., pl.* **-dies.** Something used to relieve an illness or solve a problem. —*v.,* **-died, -dy ing.** To cure (an illness) or solve (a problem). [< L *remedium* < *re-* again + *mederi* to heal]

re mit tance (ri mit′əns), *n.* A sending of money; also, money that is sent. [< L *re-* back + *mittere* to send]

re nown (ri noun′), *n.* High reputation; fame: *men of renown.* [< OF *renon* < *renomer* to name repeatedly < L *re-* again + *nominare* to name < *nomen* name]

re pel lent (ri pel′ənt), *adj.* 1. Tending to repel; having the ability to drive back or turn away. 2. Disagreeable; disgusting; repulsive. —*n.* Something that repels: *an insect repellent.* [< L *re-* back + *pellere* to drive]

rep tile (rep′til, rep′tīl′), *n.* A cold-blooded creeping animal such as a turtle, a snake, or a crocodile. [< L *reptilis* crawling < *repere* to crawl, creep]

re pub li can (ri pub′li kən), *adj.* 1. Of or like a system of government in which the citizens elect the government leaders. 2. **Republican.** Having to do with the Republican Party. —*n.* 1. A person who promotes a republican system of government. 2. **Republican.** One who is a member of the Republican Party. [< L *res publica* a public thing, interest]

adj.	adjective	*pl.*	plural
adv.	adverb	*prep.*	preposition
conj.	conjunction	*pron.*	pronoun
interj.	interjection	*sing.*	singular
n.	noun	*v.*	verb

re pul sive (ri pul′siv), *adj.* Arousing strong dislike, disgust, etc.; grossly offensive. [< L *repulsus* < *repellere* < *re-* back + *pellere* to drive] **—re pul′sive ly,** *adv.* **—re pul′sive ness,** *n.*

re quest (ri kwest′), *v.* To ask for, usually in a polite way. *—n.* An act of asking for something; petition; also, the thing asked for. [< L *requisitus* sought again < *requirere* < *re-* again + *quaerere* to ask, seek]

re quire ment (ri kwīr′mənt), *n.* Something required; necessity. [< L *requirere*]

req ui si tion (rek′wi zish′ən), *n.* 1. A formal written request, as from a government. 2. The condition of being required: *Water is in constant requisition by living things.* *—v.* To make a demand upon; require or take by or as by authority. [< L *requirere*]

res i dence (rez′i dəns, rez′i dens′), *n.* 1. A residing; dwelling at a place. 2. The place where one resides; home. 3. The length of time that a person lives at one place. [< L *residere* to abide < *re-* back + *sidere* to sit]

re solve (ri zolv′), *v.,* **-solved, -solv ing.** 1. To be determined (to do something); decide firmly. 2. To decide formally by voting. 3. To clear up; solve, as a difficulty. *—n.* A fixed determination; resolution. [< L *re-* again + *solvere* to loosen]

re spect a ble (ri spek′tə bəl), *adj.* 1. Worthy of respect; having a good reputation. 2. Fairly good; acceptable. [< L *respectus* < *respicere* to look back, consider < *re-* back, again + *specere* to look] **—re spect′a bly,** *adv.*

re sponse (ri spons′), *n.* An answer by word or action; a reply. [< L *respondere* < *re-* back + *spondere* to pledge, promise]

re strain (ri strān′), *v.* To hold back; keep in check. [< OF *restraindre* < L *restringere* to restrict < *re-* back + *stringere* to draw tight] **—re strain′er,** *n.*

res ur rec tion (rez′ə rek′shən), *n.* 1. A coming back to life; a rising from the dead. 2. The rising of Christ from the dead; also, the rising again of the dead on the Judgment Day. [< L *resurrectionis* < *resurgere* < *re-* again + *surgere* to rise]

rev o lu tion (rev′ə lo͞o′shən), *n.* 1. An act of revolving; also, the circular path of an object that travels completely around something. 2. An uprising that results in the overthrow of a government. 3. Any drastic change that has widespread effects: *the Industrial Revolution.* [< L *revolvere* to turn around < *re-* back + *volvere* to roll]

rhu barb (ro͞o′bärb′), *n.* A plant of the buckwheat family, having large leaves and tall stalks; also, the stalks of this plant, which have a tart flavor and are used in cooking. [< Gk. *rha barbaros* foreign rhubarb]

ring let (ring′lit), *n.* 1. A small ring. 2. A spiral lock of hair. [ring + -let (little)]

rite (rīt), *n.* A solemn ceremony, usually one that has religious significance: *the rite of baptism.* [< L *ritus* ceremony, rite]

ru ral (ro͝or′əl), *adj.* Having to do with the country as distinguished from the city; not urban. [< L *ruris* country] **—ru′ral ly,** *adv.*

S

sac ri fice (sak′rə fīs′), *n.* 1. The act of offering (an animal, etc.) to God or an idol; also, the thing offered. 2. Any cherished thing that is given up in hopes of gaining something more valuable. *—v.,* **-ficed, -fic ing.** 1. To offer (an animal, etc.) to God or an idol. 2. To give up (something cherished) so as to gain something more valuable. [< L *sacrificium* < *sacer* holy + *facere* to make] **—sac′ri fic′er,** *n.*

sac ri lege (sak′rə lij), *n.* An act of profaning something sacred; disrespectful treatment of something holy. [< L *sacrilegus* temple robber < *sacrum* sacred object + *legere* to pick up, steal] **—sac′ri le′gious,** *adj.* **—sac′ri le′gious ly,** *adv.*

sal a ry (sal′ə rē), *n., pl.* **-ries.** A fixed amount paid each week or month for regular work, not dependent on the number of hours worked. —*v.,* **-ried, -ry ing.** To assign a salary to. [< L *salarium* the part of a Roman soldier's allowance paid in salt < *sal* salt]

sanc ti fi ca tion (sangk′tə fi kā′shən), *n.* The act of sanctifying or the condition of being santified; a setting apart by God, or a being set apart, for His exclusive service. [< L *sanctificare* < *sanctus* holy + *facere* to make]

sanc tu ar y (sangk′cho͞o er′ē), *n., pl.* **-ies** 1. A sacred place. 2. The main part of a church building. 3. A place of protection; refuge: *a wildlife sanctuary.* [< L *sanctus* holy]

sched ule (skej′o͞ol; *British* shed′yo͞ol), *n.* A form on which details are listed, especially a table listing things that are to take place and the time when each thing is to happen. —*v.,* **-uled, -ul ing.** To appoint a certain time to do something. [< L *schedula* small sheet of papyrus < *scheda* sheet of papyrus]

scis sors (siz′ərz), *n., sing.* or *pl.* A cutting instrument with pivoted blades that are brought together on the paper, cloth, etc., that is to be cut. [< L *cisorium* cutting tool < *caedere* to cut; related to L *scissor* one who cuts < *scindere* to cut, split]

se cede (si sēd′), *v.,* **-ced ed, -ced ing.** To withdraw formally from an organization, especially a political one. [< L *se-* apart + *cedere* to go] **—se ced′er,** *n.*

seize (sēz), *v.,* **seized, seiz ing.** 1. To take sudden hold of; grab; clutch. 2. To take over by force: *seize enemy territory*. 3. To overcome suddenly; attack: *Panic seized her.* [< OF *seiser* < L *sacire* to take into one's possession]

had, māde, stär, câre, red, mē, dim, hīde, not, hōme, ôr, oil, to͝ok, po͞ol, loud, sun, tûrn; ch, such; ng, sing; sh, she; th, with; t͟h, the; zh, vision

ə represents *a* in ago, *e* in open, *i* in pencil, *o* in wagon, *u* in cactus

se lec tion (si lek′shən), *n.* 1. The act of selecting; a picking out; choosing. 2. A person or thing selected; choice. 3. A variety of things from which to choose: *a wide selection of colors*. [< L *selectum* < *se-* apart + *legere* to pick, choose]

sem i con scious (sem′ē kon′shəs, sem′ī kon′shəs), *adj.* Partly conscious. [< semi- (half, partly) + conscious]

sen a tor (sen′ə tər), *n.* A member of a senate. [< L *senator* < *senex* old]

se nile (sē′nīl′, sen′īl′), *adj.* 1. Pertaining to or caused by old age. 2. Affected by the physical and mental infirmities normally associated with old age. [< L *senilis* < *senex* old]

sen ior (sēn′yər), *adj.* Older in years or higher in rank, as opposed to *junior.* —*n.* An older person: *a senior by twenty years. Abbr.* **sr.; Sr.** (after a name). [< L *senior* older < *senex* old]

sen si ble (sen′sə bəl), *adj.* Having good judgment; showing or exercising common sense; discreet. [< L *sensibilis* < *sensus* < *sentire* to feel, perceive] **—sen′si bly,** *adv.* **—sen′si ble ness,** *n.*

sep a ra tion (sep′ə rā′shən), *n.* A parting or being parted; division or disconnection. [< L *separare* < *se-* apart + *parare* to prepare]

sep tet (sep tet′), *n.* A group of seven items or persons, especially singers. [< L *septem* seven] Also **septette.**

se quence (sē′kwəns, sē′kwens′), *n.* 1. The following of one thing by another; succession.

adj.	adjective	*pl.*	plural
adv.	adverb	*prep.*	preposition
conj.	conjunction	*pron.*	pronoun
interj.	interjection	*sing.*	singular
n.	noun	*v.*	verb

2. A group of things that follow each other; series. [< L *sequens* < *sequi* to follow]

ses sion (sesh′ən), *n.* 1. A meeting or series of meetings by a court, legislature, etc. 2. A period during which a lesson is taught in a school day; class period. [< L *sessionis* < *sedere* to sit]

sex tet (seks tet′), *n.* A group of six items or persons, especially singers. [< L *sex* six] Also **sextette.**

shep herd (shep′ərd), *n.* 1. A person who cares for sheep; sheepherder. 2. A spiritual leader or guide; pastor; minister. —*v.* To care for, guide, or direct in the manner of a shepherd. [< OE *scēaphyrde* < *scēap* sheep + *hierde* herdsman < *heord* herd]

sher iff (sher′if), *n.* The chief law enforcement officer of a county. [< OE *scīr-gērefa* shire reeve < *scīr* shire (English county) + *gerēfa* reeve, bailiff]

so lar (sō′lər), *adj.* Of or pertaining to the sun. [< L *solaris* < *sol* sun]

so lu tion (sə lo͞o′shən), *n.* 1. A finding of the answer to a question or problem; also, the answer itself. 2. A mixture consisting of a liquid and a substance dissolved in it. [< L *solutionis* < *solvere* to loosen, dissolve]

spec i fy (spes′ə fī′), *v.,* **-fied, -fy ing.** To refer to in particular; mention specifically. [< L *specificare* < *species* kind + *facere* to make]

spec ta tor (spek′tā tər), *n.* One who watches something happen; onlooker. [< L *spectare* to look at < *specere* to see]

spir i tu al (spir′i cho͞o əl), *adj.* 1. Having to do with spirit, as distinguished from *physical.* 2. Concerned about the interests of the Holy Spirit, as opposed to *carnal*; controlled by the Holy Spirit and the Word of God. —*n.* A religious song originating among the blacks of the southern United States, or one written in that style. [< L *spiritus* spirit] **—spir′i tu al ly,** *adv.*

sta tion ar y (stā′shə ner′ē), *adj.* 1. Staying in one place; not moving. 2. Not easily movable; not portable. [< L *stationis* < *stare* to stand]

sta tion er y (stā′shə ner′ē), *n.* Writing materials; paper, envelopes, and sometimes pens or pencils. [< stationer (a seller of stationery) < L *stationarius* doing business at a fixed location < *stationis* < *stare* to stand]

stat ute (stach′o͞ot), *n.* An established law; decree. [< L *statutum* < *statuere* to establish < *stare* to stand]

straight en (strāt′ən), *v.* 1. To make straight. 2. To put in order; make neat and tidy. [< ME *streght* < OE *streht* < *streccan* to stretch] **—straight′en er,** *n.*

sub mit (səb mit′), *v.,* **-mit ted, -mit ting.** 1. To yield to the authority, command, or power of another. 2. To give or send (something) to another person for his consideration: *submit a poem to the editor.* [< L *sub-* under + *mittere* to send, let go] **—sub mit′ter,** *n.* **—sub mit′tal,** *n.*

sub sti tute (sub′sti to͞ot′, sub′sti tyo͞ot′), *v.,* **-tut ed, -tut ing.** To take, put, or do in the place of another. —*n.* A person or thing that takes the place of another. [< L *substituere* < *sub-* under, instead + *statuere* to establish < *stare* to stand]

sub tra hend (sub′trə hend′), *n.* In mathematics, the number that is subtracted from another. [< L *subtrahere* to subtract < *sub-* down, away + *trahere* to draw]

sub way (sub′wā′), *n.* A railroad located beneath the street level in a city. [< sub- (under) + way]

had, māde, stär, câre, red, mē, dim, hīde, not, hōme, ôr, oil, to͝ok, po͞ol, loud, sun, tûrn; ch, such; ng, sing; sh, she; th, with; th, the; zh, vision

ə represents *a* in ago, *e* in open, *i* in pencil, *o* in wagon, *u* in cactus

suc ceed (sək sēd′), *v.* 1. To accomplish what is desired. 2. To come next after (another person or thing): *Solomon succeeded David as king.* [< L *succedere* < *sub-* under + *cedere* to go]

suc cess ful ly (sək ses′fəl ē), *adv.* In a way that succeeds; fruitfully; prosperously. [< L *succedere*]

suc ces sion (sək sesh′ən), *n.* 1. The following of one thing after another; series; sequence. 2. A group of things that follow each other. 3. Order or right of succeeding to an office or rank. [< L *succedere*]

sug ges tion (səg jes′chən), *n.* 1. An act of suggesting; also, something that is suggested. 2. The calling up of an idea by the mention of a related idea. [< L *suggestus* < *suggerere* < *sub-* under + *gerere* to carry, bring]

sum mon (sum′ən), *v.* 1. To call (a person) to come, especially with authority: *summon the defendant to appear in court.* 2. To call forth; arouse: *summon all one's strength.* [< L *summonere* to suggest < *sub-* underneath, secretly + *monere* to warn]

su per fi cial (so͞o′pər fish′əl), *adj.* 1. Of, at, or near the surface: *superficial damage.* 2. Not serious or thorough; shallow: *a superficial interest.* [< L *superficies* surface < *super-* over, above + *facies* face, form] **—su′per fi′cial ly,** *adv.*

su pe ri or (so͞o pîr′ē ər), *adj.* 1. Better than average; excellent. 2. Higher in position or rank; more elevated or advanced. *—n.* A person who is of a higher rank. [< L *superus* upper < *super* above, beyond] **—su pe′ri or ly,** *adv.*

su per la tive (so͞o pûr′lə tiv), *adj.* 1. Highest; supreme. 2. In grammar, referring to the highest degree of comparison for adjectives and adverbs, indicated by the suffix *-est* or the word *most.* *—n.* 1. Something that is supreme. 2. The highest degree of comparison for adjectives and adverbs. [< L *superlativus* < *super* above + *latus* < *ferre* to carry] **—su per′la tive ly,** *adv.*

su per scrip tion (so͞o′pər skrip′shən), *n.* 1. The act of writing (a title or an address) above or on something. 2. That which is written above or on something. [< L *super-* over, above + *scribere* to write]

su per sede (so͞o′pər sēd′), *v.,* **-sed ed, -sed ing.** To cause to be put aside, usually by being superior; replace. [< L *super-* above, over + *sedere* to sit] **—su′per sed′er,** *n.*

su per sti tion (so͞o′pər stish′ən), *n.* A belief or practice based on ignorant fear. [< L *superstitionis* a standing over (in fear or respect) < *super-* above, over + *stare* to stand]

sur ren der (sə ren′dər), *v.* To yield to (another person); give up, as in defeat. *—n.* An act of surrendering; a giving up. [< OF *surrendre* < *sur-* over + *rendre* < L *re-* back + *dare* to give]

sur round (sə round′), *v.* To extend all the way around; enclose; encircle. [< OF *sorounder* to surpass, overflow < L *super-* over + *undare* to rise in waves < *unda* a wave]

syn a gogue (sin′ə gog′, sin′ə gôg′), *n.* A building used by Jews for religious services. [< Gk. *synagōgē* assembly < *syn-* together + *agein* to bring]

T

tar iff (tar′if), *n.* A tax charged on an import or export; duty; also, a list of such taxes. [< Ital. *tariffa* < Arabic *ta'rif* information < *'arafa* to inform, know]

adj.	adjective	*pl.*	plural
adv.	adverb	*prep.*	preposition
conj.	conjunction	*pron.*	pronoun
interj.	interjection	*sing.*	singular
n.	noun	*v.*	verb

tech ni cal (tek′ni kəl), *adj.* 1. Having to do with applied science; pertaining to a particular scientific or mechanical knowledge or skill: *a technical term.* 2. Determined by strict application of a rule, a word meaning, etc.: *a technical difference.* [< Gk. *technikos* < *technē* art, skill] **—tech′ni cal ly,** *adv.*

tem per a ture (tem′pər ə cho͝or′), *n.* 1. The amount of heat or cold; how hot or cold something is. 2. A body temperature that is higher than normal; fever. [< L *temperatura* due measure < *temperare* to mix in proper proportions]

tex tile (teks′tīl′, teks′təl), *adj.* Pertaining to weaving or what is woven. *—n.* A woven material; fabric. [< L *textilis* < *textus* fabric < *texere* to weave]

Thes sa lo ni ans (thes′ə lō′nē ənz), *n.* One of the two New Testament books consisting of letters that Paul wrote to the believers in Thessalonica. *Abbr.* **Thess.**

thor ough (thûr′ō), *adj.* Through and through; careful and complete: *a thorough cleaning.* [< OE *thuruh,* emphatic form of *thurh* through] **—thor′ough ly,** *adv.* **—thor′ough ness,** *n.*

threat en (thret′ən), *v.* 1. To utter a threat; express an intention to do (something undesirable). 2. To be a sign of something dangerous, unpleasant, etc. [< OE *thrēatnian* to compel, urge]

tongue (tung), *n.* 1. The muscular organ in the mouth used in tasting, swallowing, and speaking. 2. Something whose shape resembles the tongue: *tongues of fire, a wagon tongue.* 3. A language. [< OE *tunge* tongue; related to L *lingua* tongue, language]

trans fer (trans fûr′, trans′fər), *v.,* **-ferred, -fer ring.** 1. To pass or cause to pass from one place to another. 2. To change from one vehicle to another in traveling. *—n.* (trans′fər) 1. A transferring or being transferred. 2. A ticket that allows a person to change from one vehicle to another in traveling. [< L *trans-* across + *ferre* to carry]

trans form (trans fôrm′), *v.* To change from one form or condition to another; convert. [< L *trans-* across, over + *formare* to form]

trans gres sion (trans gresh′ən, tranz gresh′ən), *n.* A breaking of a law or command, especially a breaking of God's law; sin. [< L *transgressus* < *trans-* across + *gradi* to step]

trans late (trans lāt′, trans′lāt′, tranz lāt′, tranz′lāt′), *v.,* **-lat ed, -lat ing.** 1. To change (speech or writing) from one language to another. 2. To take (a person) directly from earth to heaven without death. [< L *trans-* across + *latus* < *ferre* to carry] **—trans la′tion,** *n.* **—trans′la tor,** *n.*

trans par ent (trans pâr′ənt, trans par′ənt), *adj.* 1. Allowing light to pass through in such a way that objects beyond are distinctly visible: distinguished from *translucent.* 2. Free from deceit or pretense; frank: *transparent honesty.* [< L *trans-* across + *parere* to appear, be visible] **—trans par′ent ly,** *adv.*

trans por ta tion (trans′pər tā′shən), *n.* 1. A transporting or being transported. 2. A means of transporting or traveling. [< L *trans-* across + *portare* to carry]

treas ur er (trezh′ər ər), *n.* One who is in charge of the finances of an organization. [< Gk. *thesauros* treasure house]

trip let (trip′lit), *n.* 1. One of a set of three children who are born to the same mother at the same time. 2. In music, a group of three notes that are sung in the time of two notes having that value. [< L *triplus* < *tres* three]

tri une (trī′yo͞on), *adj.* Consisting of a trinity; being three in one: *the triune Godhead.* [< L *tri-* three + *unus* one]

type writ er (tīp′rī′tər), *n.* A machine for writing, which produces characters similar to those produced by a printing press.

had, māde, stär, câre, red, mē, dim, hīde, not, hōme, ôr, oil, to͝ok, po͞ol, loud, sun, tûrn; ch, such; ng, sing; sh, she; th, with; t͟h, the; zh, vision

ə represents *a* in ago, *e* in open, *i* in pencil, *o* in wagon, *u* in cactus

U

ul ti mate (ul′tə mit), *adj.* 1. Last and greatest; beyond all others; final and utmost. 2. Most distant; extreme. —*n.* That which is ultimate; the uttermost degree, extent, etc. [< L *ultimare* to come to an end < *ultimus* farthest, last < *ultra* beyond] **—ul′ti mate ly,** *adv.*

ul tra vi o let (ul′trə vī′ə lit), *adj.* Of light rays, having a wavelength shorter than that for the color violet. [< ultra- (beyond) + violet]

u nique (yo͞o nēk′), *adj.* 1. Different from anything else; being the only one of its kind. 2. Uncommon; unusual; rare: *a unique privilege.* [< F < L *unicus* < *unus* one] **—u nique′ly,** *adv.*

un nec es sar y (un nes′i ser′ē), *adj.* Not necessary; needless. [< un- (not) + necessary < L *necesse* needful < *ne-* not + *cedere* to go, withdraw, yield] **—un nec′es sar′i ly,** *adv.*

V

va can cy (vā′kən sē), *n., pl.* **-cies.** 1. The condition of being vacant; emptiness. 2. A place or position that is vacant; unfilled space or office. [< L *vacare* to be empty]

vac cine (vak sēn′, vak′sēn′), *n.* A preparation of dead or weakened bacteria or viruses used to make a person or animal immune to a disease. [< L *vaccinus* of cows (because the first successful vaccine consisted of cowpox germs used to immunize against smallpox) < *vacca* cow]

vein (vān), *n.* 1. A blood vessel that carries blood flowing toward the heart. 2. A structure that forms part of the framework of a leaf or an insect's wing. 3. A deposit of ore between layers of rock; lode. —*v.* To fill with veins or cover with markings that resemble veins. [< OF *veine* < L *vena* blood vessel]

ver bose (vər bōs′), *adj.* Using or containing many unnecessary words; wordy. [< L *verbosus* full of words < *verbum* word] **—ver bose′ly,** *adv.* **—ver bose′ness,** *n.*

ver sa tile (vûr′sə təl, vûr′sə tīl′), *adj.* Able to perform many different tasks well. [< L *versatilis* turning < *vertere* to turn] **—ver′sa tile ly,** *adv.* **—ver′sa til′i ty** (vûr′sə til′i tē), **ver′sa tile ness** (vûr′sə təl nis, vûr′sə tīl′nis), *n.*

vice-pres i dent (vīs′prez′i dent, vīs′prez′i dənt), *n.* An officer of the next rank lower than the president, who takes the president's place when necessary. [< vice- (substitute) + president < L *praesidere* to preside < *prae-* before + *sedere* to set]

vir tu ous (vûr′cho͞o əs), *adj.* Full of virtue; morally pure and upright. [< L *virtus* manliness, bravery < *vir* man] **—vir′tu ous ly,** *adv.*

vis i ble (viz′ə bəl), *adj.* Capable of being seen. [< L *visibilis* < *visus* seen < *videre* to see] **—vis′i bly,** *adv.* **—vis′i ble ness,** *n.*

vi sion (vizh′ən), *n.* 1. The ability to see; sense of sight. 2. The ability to see ahead; foresight. 3. Something seen in the mind, especially by revelation from God. [< L *visionis* < *visus*]

vi su al (vizh′o͞o əl), *adj.* Pertaining to the sense of sight: *a visual handicap.* [< L *visualis* < *visus*] **—vi′su al ly,** *adv.*

adj.	adjective	*pl.*	plural
adv.	adverb	*prep.*	preposition
conj.	conjunction	*pron.*	pronoun
interj.	interjection	*sing.*	singular
n.	noun	*v.*	verb

W

wel fare (wel′fâr′), *n.* 1. The state of being or doing well; health and prosperity. 2. Government aid for the needy. [< ME *wel fare* < *wel* well + *fare* a going < OE *faran* to go]

wher ev er (hwâr ev′ər), *adv., conj.* In or to whatever place.

who'd (ho͞od), Contraction for *who had* or *who would.*

world li ness (wûrld′lē nis), *n.* 1. The condition of being motivated by natural, worldly interests rather than spiritual interests. 2. That which is worldly, as a fashion. [< OE *woruldlic* < *woruld* world]

wor thy (wûr′thē), *adj.,* **-thi er, -thi est.** 1. Having worth or merit. 2. Deserving; meriting. —*n., pl.* **-thies.** A person of outstanding faith, courage, etc. [< ME *worthi* < OE *weorth* worth] **—wor′thi ly,** *adv.*

wres tle (res′əl), *v.,* **-tled, -tling.** To struggle with (a person or thing) in order to gain the mastery. —*n.* A wrestling; struggle. [< OE *wrǣstlian* < *wrǣstan* to wrest, twist]

wrought (rôt), *v. Archaic.* Past form of *work.* —*adj.* Shaped by hammering. [< ME *wrogt* < OE *geworht* < *wrycan* to work]